IN THE PALM OF
GOD'S HAND

Text copyright © Wendy Bray 2000, 2002, 2007
The author asserts the moral right
to be identified as the author of this work

Published by
The Bible Reading Fellowship
First Floor, Elsfield Hall
15–17 Elsfield Way, Oxford OX2 8FG
Website: www.brf.org.uk

ISBN-10: 1 84101 539 3
ISBN-13: 978 1 84101 539 2
First edition 2000
Second edition 2002
Revised edition 2007
1 3 5 7 9 10 8 6 4 2 0
All rights reserved

Acknowledgments

Unless otherwise stated, scripture quotations are taken from the Holy Bible, New International Version, copyright © 1973, 1978, 1984 by International Bible Society, are used by permission of Hodder & Stoughton, a division of Hodder Headline Ltd. All rights reserved. 'NIV' is a registered trademark of International Bible Society. UK trademark number 1448790.

Scripture quotations taken from The New Revised Standard Version of the Bible, Anglicized Edition, copyright © 1989, 1995 by the Division of Christian Education of the National Council of the Churches of Christ in the USA, are used by permission. All rights reserved.

Scriptures quoted from the Good News Bible published by The Bible Societies/HarperCollins Publishers Ltd, UK © American Bible Society 1966, 1971, 1976, 1992, used with permission.

Extracts from the Authorized Version of the Bible (The King James Bible), the rights in which are vested in the Crown, are reproduced by permission of the Crown's patentee, Cambridge University Press.

'Safe in the shadow of the Lord' is copyright © Timothy Dudley-Smith, and is used with permission.

'My redeemer lives': Words and music by Eugene Greco, © 1995 His Banner Publishing, PO Box 30044, Portland, OR 97294. Email: hisbanner@juno.com.

'Blessed be Your name' by Matt Redman and Beth Redman. Copyright © 2002 Thankyou Music. Adm. by worshiptogether.com songs excl. UK & Europe, adm. by kingswaysongs.com tym@kingsway.co.uk. Used by permission.

A catalogue record for this book is available from the British Library

Printed in Singapore by Craft Print International Ltd

IN THE PALM OF
GOD'S HAND

A diary of living against the odds

WENDY BRAY

To Lois and Benjamin, as ever, with big hugs

ACKNOWLEDGMENTS

A very small, select band have helped me prepare these diaries for publication. A much larger band have been part of them. Sadly I haven't the space to thank them all here. But I must include a few.

Special thanks to Archie Prentice, Bet Leppard and *all* the team on Birch Ward at Derriford Hospital in Plymouth, who continue to perform medical gymnastics in order to save my life. Their kindness, dedication and professionalism are exceptional.

Thank you, everyone at *Care for the Family*, especially Lisa and Sheron; also Rob and Jonathan who have little time to spare but have always found some to show their love and care for me. I thank God for them often; life would also be a lot less fun without them.

Thank you to the St Andrew's Wednesday Bible study group and friends at my own church, Mutley Baptist, especially Jacqui, Liza, Chris and Kate, who keep on praying—and little Peter and Timothy Wall, who talk to Jesus about making me better.

Thank you, Fiona, for your foreword, long phone calls and understanding; Gill, for our 'picked up again' friendship; Margaret and Diane, for two very special new ones; and Amanda, who has sent a card *every* week without fail since I first became ill.

Thank you, Mum and Dad and Granny, who have wielded the cleaning cloths, vacuum and iron on numerous occasions, and watched over the children.

Most especially, I want to thank my friend and 'unofficial agent', Jill Worth, who encouraged me, more than anyone else, to publish this diary. Our friendship has been glued by tough times. We have shared tears, cream cakes, metaphorical crutches and big hugs across miles. You're a star, Jill.

Thank you to Naomi and the team at BRF, who have believed in what God might do with my words and worked so hard to see them published.

And, of course, thank you, Richard, Lois and Benjamin, who have had Mrs Blobby to live with for so long. I love the three of you more than you'll ever know.

PREFACE

Most of us do not want valleys in our lives. We shrink from them with a sense of fear and foreboding. Yet in spite of our worst misgivings God can bring great benefit and lasting benediction to others through those valleys. Let us not always try to avoid the dark things, the distressing days. They may well prove to be the way of greatest refreshment to ourselves and those around us.[1]

Sharing a diary like this is about more than baring your soul. It's like taking your clothes off in public in mid-January and asking passers-by to throw snowballs at you. Not something you would do unless you hoped an awful lot of good would come out of it.

But here I am, doing it (sharing the diary, that is—I'm too much of a coward to attempt the illustration!) So I must believe in the good. Whatever good might result is God's to reveal. I hope that it will involve glory to him and comfort and encouragement to others—as well as providing the occasional laugh.

Laughter has been almost as important as chemotherapy in bringing me this far on what is really a journey with cancer (although I can think of others I would rather make a journey with!) It has often saved me from a dive into the destructive depths of self-pity and made things easier, I think, for those I care about, who, when faced with my illness, just did not know what to say. It has often been easier for them to laugh.

The words that follow have been lifted from the diary I kept during 1999 and early 2000. Because it is mainly my *prayer* diary I have had to make considerable omissions and alterations, both to make it readable and episodic and to protect other individuals and situations I prayed for during that time. As a result, it may seem as if I thought of little else except my illness and myself during those months. I do hope that wasn't the case! I trust that the gaps between dates and the fragmented entries will remind the reader that 'ordinary life' carried on as much as possible around hospital visits and trips to the bathroom. I also hope that this necessary editing has not excluded my honesty about my experience of cancer. It has been important to be real, if only to connect with other members of this exclusive club! We are none of us alone, however we might feel at 3am.

I have included some of the words I read during this time which seemed to say what I needed to 'hear'. I am so grateful to the writers of those words. I am particularly grateful for the words of David Watson (whom I'll get to thank personally one day) and James Jones (whom I already have). And to Fiona Castle, whose book *Rainbows through the Rain* kept me going when I could read very little else.

Whilst I could not possibly have recorded all my prayers—indeed many could not be put into words—I have included those I wrote simply and instinctively at the time. Even in this scanty form they remind me that I have known, and continue to know, a wonderful dialogue with the God who knows where this journey will end. From the very beginning it was clear that a tough time lay ahead, but that God would ultimately be glorified. I want this book to do just that, to say, 'Look at all that God has done.' And, more deeply, just to say, 'Look at God.'

CONTENTS

FOREWORD

When Wendy sent me the first draft of this book, I knew at once that it should be published. Its diary form, written over many months, means that it is an honest daily account of real, often raw, emotions. In facing up to cancer without pretence, Wendy articulates her fears for her husband and young family and, in coming to terms with what it means for all of them, she takes, and writes, one day at a time.

Cancer, possibly the most dreaded illness, tends to be talked about in hushed tones and code words: 'your illness', 'your little problem' or 'the big C'. Wendy seeks to break that hushed code with honesty and humour, and through listening to what God might be saying in the midst of confusion and pain.

It is good to see Wendy, already an accomplished writer working with *Care for the Family*, writing simply from her own heart. I am sure this book will give encouragement to sufferers and insight to their friends and family. It offers hope for all of us who may have a brush with cancer in some way, which—let's face it—is most of us!

Fiona Castle

INTRODUCTION

When I was a small boy in Sunday school, we sang the same song almost every week. Even now, over 40 years later, if I close my eyes and imagine, I fancy I can hear its strains coming from the little chapel on the corner of my street:

Climb, climb up sunshine mountain, heavenly breezes blow;
Climb, climb up sunshine mountain, faces all aglow.
Turn, turn your back on doubting, looking to the sky;
Climb, climb up sunshine mountain, you and I.

It's a lovely picture: you can feel the sun on your back as you journey, and just in case it gets too hot there's an occasional heavenly breeze. There are two of us, so there is no loneliness and, for good measure, doubts are a thing of the past.

I am glad my Sunday school teacher taught me that song—children need images that convey security and safety. What is a little harder to understand is why some of us can go through a whole adult life of Christian teaching—hundreds of sermons, conferences and books— without anybody telling us that sometimes, halfway up the mountain, the weather changes to an icy wind, doubts come hurtling over the horizon and, just as they do, we turn around to find that the friend who had been at our shoulder a moment ago has slipped back down the mountain during the storm. We are isolated, hurting, scared and seemingly alone.

But are we really alone? And here is where the crucial issues begin to surface. If God is just the Lord of 'sunshine mountain', if he exists to make me happy, to answer all my prayers with 'Yes', ensuring that my friends or my children never break my heart, that my firm never 'down-sizes' me, and that my body remains healthy, I can only love him when times are good.

But what if there is another possibility? What if he is the God not just of the mountain but of the valley? What if there are times in life when he allows me to know crushing pain, when my prayers seem unanswered and when the darkness seems suffocating? What if he not only loves me but suffers with me—cries with me, holds me sobbing to his chest as I cry out, 'Even in the valley of the shadow of death, you are with me'?

There will come times for each of us when we will find out for ourselves whether we love God because he looks after us, or simply because he is God.

We may find ourselves among those who say, 'I can't believe in a God who would let our holiday be ruined' or, at the other end of the spectrum, we may find ourselves with those who, like Job of old, see their life broken and yet manage to stutter out, through the grief that racks their body, 'Even though he slay me, yet will I trust in him.'

Occasionally God gives us a rare privilege. He allows us to gaze for a while into the life, even the soul, of another person. He did it with Job. As we watch life unfolding for that man, we catch ourselves holding our breath as we wonder how he will react. We ask in our hearts, 'What would I have done?' Well, here is another privilege. Wendy Bray has decided to open her life and soul to us. As she says herself, there are no guarantees; she does not know how all this will turn out. And her diary is deliberately published without a happy end. You and I can watch daily how somebody who loves God copes with the massive shock that he has allowed her to contract cancer and, along with it, to have to bear the everyday frustrations, like delayed scan results, or the people who assume her baldness is the protest of an anarchist instead of the evidence of a woman battling for life.

There are often passages of incredible poignancy. One day she writes, 'I have just read two whole chapters of *Charlie and the Great Glass Elevator* to my son… without coughing once! What an achievement. I haven't been able to do that in months.' And, as one would expect with Wendy, there are moments of helpless laughter: 'What a hilarious morning. The wig fits. But it swings round my cheekbones like a final curtain at the opera. The children took one look at it, burst out laughing and chuckled all the way through *Blue Peter*. I'll put it on when we need a laugh.'

Near the end of her diary we read this: 'I feel very fragile today. Bewildered. Yet I cannot shut you out. I can do nothing but trust you.'

And I suppose, at its heart, this is a book about trust. Not the kind of trust that says, 'I know that soon it will be all right again', but rather the kind that trusts God—anyway—sometimes because there is just nowhere else to go.

Wendy makes me laugh, and she makes me cry. And when life is so hard that it almost crushes me, she asks me if I love God... *anyway*. Wendy, I pray with all my heart that you will be well again. I want you to know the strength and energy you had when you ushered Jonathan Booth and me on that ridiculous bike ride from John O'Groats to Land's End. But whatever the future holds, I want to thank you for sharing your journey with me; I will remember it in my valley. It will encourage me to press on. And it will bring me hope.

Rob Parsons

—— *Part One* ——

THE BEGINNING

HOW IT ALL BEGAN ...

During the early months of 1999 I began to take seriously some niggling symptoms—mainly because my husband Richard and my two children Lois and Benjamin nagged me! During the previous summer I had co-driven the support van for a nationwide cycle ride for *Care for the Family*, the charity for which I work. I'd had the time of my life, but struggled throughout with a dreadful virus which left a persistent dry cough and tiredness. At the end of the ride I asked God for the next challenge.

I would never have imagined that challenge would be cancer! I was not in any high-risk group and had generally been healthy. Cancer was an illness which 'other people' got. But God knew otherwise. And out of his knowledge has unfolded a time of tears and frustration, unexpected laughter and joy, and an intimate dialogue with a loving heavenly Father. But there have also been times of deep confusion, emotional rawness and physical pain which have left me shocked by their intensity.

I am sure there will be more to come, for this journey is not yet at an end. The days ahead may seem filled with uncertainty, but they are not uncertain to God. The truth is that we can only ever assume that we have a certain number of days ahead. Our times really are in God's hand.

The last months have also been something of a learning curve. I have learnt that I haven't truly been living with a heavenly perspective, that I need to face earlier death and accept its strong possibility in order to really live. I have also learnt just how much I am loved. Not just by friends and family but most importantly by the God who continues to sustain me throughout and who keeps me 'in the palm of his hand'.

WEDNESDAY 24 FEBRUARY, EVENING

Richard's concern is justified, I think. This pain has continued on and off for weeks and the parade of symptoms marching with it are not very smart. I needed to do something, so I saw a GP at the surgery this morning. She couldn't find any signs or sounds of infection but gave me some antibiotics and sent me to Derriford Hospital in Plymouth to have a chest X-ray 'just in case'. The results will be with her in a week or so.

Doubtless by then the antibiotics will have done their job. She also suggested that some indigestion remedy might be all that's needed. I am obviously not communicating this well. I don't know what this is, but I *can* tell her it isn't the result of one too many onion bhajis last night!

THURSDAY 25 FEBRUARY

It's 9.30am. Half an hour ago the telephone rang. It was the chest clinic at Derriford. I thought maybe they'd accidentally X-rayed my knee or forgotten to put film in the 'camera', but it's worse than that. They have 'found something' on the X-ray. (Found what? A mouse? A cheque for a cool two million? An onion bhaji?) Would I please attend for an emergency appointment at 3.40pm on Monday, when they'll tell me what it is. Bye for now. Have a nice day. Obviously the staff at the chest clinic don't have weekends as we know them in which to worry, panic and generally imagine the worst! I have phoned Lisa in the office and asked her to pass on the message to pray. (Perfect timing that the office have a prayer time on Thursday mornings!) Also rang Richard in floods of tears, doing a convincing impersonation of a gibbering wreck. Won't really help him feel much better. I'm sure the 'found something' is just a little something. (Am I?) It is a mouse, then. This wait will give an alternative meaning to the phrase 'long weekend'.

FRIDAY 26 FEBRUARY, MORNING

Woken by pain in the night. It was so bad that I was sitting up in bed, rocking and doing the breathing exercises I had used in labour. Staggered out of bed and found some high-strength pain-killers. They didn't even touch the pain! Got back to sleep about four when it eased off. Felt very frightened indeed. Eyes kept filling with tears as I muttered to myself to stop being silly. Dear R slept on beside me. Really should have woken him up, but couldn't see the point in both of us being scared. Just kept praying, 'Lord, whatever this is, give me what I need to cope with it.' I think the cup of tea just before four probably did the trick in the end!

Ought to get the house cleaned today and do some work, but it's hard to concentrate. I did manage to write a book review last night. Getting involved in writing does help to take my mind off things. We're out to the Lord Mayor's dinner tonight. (R's charity contacts!) Then tomorrow R is to stay overnight in Bristol for Julian's stag do. He's hesitating about leaving me as he's so worried, but I've urged him to go and enjoy himself. It will be good for him and I'd hate Julian to be disappointed.

Rebecca Manley Pippert's book[2] this morning refers to a couple of verses from Deuteronomy (20:3b–4) that I maybe ought to adopt as mine: 'Do not be faint-hearted or afraid; do not be terrified or give way to panic. For the Lord your God is the one who goes with you to fight...' Terribly out of context, as I'm not exactly about to enter a battle—as far as I know. But it seems appropriate. Especially the giving way to panic. Keep seeing a little picture of Corporal Jones in *Dad's Army*, waving his arms and shouting, 'Don't panic! Don't panic!'

Lord, I'm wondering what's ahead. It's beginning to be apparent that you may know something about this that I don't. But I won't panic.

SATURDAY 27 FEBRUARY

No pain last night. Thank you, Lord! There is still a strange sensation and the odd twinge, but nothing like before. I had a good lie in this morning after our late night with the Lord Mayor(!) and because I'm still feeling dreadfully tired. The odd bit of socializing wears me out. The not so odd socializing does too! Not good for my image as 'Original Party Girl' at the office! The meal last night was good and it was rather amusing to see all the pomp and circumstance. Prayed a quick, silly prayer that I would win a raffle prize—and I did! Not the TV or the champagne, the holiday vouchers or the painting, but a 1/4lb box of chocolates. It cost less than the ticket. R was very amused, as I always moan that I never win... then I win the very last prize on the list of about two hundred. Lord, your sense of humour is beyond a joke sometimes. Please stop it. (Don't mean that really!)

SUNDAY 28 FEBRUARY

Only minimal pain last night. And no R to disturb with my tossing, turning and sweating, anyway. He was busy terrorizing the streets of Bristol with Julian on his stag night. Will seem odd going to church without him this morning. Especially in this limbo state.

I realize what a quiet tower of strength he is to me on days like this.

MONDAY 1 MARCH, MORNING

Church yesterday seemed like a social club we weren't members of. Maybe because I was absorbed with sticky issues and found it superficial. R is back, safe and sound. Bristol is still standing.

Nice big row with Lois this morning. She seems to think that when she runs out of tights she can just help herself to mine. Oh, how comforting that the little irritations of life still dominate. That whatever the news is today I will still have a twelve-year-old daughter who pinches my tights! I'm not worried about the chest clinic appointment. (You're not?) Surely they'll just confirm the end of a chest infection or an empyema. Seven years ago I had pneumonia which developed into an empyema. It's possible that this condition—a fluid-filled sac on the lung—might be the 'found something' on my X-ray. Dr JR looked after me well then; maybe he will now.

Maybe I need a week or two's rest. I certainly feel pretty tired and unhealthy. It's crept on so gradually that it's been easy to dismiss it. But when I think about it, I do look and feel awful!

TUESDAY 2 MARCH, MORNING

R came with me to the chest clinic and waited in the waiting-room. I saw a not terribly communicative young doctor who talked to me (but mostly to the desk) about the choice of possible diagnoses almost as if he was asking me to choose a holiday. He showed me the X-ray. It was very pretty! But I suppose it isn't meant to be. My lungs are decorated with lots of white, fluffy dandelion clocks. The dandelions are not good news, evidently.

A nurse took some of my blood and gave me a Mantoux test for TB. In a daze, I wandered out of the examination suite to R. My thoughts were, 'I love you, darling, and now I'm about to drop us both in something worse than we've ever been through together before...' And we've been through some: post-natal depression, my pneumonia with complications, bereavement, worries about work and the children. But nothing like this. My words as I reached him were, 'I think we're in trouble, love.'

It seems it's either a high-grade infection (they make it sound like a privilege), TB or malignancy. The dandelions are little glands swollen all around my lungs and heart and under my arms. They're possibly in my neck and beneath my diaphragm too. I'll have a CT scan next, to view the extent of the swollen dandelions, and an op in a couple of weeks, to remove one and test it. JR will do it, which makes me feel a lot better already. He's an old hand at messing about with my lungs, having been in charge of my successful treatment for pneumonia and empyema before. I'm not feeling well, and at least I now know there's a reason. Well, one of three, anyway. I know where this peace has come from, Lord. And miraculously you've taken away fear in exchange. My main concern now is R—that he won't worry too much. I'm OK. I'm on autopilot.

My Bible reading this morning, using James Jones' *People of the Blessing*,[3] is based on Psalm 34: 'For I sought the Lord's help and he answered: and he freed me from all my fears.' I can remember reading that 'Don't be afraid' appears 365 times in the Bible. One for every day of the year. Scared lot, aren't we? Why? 1 John 4:18 tells us: 'There is no fear in love, but perfect love casts out fear' (NRSV). Slightly out of context maybe, but that is what has happened, at least for now, when I most need it. Lord, your perfect love has cast fear out. Or numbed it.

TUESDAY 2 MARCH, EVENING

Have spoken to Chris (our surgeon friend) who thinks TB is possibly the 'best' of the three options. (Whoopee!) He also said that the drug treatment for it is very aggressive. (Whoopee again.) It's very likely I've got TB, as I didn't have the jab as a teenager. Also, of course, I was around Newcastle, Liverpool and London back in the summer on the bike ride. However, I haven't got all the symptoms. The Mantoux (sounds like a French spy) test means watching a little ring of spots react, so we'll see what they do.

Lord, it's easy to be 'brave' now, because I hardly know what I'm being brave about. Give me as much of your understanding of the situation as I need. I so much want to carry on with my work. I'm determined not to let this stop me. Keep me in the assurance that you have everything under control. You've certainly done that these last few days. I've rarely known such peace. But I worry about R. He's so busy. This is an enormous extra burden for him. You know also my fear of being the source of others' pain. Especially that of R and the children. Please help me get everything in the right perspective and cope with feeling unwell, to get as much work done as I can before things get difficult.

WEDNESDAY 3 MARCH, MORNING

Well, the little spy ring of spots is developing. It's visible, but not raised yet, although it's supposed to take between 48 and 72 hours. The hospital don't check it until next Monday. I'm concerned that TB is the best of the three options. I thought the high-grade infection would be. But evidently that's sarcoidosis, which isn't terribly pleasant. I can't believe I've got cancer. I've never smoked and I've spent virtually no time in smoky atmospheres. There's no point speculating. Just hope the CT scan appointment arrives soon. I've mentioned that R has private health insurance through work, so that might speed it up. I just don't feel well enough to keep going sometimes. Even as I sit up here in bed at 7am after a night's sleep, I feel as if something's giving my whole system a real going over, fighting in my veins. Very odd. Quite a lot to do today. Some work to finish. Off to town to pick up R's very glamorous dinner jacket. It's a cream one. R has to be master of ceremonies at Ian P.'s 40th birthday. Ian and R shared an office and a similar brand of insanity a few years ago. Ian has moved on job-wise, and although they no longer share an office, they'll always share the insanity! Later, it's Lois' parents' evening and back to a huge pile of ironing. Will I make it beyond the jacket? I would still love to go to Oxford for the *Promoting Parenting* conference tomorrow. I might see how I cope today. It would mean getting up at some unearthly hour!

THURSDAY 4 MARCH

Well, against my better judgment, I'm off to Oxford today. I think it will be good for me psychologically, if not physically. It's 5.20am and I feel really quite well. A long journey to Oxford ahead. Must be mad. Does anybody else love his or her job this much?

FRIDAY 5 MARCH, MORNING

Absolutely shattered. Apart from a nasty headache at lunchtime yesterday, I felt more or less OK all day. It was a really good day and fun to meet everyone, to hear some brilliant speakers on family issues and have a good chat with my pal Jill W. over *very* large cream cakes! The Mantoux mark seems to have almost disappeared. (It's behaving like a French spy too!) One minute it's obvious, the next it's nearly gone. ('We seek him here... we seek him there...')

Waiting for scan appointments and test results is the worst thing. However, we've got a busy weekend ahead: our friend and Ian's, Peter, is staying with us for Ian's party on Saturday night. R is the master of ceremonies in his smart, new, cream DJ. So there's plenty to distract us.

FRIDAY 5 MARCH, EVENING

Felt quite low today. Was grateful that I was on my own and didn't inflict it on anyone else. Frustrated at not being able to get any info out of a very patronizing doctor whom I finally managed to get on the phone. I was trying to chase up my scan appointment and find out what I'm supposed to be doing to look after myself and protect other people if this *is* TB. She just thought it was all very funny!

Have discovered that it could be another form of cancer called lymphoma. There are two main types—Hodgkin's and Non-Hodgkin's. I've had tenderness under my right arm for ages and thought it was PMT. But it's very likely to be a symptom. Itchy skin and night sweats can also be symptoms of Hodgkin's. I can remember a while ago thinking rather smugly that probably cancer was one illness I was unlikely to suffer from. There hasn't been any in our family and I'm not in any other high-risk group. I still can't believe it could happen, really. It's so easy to believe that cancer is something that happens to other people.

I have an appointment next Thursday with JR at the Nuffield hospital. Maybe he will be able to hurry up my scan appointment. By then the Mantoux result will be known and my blood test will be back. Just want the days to go by until I find out. It figures that it might be something to do with the lymph glands because of how I've been feeling.

Deuteronomy 20:3b–4 is still good to hang on to.

SUNDAY 7 MARCH, MORNING

R has found a new vocation! He was absolutely brilliant as the master of ceremonies at the party last night. Directed operations smoothly. Milled around chatting to people like a regular Hughie Green (that dates me). Gave an excellent presentation on Ian's life and work—excellent enough to have Ian squirming and his kids laughing (and taking notes!) He really is very good at that kind of thing. It's one of his hidden and under-estimated gifts. (Speaking, that is, not getting people squirming!)

MONDAY 8 MARCH, MORNING

Off to the hospital for Mantoux test result today. Will the spy ring reveal itself?

THURSDAY 11 MARCH, MORNING

Have been too tired to write this. Mantoux test was negative. The nurse took one quick look at it and said, 'That's negative.' I was so shocked that I burst into tears. She seemed taken aback that I was distressed that it was *negative*. So I briefly explained my scenario to her. She tried to find a doctor to talk to me and help speed up the CT scan appointment, but couldn't. I felt sorry for her because she obviously felt so helpless.

Once I'd pulled myself together I trundled off to get the bus. It brought home to me how many people must get bad news in huge, busy hospitals and then have to carry it home alone. At least I had R to tell later. He is always there for me. So, one down, two to go. Sarcoidosis sounds positively horrible. But then, lymphoma doesn't exactly sound like a party either. I'm off to see Jacqui soon, who is always a tonic. At least, being a hospice nurse, she knows something about all this. (Is that a black sense of humour I see developing before me?)

PS. Post has just arrived and I've finally got my CT scan appointment... for two weeks' time. A long way off, and another wait. Especially considering the need for scan results before a biopsy is possible. I'll mention it to JR at the Nuffield this afternoon. If anybody can make things happen faster, he can.

FRIDAY 12 MARCH, 1.25AM

(Can't sleep.)

Very glamorous at the Nuffield. More like waiting at a beauty parlour. Sadly didn't get a manicure, but a probable diagnosis. JR examined me and found a lump in my neck. He promptly stuck my fingers on it so that I could enjoy that same experience of discovery! It's the size of a large marble. I would never have found it myself without a mine sweeper. It's deeply buried away. But, just like me when Benjamin has lost something, JR knew where to find it! There's an outside chance that it's sarcoidosis but he's 99 per cent sure that it's a lymphoma of some description. 'That'll be a challenge for you!' he quipped. I suddenly remembered my prayer after the bike ride. I'd prayed for the 'next challenge'. My scan appointment letter was tossed aside, the CT scan department contacted and arrangements made for me to have the scan about half an hour later. They couldn't 'do' my stomach because I hadn't drunk dye the night before but they 'did' my neck and chest.

I rang R and he met me. He was visibly shaken by the news. I've never heard him say 'Why?' He always takes things on the chin much more than me and remains philosophical. So far, at least, I'm not asking 'Why?' I think I feel a bit like Roy Castle did. Why *not* me? Cancer is indiscriminate, unfair and ruthless. There are precious few criteria for safety in the selection process. It may even be random. But for us, God is in control. Doesn't that make all the difference? I can remember David Watson writing that 'What?' rather than 'Why?' should be the question.[4] It seems fruitless to have to ask God why. He doesn't have to explain himself to us! He knows and that's all that matters. But 'What?' Yes. 'What are you telling me, asking of me, planning, saying to others beyond me?' I need to *listen*.

Chris and Kate came round last night so we were able to ask Chris about both diagnosis 'options'. Chris was grave and serious. Unusual for him. Maybe he felt he shouldn't laugh. I just wanted someone to laugh. Couldn't bear it. And I just want to get on with getting it sorted out. My main concern is how this affects the children. Benj with his secondary school decisions coming up. Lois at her tender twelve-going-on-twenty. I'm obviously going to be very ill. What is it going to mean for them? Lord, I really need a lot of faith to let go of them into your hands. Don't let me give up on anything. I know you won't give up on me. The remaining CT scan is next Thursday and the biopsy op on the following Saturday, if JR can manage it… or faster. He has been brilliant. Of course, he'll eventually turn me over to a haematologist (makes me sound like an omelette) but he's doing the biopsy at least. R says he thinks I am coping too well. Maybe the shock will kick in later. But to be honest I'm just gritting my teeth and thinking, 'These lumps are everywhere! How dare they?' (A lumpy omelette, too.) Surely between us all—you, Lord, the medical team and my determination—we can deal with a few lumps!

2am

Have just read my Bible reading for later today: Psalm 84:5–7. It is so right for now. 'Blessed are those whose strength is in you, who have set their hearts on pilgrimage. As they pass through the Valley of Baca (the valley of tears), they make it a place of springs; the autumn rains also cover it with pools. They go from strength to strength, till each appears before God in Zion.' Alongside this passage, James Jones writes of his experience in hospital:

As I sat in the abandoned wheelchair I knew that God was with me. In the cavernous corridor lined with empty seats God filled my heart with a desire to serve him. In that sterile atmosphere I was transfused with a life that had little to do with breathing… Weakness exposes us to God in a unique way and this is what the apostle Paul experienced: it is human weakness that opens up the gates to the energy of God. The Lord said to Paul: 'My grace is sufficient for you, for my power is made perfect in weakness.' (p. 76)

Your timing is perfect, Lord. Can I make the 'valley of tears' a 'valley of springs'? With that in my heart I will turn over and try to get some sleep again.

6.41am

Finally dropped off at about 4am. Then R was noisily awake at 6.15! But I didn't mind. There is something very precious about all the familiar little morning rustlings, footsteps and flushings. Still a lot to do today. It's as if I'm trying to cram in as much as possible before it all gets stopped by the lumps!

'Lumps' up until now were associated with 'One lump or two?' at Victorian tea parties—or, at the very worst, molehills! Will I ever enjoy such innocent word association again? I love you and trust you in all this, Lord. I know that my faith is a gift right now, as is this remarkable freedom from fear. An extra special gift for someone who is such a coward! To be honest I think I need three-birthdays-and-four-Christmases-rolled-into-one's worth of gifts of faith at the moment. But I trust you, that's all that matters. I know you will not let us down.

I remember David Watson saying that faith is the opposite of fear: 'in one sense, fear is faith in what you do not want to happen'!

The words of Rebecca Manley Pippert were bang on time this morning: 'When crisis comes… the issue is not whether we can remain positive but whether God remains in control. He does! Therefore we do not have to be self-confident to possess hope. We only need to be God-confident.'

FRIDAY 12 MARCH, EVENING

The biopsy has been brought forward to Wednesday. Faster and faster comes the fun! Funny the stages you go through with this. Yesterday was like being on Coping Auto-Pilot. Last night saw me a bit weepy in the darkness and today I had a good cry with Liza, which was good to do, I think. I spilled red wine all over my new trousers and said to Liza, 'Never mind, Lize, I might not need them for long!' which made us both cry and laugh at the same time. We then had a good talk about dying, leaving the kids and so on. It's not something to dwell on but it has to be glanced at, at least. (Poor old Liza, she's been through so much with me!)

At the moment it's as if I'm shining a spotlight around all the issues concerning this illness and catching each one in the light. What's disconcerting is that what's important about it seems to differ from moment to moment. But maybe that's the nature of coming to terms with things. And we haven't even got a definite diagnosis yet. My right underarm is very sore tonight. I think I must be full of these things. I feel like a bag of marbles. I must be getting neurotic, because I've had an odd pain in my head and twinges at the back of my neck, but I haven't got lymph glands in my head!

We've decided to move bedrooms. We'll move down to the spare room next to the other bathroom. That way I'm closer to downstairs and all that's going on. And there aren't as many stairs to climb for bed every night. Goodness, I feel as if I ought to order my stair-lift now. It's a bit like preparing for a siege. It seems that chemotherapy (if that's what I'll eventually have) knocks you out a bit.

Found the cancer charity BACUP's site on the Internet. It's excellent. I'm trying to avoid the ones about dodgy 'cures' (such as: to cure cancer, swing from the chandelier daily and rub raspberry jam into your left kneecap). There are also one or two very sad ones from the States, where cancer patients are letting rip at the medical profession which has failed to cure them.

Jill W. phoned today and said she would like me to include my current predicament in the Mothers' Union *Home and Family* magazine column which I've just started writing for her. I'm no John Diamond, but maybe it's OK as long as I do it in a relevant and constructive way. It shouldn't be self-therapy. Poor John Diamond has had enough stick for his columns.[5] Talking of which, isn't it ironic that it was only a few weeks before my diagnosis that *The Times on Saturday* magazine printed my letter in response to his column? Maybe cancer is catching! Perhaps reading his column has prepared me for this. (Can anything prepare you for this? Forget about the marriage prep course we were thinking of writing. We could do a cancer prep course instead: shave your head; find your favourite way of inducing nausea; gain or lose three stone; become intimate with needles; spend a day every so often being scared beyond belief—Alton Towers will do. Will my sense of humour become blacker?)

There is a genuine sense of 'This isn't really happening to me' about life at the moment. Like watching your football team lose hopelessly from the sidelines. But that feeling is fading slowly, as if the dream world is slowly melting into reality and a realization that it's permanent. This *is* real life. I think trying to 'be positive' all the time will create stress in itself. The important thing is to be honest. I need to get a good balance between being optimistic, knowing God's in control and being real about how I feel.

The biopsy on Wednesday means that I can still see Ian C. about work projects on Monday and will be able to go to Cardiff for meetings on Tuesday, which will be a treat! I want to see all the lovely gang at *Care for the Family*!

SATURDAY 13 MARCH, MORNING

Woke up feeling sweaty, but positive. Positively sweaty, then, we conclude. I'm sitting up in bed and the sun is shining through the grey clouds outside. Maybe that just about sums it all up. Lord, I marvel at your gentle blessing and the way you assure me of your love.

Telling people about this illness before they find out the wrong way has been tricky. I don't want to keep on or shout about it but people do need to know. Their reactions are so difficult to cope with. I feel as if I need to reassure them, but I haven't always got the resources to comfort them too. The other thing that's interesting is that people always immediately want to tell you about their Great-aunt Annie who also had what you think you've got and how she recovered 30 years ago and is now world pole-vault champion. And, by the way, went on to have ten children. I know they think it should help, but for some reason it doesn't. It just puts pressure on me to do the same. I'm really only encouraged by the black-and-white medical research and statistics that give me a hopeful survival rate. Maybe I'll change. I keep being told about the relatively high survival rate for Hodgkin's, too, as if I wouldn't have found that out for myself already! It seems mean, but it makes me kind of impatient and it doesn't help.

It's difficult for Mum and Dad. A real shock for them. Mum's reaction is very emotional. But I must let them react and cope in their own way. I'm also anxious that people don't stop sharing their own problems with me. It would be awful to become so self-centred about this that I miss everyone else's needs. Problems are still problems whatever they are. I suggested to Jill W., struggling with her own family problems, that we ought to join forces on a book entitled *Life… it's like walking up a wall in wellies and a ballgown*.

James Jones today included a lovely hymn by Timothy Dudley-Smith, based on Psalm 91.

Safe in the shadow of the Lord,
beneath his hand and power,
I trust in him,
I trust in him,
my fortress and my tower.

My hope is set on God alone
though Satan spreads his snare;
I trust in him,
I trust in him,
to keep me in his care.

From fears and phantoms of the night,
from foes about my way,
I trust in him,
I trust in him,
by darkness as by day.

His holy angels keep my feet
secure from every stone;
I trust in him,
I trust in him,
and unafraid go on.

Strong is the everlasting Name,
and in my Father's care,
I trust in him,
I trust in him,
who hears and answers prayer.

Safe in the shadow of the Lord,
possessed by love divine,
I trust in him,
I trust in him,
and meet his love with mine.

Lord, it's amazing that this book of readings I bought before the diagnosis has been so appropriate. You've used them so well to encourage me. Maybe one day I'll get the opportunity to say thank you to James Jones. Thank you for the way you prompted me to buy it. Your attention to detail is awesome.

MOTHER'S DAY, SUNDAY 14 MARCH

Am trying not to wonder how many more of these special days I'll see. Coughing and discomfort meant I woke up constantly through the night and then R's alarm went off at 5.45am, just after I'd finally drifted back to sleep. He moves so fast to try to turn it off before it wakes me that I end up silently giggling! R has been so sensitive today, understanding how I feel. Especially when I had a little weep as the kids gave me their presents and cards. Best to be honest about that. Benj gave me a card with 'Mum for the Millennium' on it. Will I make it that far?

Church was extraordinary. One or two people who'd heard the news about the cancer were very kind; others just 'looked' at me! I guess they just didn't know what to say, if anything, but it felt dreadful from my perspective. Must remember that. Wonderfully, there was a family communion today and Benj decided, quite of his own accord, that he' like to take communion for the first time. He said he understood it all and felt he was ready to take that extra step. So *all* of us took communion together on Mother's Day. An extra special bonus for a lovely day.

R has phoned my brothers so that they know our situation, partly because I'm feeling very fragile today and partly because I'm just getting fed up with talking about cancer. I want to get on and enjoy what is a beautiful sunny day with the children. Lois worked very hard cooking a beautiful meal. I am so proud of her.

James Jones' reading was perfectly apt again today. It's amazing. Reflecting on Psalm 89, he writes:

God is not a spectator of human suffering. In Jesus we meet the God who cries and suffers pain… Jesus sets the life of each of us in the context of eternity… This greater reality—heaven—offers a new perspective on this life, inviting us to keep a sense of proportion about all that befalls us… I am not suggesting the mouthing of pious platitudes to people in pain but I am encouraging myself and all disciples of Jesus to break out of the contemporary mould of reacting to calamities and disasters as if we lived for this life only… To know God means that, even in suffering, there is blessing. (pp. 85, 87)

MONDAY 15 MARCH

I'm due to see Ian C. today about a work project he might be involved in. Trouble is, I feel so groggy that I don't feel I can be either intelligent or articulate (any different from normal, then?)—yet I need to be both in order to get the best from that time. I also don't want the time to be dominated by cancer talk, yet Ian is bound to ask me how I feel about it all. And of course we still haven't got a definite diagnosis. It could still be something else. Fowl pest, or foot and mouth, or some incredibly rare illness that scientists will pay me thousands to learn about. Dream on.

Evening

Today's meeting with Ian was fine. I don't think I was *that* muddle-headed. But then, I'm so muddle-headed I probably wouldn't notice, would I?

Rob P. phoned tonight. He is such a darling, so gentle on the phone. 'Make her well, Lord,' he prayed. I think we were both in tears by the time he'd finished. Andrea phoned too, as Lois had mentioned something to Anna at school. I hardly see Andrea, yet she took the trouble to phone and realistically offer help and support and someone to talk to. I'm glad Lois is talking to someone. I'm so concerned about R, L and B and how they'll cope. R is sometimes quite 'detached'. He needs to find his own way through and I need to give him space to do that, but it's hard sometimes.

Practically, the plan at the moment is that I'll stay in the hospital overnight on Wednesday as I've got the second CT scan on Thursday. I'm looking forward to going to Cardiff tomorrow and seeing everyone, but I'm also a little apprehensive. I'm bound to be met with lots of love and care, which will doubtless make me weepy.

Lord, all I need to know right now is that you love us all.

TUESDAY 16 MARCH, 3PM

Have left the office after my round of meetings and am just about to leave Cardiff station *en route* for Bristol. Can't help wondering when I'll be back. Jonathan B. (known as 'our intrepid Director' since the bike ride) was brilliant and walked me to the station. He was as practical as ever in the suggestions he made for how things might go in the months ahead. It's lovely knowing I've got so much support from them. My wonderful team gave me the most beautiful bouquet of white lilies. I hope they know how much I love them all. I feel as if I just want to get on with it now.

WEDNESDAY 17 MARCH

Biopsy day. Ho hum. (Why do I feel like whistling 'Mac the Knife?' under my breath?) I'm meant to be staying in tonight, but in retrospect that seems a bit pointless when my CT scan isn't until 4.30pm tomorrow. I'll be sitting around, twiddling my thumbs all day. Unless the op leaves me feeling so ill that I have to stay in. (The other singing alternative could be 'I've got you under my skin…' But not for long, if I can help it!)

Please just give me your peace today, Lord. Be with JR as he does this op, and with all the staff who assist him. Keep me positive, even when the op site is sore later.

10.11pm

Biopsy all done and I'm home again! Didn't need to stay in after all. Felt rough when I first came round in recovery and couldn't stop coughing. I've got a sore throat and wonder if a tube or something was rammed down a bit hard. My armpit is very sore, with the occasional digging pain, but not half as bad as I was expecting. They've given me enough pain-killers to last until the end of the year (that's private health care for you!) JR only let me go home on condition that I get lots of rest. He even knows me well enough to accompany the warning with a wagging finger! (His stitching is very neat, by the way.)

The private ward was quite a revelation! Like being in a four-star hotel. The nurse told me to take advantage of the food. So, seeing as taking proper medical advice seemed important, I decided to book myself in for dinner. Before I went down for the op, the chef paid me a visit. Important to get priorities right. (He was there longer than the anaesthetist!) I chose an evening meal from a menu that looked as if it should be on a table at the Dorchester. My goodness, the nurse was right! Not wanting to miss out on anything, I chose smoked salmon to start—yes, smoked salmon —then chicken with grapes.

'What vegetables would you like?' he asked.

'What have you got?'

'Anything; you choose.'

So I chose broccoli and carrots. Then summer pudding and clotted cream for dessert. It's worth being ill for! I'm just so glad that I felt like eating by supper-time. At least my appetite's not gone. I tried not to think about the wide divide between food in private health care and the NHS. But anyway, thank you, Lord!

THURSDAY 18 MARCH

Really good night (all that food, no doubt) with very little soreness. Only had one dose of pain-killers. Throat is still stiff on swallowing, but it's getting better. Thank you, Lord; it could have been so much worse. Feel weak and funny, so I'll stay in bed this morning and have a slow start later, before going back to the hospital for the scan.

9.50am

My friend Mandy has just phoned. She's going to see our mutual friends Amanda and Victor in Bristol tomorrow and wanted to know if I had a message. Not quite the kind of message I wanted to send, really, but Mandy can do it well. She's been through all this herself so often, so she'll even know the best way to tell them. The timing of her call was perfect. I'd felt I wanted to ring her, but feared upsetting her. Mandy has lived with her own cancer on and off for years. I didn't want to give her mine to live with too. But, knowing Mandy, she'll want to live with it.

Lord, I feel as if you are attending to all the details around the edge as a larger picture unfolds. I know such peace and security at the moment. It's as if I am balanced safely in the palm of your hand, and anxiety seems so diluted by your peace that it's hardly noticeable. You are giving such a sense of your love and protection and the clear knowledge that we can rest in it. Thank you, Lord.

Evening

Second scan over. It was hilarious waiting for it. Had to drink vast (and I mean vast) quantities of white, glutinous drink with a very odd, sweet taste. Three of us were at it together, our glamorous plastic beakers balanced precariously on the side of the table. We were under strict instructions from a very officious, humourless assistant to make each drink last an hour. There was a large pot plant in an enormous container just next to the seats. I couldn't help wondering how many beakers of the glutinous stuff it had been given over the years. That's probably why it looked so healthy. The choice of piped music wafting across the waiting-room was priceless. When I first arrived, it changed from a Tina Turner sound-alike to Latin American dance tunes. I was told with amusement by the others not to complain as the music I'd missed earlier had sounded like something written for Brezhnev's funeral!

'The others' had been waiting for nearly two hours, as an emergency patient was being scanned. They were scared they might have to drink another load of the white stuff because of the delay. When the emergency patient was wheeled out from the scan room, we realized that we should have been happy to wait days for her. She was unconscious and full of so many tubes that I can't imagine how they got her on to the scanner. We silently counted blessings. The scan was very straightforward. Coloured dye injected into my arm as a bonus today. Am now blue-blooded! Have developed that skill called 'waiting' now. No wonder we're called 'patients'.

FRIDAY 19 MARCH

Have 'waited' all day, hoping JR will phone with the CT results. I'm selfishly behaving as if I'm the only patient he's got! He's doubtless seeing dozens in a worse state than me every day. I've had so many calls from holiday companies, time-shares, investments companies and replacement window salesmen, yet all I want is information about lumps! Have these people got any idea what slow torture it is having to talk to them? Once the last window salesman had finished running through every available window and door combination, I asked, 'Have you got any CT scan results?' to which he replied, 'No, I don't think so.' Maybe I should ask JR if he does conservatories as well as biopsies.

Made the mistake of looking up sarcoidosis on the Internet and wish

I hadn't. It seems a dreadful debilitating disease, which does nothing but make you feel and look progressively awful. Feel quite low tonight. Help me to hang on in there, Lord. There are bound to be bad days. But having to wait again for results is almost a symptom. 'Not Knowing' syndrome is painful too.

Later

Had a good cry in the bath, which made me feel a lot better. Best to have a good weep and then move on, I think. It's just as well that I encouraged R to go to his Lib Dem meeting and the kids are glued to the TV. I'll just have to make the weekend busy, so that Monday comes faster.

SATURDAY 20 MARCH

Worrying in the night. Silly things. Like, if this is sarcoidosis everyone will think, 'Thank goodness it's not cancer', and not understand how awful it is. I even worry that they'll think I was making the cancer up! Why are the night hours such a prime time for sensationalism and scariness? It's as if they stretch on and on long enough to allow your imagination to entertain every worst scenario! It's like being trapped in a horror movie cinema for a very long programme—and without any ice-creams in the interval. This has got to be the longest weekend in history and it's not even Saturday night yet!

R has gone back into work this morning. I felt like screaming at him when he went out of the door, 'Excuse me—remember me? I'm your wife and I'm sitting here waiting for a cancer diagnosis!'

He's not being uncaring. Just coping as he needs to. And, after all, if I don't tell him that's how I feel, how will he know? Talked to our surgeon friend, Chris, earlier on the phone, which was helpful, as he said the up and down reaction is quite normal at this stage and not to worry. I've almost had a touch of the 'Why mes?' which hasn't happened before. I just feel as if I'm carrying it all on my own today. I wish there was someone to cuddle! Last night I cuddled my pillow to sleep as R was late back. Now is all that self-pity or what?

Sorry, Lord. Today, I'm finding it Tough with a capital T.

SUNDAY 21 MARCH

Had a dreadful coughing fit, which left me exhausted before I went to sleep last night. This happens often. I had tried to read the next instalment of Benj's bedtime book to him earlier. Poor old Benj. It's months since I've been able to read more than a paragraph of his book without coughing and spluttering. But I woke feeling brighter. We're off to Truro today to see R's mum's new flat, which will be something positive to do.

Evening

It was good to see Granny's beautiful new flat. But for the first time I experienced what it feels like when you don't know if you'll live to see things in the future. R's sister Hilary was talking about the long-term future of the flat, and about holidays for next year. I just didn't know if I'd see either. It was as if it wasn't my world. Felt very odd. I'm not sure if Hilary has really grasped the implications of our situation, or maybe it's just her way of coping. She seemed to think we should have a party for R's 40th. It's about the time I'm likely to be starting chemo! It was as if she'd just pushed reality away. Or maybe it's optimism. What I'm learning fast is that for everyone, family member, friend or patient, there is no predictable or right or wrong way to react to cancer.

Driving back in the car, we talked about Coln St Aldwyns in the Cotswolds, where we spent our honeymoon. We're due to go up to Julian's wedding in Cambridge in a couple of weeks, so maybe (if I'm allowed to go) we'll be able to return via the Cotswolds. I so want to see it all again. The beautiful walk by the mill house and the little cottage we stayed in. It suddenly seems very important to go.

Hopefully someone will phone with the test news tomorrow. ('Test' is another one of those words with changing connotations. It always used to mean academic test at worst, Test Match at best, and pregnancy in between!)

MONDAY 22 MARCH

Cough still very annoying. There must be a tumour pressing on my lungs and windpipe. Don't feel terribly bright. Legs ache. Very tired. Boring, boring. Must keep busy.

Evening

No call all day. Rang JR's secretary at lunch-time. She said the results weren't 'up' yet (whatever that means) but that she'd chase them and that he *might* phone early this evening. I waited until 8.15pm; no call. By this time I was getting very anxious and just sat on the lounge sofa praying for some peace in it all. Into my head came the words of the first and second verse of one of the songs we occasionally sing at church:

> *Be still and know that I am God.*
> *Be still and know that I am God.*
> *Be still and know that I am God.*
>
> *I am the Lord that healeth thee.*
> *I am the Lord that healeth thee.*
> *I am the Lord that healeth thee.*

Well, what more could I say? Or pray. Thank you, Lord.

Later

Liza phoned tonight. She's so good for me. She told me that maybe they haven't phoned today because they can't find anything! She had my 'reading list' for going into hospital all worked out. Everything I'd always wanted to read and never got round to. Made me feel like I was going on holiday! The friends who know me best really are the most helpful. Thank you so much for them, Lord. So now I'm sitting up in bed feeling a lot more philosophical about the whole thing and thinking, 'Tomorrow is another day (to wait for phone calls…).' Also thinking that if it's cancer I don't want to 'fight' it. That may be a metaphor that helps some people but I really don't think it's me. I've never fought anything in my life and I'm not convinced that fighting is the best tactic with this now. I shall just ask it very nicely if it would mind shifting, try to get to know it a bit and give it a polite shove if it doesn't respond. I'm not a combat soldier. Yet I also agree with John Diamond who says:

I despise the set of warlike metaphors that so many apply to cancer. My antipathy to the language of battles and fights has nothing to do with pacifism and everything to do with a hatred for the sort of morality which says that only those who fight against their cancer survive it or deserve to survive it—the corollary being that those who lose the fight deserved to do so.[6]

TUESDAY 23 MARCH

Felt a bit rough during the night. Chest is aching a bit and I feel out of sorts. But it's special sitting here, writing this, listening to the kids downstairs laughing and chatting. Lois made the most gorgeous chocolate cake last night! So, we just get on with today and see what it brings. Trying very hard to avoid the pent-up *angst* of yesterday. Whatever the news, Lord, help me to hear it in your peace; help me to accept it and act on it as you would want me to.

James Jones is very appropriate again; he suggests reading Psalm 119 as a source of images of God to use for meditation. I think that's really what I need to do. Lord, keep my focus on you instead of the illness.

Evening

Still no call from JR. Gave up expecting it in the end, especially as I had a call from Dr P's secretary (he's the top consultant haematologist; nothing but the best for me!) at 9am this morning asking me to go for an appointment with him at 11am tomorrow morning. Gosh! No hanging around there! Is it worrying or reassuring that it's fast? Both, I guess. Jacqui says she's 90 per cent sure that if it's Dr P it must be lymphoma.

Had a good time with Lois tonight, talking it all through.

Funny what it all does to you. Suddenly I'm noticing how wonderfully expressive people's faces are. Especially old ladies! And the tiniest, simplest things take my breath away. I've read about finding new joy in what was previously mundane in this kind of situation. It's as if everything is precious, worth taking the time to look at and appreciate. Almost as if life is being experienced for the first time. Strangely enough, not as if you're about to lose your sight of the world, but as if you've just gained it.

It will be a month almost exactly tomorrow since I went to the GP and had the chest X-ray.

—— *Part Two* ——

THE VALLEY OF BACA

WEDNESDAY 24 MARCH. D-DAY

So much to pray about this morning. The consultation; the fact that R is so busy, without all this on top; the children and how they'll cope; the right questions to be asked and the right way of telling other people what's likely to be bad news. Again, James Jones is so appropriate, on 'The Lord our Keeper'.

The eyes of faith enable us to see that every situation is within God's mysterious purpose and no situation is beyond God's power to change… For us as well there will be any number of situations, such as illness… that will make us doubt God's love for us. But however bad and tragic all these things are, when we are 'in Christ' they can never ever separate us from God. (p. 131)

He also includes the same verses from Habakkuk that I wrote up for R some time ago, to pin on the study wall for when things were tough for him.

> *Though the fig tree does not blossom*
> *and no fruit is on the vines;*
> *though the produce of the olive fails*
> *and the fields yield no food;*
> *though the flock is cut off from the fold*
> *and there is no herd in the stalls,*
> *yet I will rejoice in the Lord,*
> *I will exult in the God of my salvation.*
> (Habakkuk 3:17–18, NRSV)

Evening

It's definitely cancer. 'Yet I will rejoice in the Lord.'

It's Hodgkin's lymphoma, which (evidently) is 'good'. Better than Non-Hodgkin's anyway. Basically cancer of the lymphatic system. A few more tests are needed to 'stage' it properly, so that the doctors know how far it's gone. Stage one means early days, two further on, three pretty desperate and four very desperate. They also add any symptoms I've got to the equation (the glamorous night sweats, itchy skin and so on).

I liked Dr P. Very Scottish, very straight-talking. No nonsense, which I appreciate. And, hooray, a black sense of humour there somewhere. (How else would you cope in his job?) He mentioned that I would lose hair from everywhere as a result of chemotherapy. 'What, everywhere?' I asked. 'Yes, I'm afraid so,' he replied. So I turned to R and said, 'Well, at least I won't have to shave my legs this summer!' Dr P. seemed to approve of that reaction. He also checked that we've had enough babies, as I'll have such vast doses of chemo that all my baby bits will shut down and I'll have an early menopause. Two will have to do! He cannot treat me privately as cancer treatment needs a team approach, so it's back on the NHS. As John Diamond says, 'Private hospitals are wonderful places if you're slightly ill and need a reasonable hotel with nurses in attendance, but they tend to come second-best *in extremis*.'[7] Whether that's true or not, I'm not bothered, as long as God's the Medical Director.

I'm on auto-pilot for R's and the kids' sake. I think the diagnosis may take some time to sink in, but it's a relief that I now know what it is. I've got a bone marrow biopsy tomorrow, which is supposed to be a picnic-and-a-half, so I'm not looking forward to that! A lung function test is happening before that and a cardiogram on Friday or Monday. That completes the 'staging'. Then I can start chemo.

As I'm going to lose my hair, they advised me to have it cut short. Firstly, so that it's less of a shock and also so that I don't have to vacuum the bed for long strands. (Will I have to vacuum up my trouser legs too?) I'll obviously have to get into bohemian clothes to go with my headscarf fashion for the next nine months. Not really me, but it might be fun to indulge that arty side of my personality! And, of course, I can indulge my penchant for hats!

All this has stunned R. In the car on the way home he was again saying, 'Why us?' I think he was really meaning, 'Why us *again*?' It does seem we've had more than our fair share of illness in 14 years of marriage—but what's anybody's 'fair share'? I feel a bit fragile, but OK. Had a lovely lunch at the 'Who'd Have Thought It' to celebrate the diagnosis. Discovered Salcombe Dairy coffee ice-cream. Yum. We'll have to go back to celebrate the outcome one day, too.

THURSDAY 25 MARCH

Lots of 'little things' seem to be annoying me that I really can't do anything about. I thought I'd stop worrying about the 'little things' (like Lois' lost brace, my sniffles, a dirty kitchen floor already) but they just seem to get irksome and irritating. Maybe it's because subconsciously I want to get rid of them all so that I can concentrate my energies on the 'big thing'. At the same time, I'm already feeling that we can't let cancer dominate our lives. Yes, it will dictate to a certain extent, and change our lifestyle, but it shouldn't be allowed to yell at us all—not unless we're allowed to yell back! I dug out some of my old scarves this morning and tried them on; very chic (if you try hard and squint)!

Evening

Felt very low and fragile this morning. Andrea invited me round for toast and coffee at lunch-time, which was thoughtful. Took my mind off the tests, and she drove me to the hospital afterwards. The lung function test was hilarious—lots of puffing and blowing into tubes and bottles which looked like something designed by Heath Robinson. I breathed in the wrong place at one point and nearly got my knuckles rapped by the very efficient technician. Wish I could say that the bone marrow biopsy was as much fun. The least said about that the better. Let's just say that I can think of a million better ways to spend a Thursday afternoon!

Had a chat with the nurse about chemo. It takes between two and three hours to give each dose through a small tube called a cannula, with drugs to take alongside at home. She also said it's best to get your hair cut so that when it starts to go thin and fall out you're quite glad to get rid of it all. (Oh really?) She mentioned that the 'appliance lady' would pay me a visit. So enraptured am I by the idea of an 'appliance lady' that even though I don't want a wig I must see this woman. My mind is boggling! I can see there is plenty of scope for hilarity in all this. Although my back is a bit sore from the biopsy this afternoon, I'm feeling much more positive tonight. Lord, I just pray that the cancer will stay where it is. It's already in two sites. As I already have some symptoms, it's stage two—hence chemotherapy rather than radiotherapy (it's too extensive for that). And, Lord, I pray that my lungs and heart won't be too damaged by the drugs. Thank you for being with me today. I have a sense that in these last days you have never left my side. It's as if you've been in every spare chair next to me, so I've never been alone.

FRIDAY 26 MARCH

A beautiful, sunny morning. And, hooray, a day ahead without being prodded, poked or having a needle stuck somewhere! (R said he could arrange it if I'm missing it!) I'm planning a 'pre-siege' shopping trip to town. (I bet R's twin credit card is twitching in his wallet!) Dr P. says I must keep away from crowds for a bit because of the risk of infection, so it might be my last shopping trip for a while. Will look for hats. Must also get R another wedding anniversary card, as Lois has pointed out that the one I've bought is exactly the same as last year's!

Evening

I think I overdid it today. Exhausted after my trip to town. Chest pain and other aches. Must pace myself. Had a hilarious time buying hats. One of the big stores conveniently had a '20 per cent off' sale, so I thought I would take advantage of it. Just chose simple, cheap, pull-on ones. I spent about half an hour trying on various styles, much to the interest of the assistant behind the nearest perfume counter, who must have thought I was some kind of mad eccentric. (What perception!) Her face was a picture when I walked off with a pile of six to buy!

The booklets have arrived from BACUP today. They're very impressive. Easy to read, well written and informative. Spoke to my brother Chris on the phone tonight (talking of mad eccentrics!). He is incredulous that I am being treated by a doctor who he thinks sounds more like a Scottish alternative comedian. I guess he could be described as that. Chris has also enjoyed the delights of bone marrow biopsies because of his MS, diagnosed last year, so we could swap notes. He has more juicy, gruesome adjectives in his!

SATURDAY 27 MARCH

Another uncomfortable night coughing, retching and feeling ill, complete with night sweat. Thank goodness R sleeps through more or less anything. I really am a textbook Hodgkin's case! It was interesting reading the John Diamond column in *The Times* today. His honesty is so refreshing, and no matter how much flak he gets for 'self-therapy writing', I think he's brilliant. In a wildly different philosophical vein, today James Jones' reading is about overcoming obstacles on a path to maturity, with the verse from Job 23:10: 'He knows the way that I take; when he has tested me I shall come out as gold.' Will I, Lord?

Evening

Had a good weep while hoovering our upstairs bedroom before moving down to the guestroom. R sat on the bed hugging me while I howled! I was wondering if I'd ever sleep up there again. Our pretty pink bedroom with beautiful views of Plymouth Sound. Now I've set up the room downstairs it looks fine. I just feel a bit daunted at the thought of how ill I'm likely to be in there!

PALM SUNDAY 28 MARCH

First morning waking up in the new room. I can still see the blue sky above the curtains, just a slightly lower bit of blue sky! It is a calm and restful place to wake. I'm thankful we had the option to move rooms. I booked a meal out for us today, as it might be some time before we can do that if I'm supposed to keep away from crowds. I honestly don't see how practical or necessary that will be. But I guess I should do what I'm told! I am beginning to compile in my head a list of 'Tips for Dealing with People with Cancer'.

- I know I've said it before, but don't tell us about your great-aunt who survived the cancer we've got and went on to become pole-vault champion, had ten children and wrote four novels. It doesn't help. It puts pressure on us to do the same. (And there's only enough room in the world for so many pole-vault champions, novels and children!)

- A cancer diagnosis does not mean we suddenly get a reduction in our IQ or life expectancy. You don't have to talk to us (a) as if we are two years old or (b) as if we are about to die. Neither do you have to try out your Joyce Grenfell impersonation on us.
- Life goes on. Sometimes we need to talk about every minute detail of the cancer, but most of the time we'd prefer not to. It's still fun to talk about the things we always used to talk about—books, art, shopping, food, *EastEnders*, the guy up the street and his string of women and especially, oh especially, the things that bother *you*. Just because we've got one or two lumpy problems of our own it doesn't mean we can't share the burden carried by somebody else!
- Ordinary things become very beautiful and strangely moving. Colours are vibrant. Faces are wonderful, especially babies', and old ladies carrying years of wisdom and experience in their faces. We might tend to flip at nature, beautiful views and clouds. Humour us a bit, please. Sometimes we can be surprised by the things that make us cry, laugh, get irritated, get angry or lose patience. Life has a changed perspective and emotions and priorities tend to change with it.
- We *do* usually notice when you cross the road or the room to avoid talking to us. Please don't. It hurts us and it's cowardly of you. If you don't know what to say, then say just so, but say *something*. Even just the first few words. We'll help you say the rest.

Evening

We've just had a lovely meal out together. Watching Benj and R share a huge chocolate ice-cream sundae was very special! Can hardly bear to watch the children. They're so precious. Please, Lord, let's get on with this treatment soon. I want to LIVE, LIVE, LIVE. (And I want to be able to eat the ice-cream sundae with them next time—tonight I felt too ill.)

MONDAY 29 MARCH

A good night's sleep, but very odd dreams. I dreamed I was back at school and planning to take Friday off in a very blasé manner. I wanted to shout at myself, 'Don't you dare; get working!' R and I talked about writing wills this morning. (Aren't we cheerful?) Trying to be practical. I also want to write a 'living will' about what I want 'done' with me if I become really ill. I suppose that really *is* cheerful. Seems best to do it in a clear frame of mind. But it's such a big 'if' at the moment, I don't think I need rush for the pen yet.

Evening

There was a wonderful piece in *The Times* this morning, profiling Donna Marie Keyes, one of the Omagh victims, at her wedding, with a beautiful photograph alongside. Puts things into perspective somewhat.

Fiona rang today. Obviously shocked at my news, but very supportive and caring. Also got me laughing, as usual! She said that when Roy lost all his hair Don McClean told him not to worry: he could always go to a fancy-dress party as a roll-on deodorant! She also told me of others who'd made it. It's clearly meant as an encouragement and it seems ungrateful to dismiss it, but I feel I almost need to in case I can't match up. Cancer is exclusive and individual (makes it sound like designer wear... if only). What goes for someone else won't necessarily go for me.

Cardiogram tomorrow. That completes the full set of tests. Wonder if I get a badge.

TUESDAY 30 MARCH

Waited one-and-a-half hours for the cardiogram—they forgot me! Bit embarrassing having this guy run something like a microphone all over my jelly-covered boobs. (Well, under and around them.) Especially as he seemed to have stopped off for a sense of humour bypass on the way in. But hey, so what? Dignity will disappear with my hair, I expect.

I saw JR as I was walking into the hospital but could hardly say hello, as my mouth was full of Mars bar. He seemed quite amused by that! I wasn't really pigging out—just keeping my energy levels up!

Watching the news about Kosovo tonight also puts things into perspective. Refugee numbers are frighteningly large. And all just wandering aimlessly. How many mothers among the throng have as yet undetected cancer, complicated pregnancies, or will lose babies *en route*, before or after birth? How many will not survive because they won't have organized medical care? Most are without the support of their partners, whom they've seen driven away to unknown destinations which are probably too terrifying to think about. Yet they are ordinary women, like me, who wanted ordinary motherhood. But motherhood is about facing pain and mothering on, regardless. These women are unsung heroines, and mostly we don't give them a thought. What a contrast to the woman in front of me in the Post Office yesterday who moaned at the assistant behind the counter, 'Oh, I hate Mondays!' I wanted to shout, 'Oh, I love them; give them to me every day!' We're alive, safe, fed and healthy (almost), aren't we?

Dr P.'s secretary has made an appointment for my chemo to start on Thursday.

Wig joke: A lorry load of wigs was stolen from a lorry in Plymouth today. Police are combing the area. (Benj read it somewhere!)

WEDNESDAY 31 MARCH

Touching cards and letters in the post this morning. Some from people I've not heard from for years, lending their support. I only hope I get the opportunity to give it back one day. They must be hard letters to write. My college friend Jenny has sent me a magazine cutting which declares that headscarves are definitely 'in' this summer. (Well, of course: I arranged it with the editor of *Vogue*!)

Treated myself to a CD in town. (My *second* 'last' shopping trip!) Didn't realize when I bought it that the *Agnus Dei* it contains is that beautiful piece of music I've been trying to find for ages. But you did, Lord, didn't you? And it was the first track on the CD! As I listened, I kept thinking about how good you are to me and said so out loud. As I did, I could almost hear you saying over and over again, 'I love you, I love you', as if it is all that matters. Of course it is. Didn't I pray a while ago: 'All I really need to know is that you love us'?

Evidently, everybody prayed for me in groups at the *Care for the Family* staff awayday yesterday. Andrew said, 'We all sat around in groups and just went for it.' I really do think that with the amount of prayer that's going on for me I should come out of all this a size 8 and looking like Michelle Pfeiffer. (R would love that!)

THURSDAY 1 APRIL

Is this really a good date to have your first dose of chemotherapy? Maybe when I get there they'll say, 'April Fool! You haven't got cancer after all.'

Part of me is glad that something is going to be done today; another part can't really believe I've got cancer. And, what's more, I'm not sure which part thinks what. I've had such a variety of reports as to what this is going to be like. Extremes ranging from, 'He drove himself to and from the hospital for chemo before ballooning around the world' to, 'I had to wheel her out on a trolley; she said it felt like four hangovers having a reunion.' I guess it will be somewhere in between. But I do really feel I ought to be sending some kind of warning and apology to all those bits of my body that are behaving so beautifully—or they might pretend they don't know me when all this is over; or, at the very least, they might feel terribly betrayed that I spent six months effectively poisoning them just to get rid of a few stubborn lumpy bits. Will I and my immune system ever trust each other again?

It's going to be pretty obvious that I'm the new kid on the block in chemo today. Is there an initiation, I wonder? Or an accepted way of behaving? Maybe there's a pecking order, or everyone has their favourite armchair.

Lord, please help me in my relationship with those around me, nurses and patients. They can teach me a lot. There's enough to learn.

I received so many beautiful cards this morning. The postman must think it's my birthday every day. So many rich words. Then why do I still feel so alone? Must remember what I read yesterday: Psalm 22, from which Jesus quoted on the cross: 'My God, my God, why have you forsaken me: why are you so far from helping me, and from the words of my groaning?' James Jones wrote:

In this psalm, and especially in Jesus quoting from it, we find permission to express our sorrows and doubts... Here is the paradox: it is in the moment of

48

desolation that the sufferer binds himself fastly to God… In spite of the catastrophes surrounding him, God was still 'my God'. And that is how he reached out to him. (pp. 154–155)

It's true that written within the very words 'my God' there is a statement of trust.

I've just read James Jones' passage for today. He writes:

In a time of loneliness our heart fills up with a sense that God loves us; in a period of confusion our mind is flooded with peace, sensing that there is a purpose at work in and through the chaos; in a moment of darkness a placid joy mingles with our tears as an unexpected light pierces the gloom, inspiring us to persevere. These experiences are intimations that God is with us. (p. 157)

God, be with me.

Evening

No chemo (but sadly no April fool either). When I arrived on the ward, there was no record of my appointment for chemo. Instead, I had to see Dr P, who explained that I needed to know more details before treatment was started. He explained the options for a four-drug or eight-drug clinical trial, or for an eight-drug regime if I don't opt for the trial. But it seems that most patients do. Then he dropped the double bombshell. There is also a tumour below my diaphragm, so I'm stage three for definite, and the cancer is behaving much more aggressively than originally thought. So it's advanced Hodgkin's. I feel as if it's advancing too—like an army, all guns blazing.

I left the hospital feeling as if I'd been given a second death sentence, and rang R from outside amid the smokers, whom I felt like murdering with my bare hands. R left the office to collect me. He said he just walked out, telling somebody simply that I needed him. I could just imagine him waving papers away and saying, 'Tough, my Wendy needs me!' We absorbed the shock together. So now R and I must chat through the options of the trial with Chris, who, being a surgeon, knows at least more than we do. I return to the hospital on Tuesday at 2.30pm when Dr P.

will ring the clinical trial office for the drug regimen to be selected at random. Chemo will then start on Thursday. It's a week behind, but Dr P. didn't like the idea of me starting chemo and maybe having problems over the Bank Holiday weekend.

We just weren't expecting any more news of this kind, thinking that the diagnosis was done and that was it. But obviously Dr P. has had more time to look at the test results in detail, and has discovered that things are worse than he thought. What must it be like for people who haven't anyone to ring, and who drive home alone with news like that and entertain it alone all evening?

GOOD FRIDAY 2 APRIL

After the trauma of yesterday, another bundle of cards and letters to cushion the blows this morning. Cards, cartoons and chocolate buttons. I feel very loved. The delay does have a silver lining in that I'll be able to go along to the St Andrew's Good Friday meditation today. Good Friday will have a different slant. By amazing God-given 'coincidence', the James Jones reading is perfect for Good Friday, perfect for me, and for now. Jesus' words in the Garden of Gethsemane: 'Now my soul is troubled. And what should I say—"Father, save me from this hour"? No, it is for this reason that I have come to this hour. Father, glorify your name' (John 12:27).

9.05pm

Those words, read out this afternoon, echoed with meaning through the meditations at St Andrew's. Although they seemed almost whispered by the reader, it was as if they bounced off the cold stone walls and hurled themselves at me. I was glad to be on my knees. I felt that if I had been standing I would have been knocked off balance. Lord, I know you are in this. What is it about? Where are you leading me? I feel in possession of a dark, fearful, unexplored yet wonderful treasure: that I might glorify your name. I can identify with those words of Jesus. Even though my suffering will be so much less, I know that mixture of feelings: of knowing you must be in the darkness with me, but also feeling abandoned.

I can remember reading that sometimes you are like someone trying to hide in the darkness who gives themselves away by clearing their throat. Will you be doing that so that I know you are there? Jesus first asked you to take it all away, didn't he, Father? But by the end of his prayer he had acknowledged that your glory is all. With that he surrendered himself, first to the suffering, but ultimately to your safe, eternal arms. I can do nothing less.

I am reminded of some words by Henri Nouwen: 'It would be just another illusion to believe that reaching out to God will free us from pain and suffering. Often, indeed, it will take us where we would rather not go.'

But I would rather go with pain and suffering where you are, than not go with you at all.

Later

Chris has just been here with us and we have prayed through the chemo options. We've decided that we'll opt for the trial, because then it gives God the option to choose. We can't believe that if we're praying the selection will be 'random'.

SATURDAY 3 APRIL

James Jones' reading this morning is about maturing through crisis. (Is God rewriting these pages each morning as I turn them? I almost feel like checking another copy to see if it's the same!) The verse at the end is so familiar: 'Yea, though I walk through the valley of the shadow of death I will fear no evil; for thou art with me' (Psalm 23:4). The notes conclude: 'Jesus, who has passed through this way, will be with us by his Spirit and will lead us out of the valley of the dying into the world of the truly alive.' Whether this journey will end in this world or the next, you have 'passed through this way' and will go with me. I found another passage in a book lent to R by Victor. It's by M. Craig Barnes, and says:

Our experiences of abandonment and unwanted change are crisis moments when we must decide whether or not to leave behind the life that has gone for ever. We can do that only if we believe in the ongoing creativity of God, who brings light and beauty to the dark chaos of our losses in life.[8]

This morning I posted a long letter to Rob and Jonathan (my 'bosses' at *Care for the Family*) to explain my situation. It will make a big difference to my work schedule. Others will have to pick up the projects I am working on. I can't imagine that they can wait for me. What all this means for the next year of my life, or the rest of my life, is starting to sink in.

On a point of vanity: I've just combed through my long fair hair. I'm going to find losing it very hard.

EASTER SUNDAY 4 APRIL, MORNING

It's so wonderful that I'll be able to go to church this morning, after all. Even if it's not for the kind of Easter Sunday we'd expected before all this. Yet somehow it's more precious.

Later

This morning we sang a new song I hadn't sung before:

> *My redeemer lives,*
> *and I will see his glory*
> *as he works all things together for my good.*
> *Whatever things occur, of this I can be sure;*
> *I know my redeemer lives.*
>
> *Even though I walk through the valley,*
> *I will fear no evil.*
> *He is with me;*
> *on the battlefield, although the pain is real,*
> *my struggles soon will fade*
> *as his glory is revealed.*[9]

Your timing is perfect, Lord; your assurance is consistent, offering an almost unbelievable security. I grabbed R's hand as we sang those words and was aware that your love surrounded all of us—Benj, who held my other hand, Lois alongside him. I can hardly imagine what is in this or what will come out of it. But there is no fear hidden in the blackness, only a strange, almost breathtaking excitement and sense of expectation… of you.

Reveal your glory, Lord.

MONDAY 5 APRIL

Easter obviously exhausted me—I slept until 9.05am this morning! My neck is very stiff (and I am still sweating buckets all night; I must be charming to sleep with!) I can feel a swelling on the right side of the base of my neck. It must be the pile of marbles that JR pointed out to me. Slightly unnerving to find them again.

TUESDAY 6 APRIL

Clinical trial allocation day today. I took the children to the hospital with me to see Dr P. They were eating crisps while we waited, which he tried to pinch, much to their amusement. I think they probably realize their mother is better off with someone slightly off-beam than a completely serious soul. I had some blood taken (Lois is fascinated and now wants to be a haematologist… until next month's idea comes along). And then Dr P. left the room to ring the clinical trials office. The children understood where he had gone and we sat quietly, praying silently. During the five minutes or so that he was gone, a sense of the most incredible peace and well-being filled the room. It was as if everything outside in the corridor had disappeared way into the distance. Sounds were muffled; no one disturbed us. Even the children sat very still, and we spoke in whispers. I'm not sure they understood, but I did. Your presence filled that room, Lord. You did not leave us alone.

So, the eight-drug trial it is, which pleases Dr P., as that's the one he would have chosen anyway. The first anti-sick drug is tonight, in readiness for chemo tomorrow.

WEDNESDAY 7 APRIL

I took Lois to the dentist at 8am. When I got back, three beautiful cards were waiting for me, filled with the most appropriate words. Particularly special, as none of the senders knew I was starting chemo today. Lord, you have prepared everything ahead. You are arranging the emotional support that I need before I realize I need it. You know I'm apprehensive about today. But because I know you, I have nothing to fear. I'll take the three cards with me—and the verses I've written out to read as I wait, which assure me of your love. They are all evidence of your care and protection, like the words these three cards contain:

'Peace be with you.'

'Be strong and take heart, all you who hope in the Lord.' (Psalm 31:24)

'Do not worry about anything, but in everything by prayer and petition, with thanksgiving let your requests be made known to God, and the peace of God which passes all understanding shall keep your hearts and minds in Christ Jesus.' (Philippians 4:6–7)

Be with R too, Lord—waiting at work and not knowing how I am. Let him know your reassurance.

Here goes.

7.25pm

Well. What a doddle!

Chemo was fine. Bit of a fiddle finding a vein. I don't feel a bit sick, so have just eaten a meal! (Takes a lot to stop me eating pasta!) But it's strange how for the first couple of hours afterwards you are just sitting around waiting to feel ill! It must be all those people I know who are praying for me. (What I mean is that their prayer is stopping me feeling ill—not that they make me feel ill!) I'm very aware of those prayers.

Have brought home a huge bag of tablets. If we combined them with all the toiletries and make-up belonging to Lois in the bathroom, we could open a branch of Boots. But I think I'd better take them. They're a matter of life and death. (I suppose Lois views her toiletries and make-up in much the same way!) Evidently, the steroids will kick in before long and I'll be extra perky and full of life! That'll make a change!

Thank you, Lord, for your wonderful peace today. I have felt so loved and cared for, with great tenderness and deep understanding. Please help me remember that in the tough patches ahead.

THURSDAY 8 APRIL

I feel a bit of a fraud. Not even a hint of sickness and I feel fine. I've been tablet-taking all day; it's quite complicated, but I'm sure it'll become second nature before long. (Most things to do with eating I pick up fairly quickly.) R says I am 'up a gear'. I am yapping away nineteen-to-the-dozen. (Rather like Joanna Lumley on speed, he says.) He has the day off today as he was expecting me to be really ill—and all I'm doing is talking. Rather more loudly than usual, and with great animation. Poor love. He'll be glad to get back to work tomorrow.

Evening

What a brilliant day. It's great to have so much energy again. Even if it is steroid-induced. I've got so much done—vacuuming top to bottom and six hours' work! This can't last, but I'll enjoy it while it does.

FRIDAY 9 APRIL

Not much sleep last night. The downside of the steroids, I guess. Woke at 2.30am and just couldn't get back to sleep again. Spent five hours working on the computer, only to lose the lot somehow or other. Was so tired I burst into tears. Have come up here to the bathroom for a rest. God, with his calm and gracious sense of humour, made sure that the first words I set my eyes on in my little book were: 'When in faith we take hold of his strength, he will change, wonderfully change, the most hopeless, discouraging outlook.'[10] That goes for my work and the wider issues. Wish it was possible to be constantly reminded of that, to have it pinned to my person with a big nappy-pin. And then, to prove that same sense of humour: 'He who numbers the hairs on your head (while they are still there, she adds) is not indifferent to your needs' (Matthew 10:29–32). Ha ha, very funny. I love you, Father.

It's Julian and Julie's wedding today in Cambridge and we're missing it. If only we'd known I would be feeling so well… but we couldn't have risked the journey.

SATURDAY 10 APRIL

R's birthday cake to make today, while he is at Saturday morning cinema with Benj.

4.45pm

R is very down. I have come upstairs to give him space. It's so difficult for him. He's 40 tomorrow and is lumbered with all this. He never complains and doesn't say very much, but it's obvious he is hurting, for all of us. He isn't taking any interest in his birthday—even in the food. I suppose we are both thinking it might be his last birthday with me. But isn't that a reason to make it special without declaring why?

In similarly morbid mood, there were three deaths from cancer out of five deaths in *The Times* obituaries this morning (I've taken to reading them). I wonder why it is that when someone dies of cancer the cause of death is mentioned? If someone dies from anything else it usually isn't. You'll see, 'Bill Brown died on 5 September from cancer…' but never 'Bill Brown died on 5 September from kidney disease,' or '… after falling from a tree'. Odd that. Maybe it's trendy or particularly dramatic to die from cancer. I'd rather not try it and find out. John Diamond, in his column, was debating the pros and cons of being 'given time' to live— what happens when the estimate turns out to be wrong and how people react. ('You still here, then?')

9pm

We've been lazy and bought boxes of Chinese ready-meals for R's birthday meal tomorrow. He is very low. My very presence must remind him of all we have to face together. I feel a burden, a disappointment and a liability. It's simply how *I* feel. Nothing he says or does implies that. He is always silently supportive. Often numb, I think.

We will have been married for 14 years on Tuesday.

SUNDAY 11 APRIL

R's 40th birthday. The children were primed to come into our bedroom at 8am, as they always do on birthdays. All these little 'always dos' are so precious. R opened up various West Ham United presents in a little celebration. Lois provided the beauty and Benj the cabaret. It's a beautiful Sunday morning. R's mum is coming about 6pm to join in the end of the celebrations. She'll stay to help until after my chemo on Wednesday at least, to see how I am.

Evening

We walked along the river near Saltram this afternoon and watched two beautiful swans and an extended family of ducklings. It looked as if they were doing exactly what families on the bank were doing: bumbling along, chatting together, rounding up children, calling for them to catch up. Benj was laughing at the way one of the ducklings was paddling hard but going nowhere—except round and round in circles. I know how it feels! We got back for the rugby, which was *ace*. Wales beat England 32–31 right at the last minute, just after R (the family England supporter) had walked out of the room grinning and saying, 'Well, we'll win now!' Benj and I were still hanging on for a miraculous Welsh victory and got what we wanted! We cheered, screamed and kissed each other for at least three hours... and teased R all this evening.

Don't count your ducklings before Neil Jenkins has scored, that's all I can say!

MONDAY 12 APRIL

My night began with a bizarre nightmare. I dreamed I was having to sleep in a long, tube-like hammock, rather like a straitjacket. It was hung in a cubicle on a train packed with hundreds of other people, and there was a pervading sense of fear and evil. It was so vivid, and infused with a sense of real panic. It now seems ridiculous in the bright light of day, but the sense of claustrophobia in the middle of the night was real enough.

Very jittery when I awoke this morning. Steroids. Pupils are dilating away like mad. Joanna Lumley wouldn't want this comparison. Perfect sense of peace again this morning as I prayed—reassuring after last night's dream. A sense of 'all will be well'. I was trying to express how I felt when I came across, 'But I will sing of your strength, in the morning I will sing of your love; for you are my fortress, my refuge in times of trouble' (Psalm 59:16), and Isaiah 54:10: 'Though the mountains be shaken and the hills be removed, yet my unfailing love for you will not be shaken nor my covenant of peace be removed, says the Lord, who has compassion on you.'

Sadly, I finished reading James Jones' *People of the Blessing* this morning. It's certainly been a blessing to this 'people'.

10pm

I have just read two whole chapters of *Charlie and the Great Glass Elevator* to Benjamin with enormous (steroid-aided) expression! American accents and everything... *without coughing once*! What an achievement. I haven't been able to do that for months. Benj is so proud! I was told the steroids would work quickly to reduce the inflammation, but that's amazing.

Bought some fabric for headscarves today. Ho hum. Will send it to Mum to sew for me. It's something she will feel able to do to help at a distance. (My sewing is legendary—the unbelievable kind of legend.)

TUESDAY 13 APRIL

Our 14th wedding anniversary. Woke up about 6am feeling strangely sad and cuddling into R. Went off to sleep again. He woke me at 7.30 with red roses and chocolate truffles. What a nice man! I think I might marry him!

We are both treading on eggshells with each other, lest we trigger the tears. Best not to think that this might be the last anniversary. (I don't think I'd die *that* quickly anyway!) I can't help wondering what we would have thought 14 years ago today if we'd known this was to come. Lord, what if, as I'd slipped into that beautiful wedding dress, there had been a knock on the door and a visitor had told me that 14 years later at the same time I would be taking cancer drugs and planning where to celebrate what might be my last anniversary with R? How would I have felt? Devastated? Disbelieving? Angry? Who knows? We were so young and optimistic. What followed has not been easy. We've had plenty of preparation for this time in the difficulties of the last few years. Illness, bereavement, work worries. Yet for that I'm grateful. If this had come to us when we had known 14 years of relative ease and calm, it would have been much worse. Our rough times together have been like an investment of the love and commitment between us. We know from experience that we can hang on, that you are there for us, Lord, always. We have tested that so often and know it to be true. And we have no reason to doubt that you will be there always through this too. R had no idea how much 'sickness' he was agreeing to stand by me for on that day. Where would I be without him? Please bless him especially today, Lord. He needs you so much.

Evening

Had the most beautiful meal at The Cott at Dartington. Fabulous food and friendly surroundings. (Even had Salcombe Dairy coffee ice-cream, which is fast becoming God's little culinary pick-me-up! This diary should double up as a Good Food diary!) The gorse across Dartmoor on the way seemed so vibrantly yellow, as if it was shouting for attention. Colours seem so much more beautiful—freshly painted—sharper, somehow. (And I don't think that's the steroids!) Icing on the anniversary cake on the work front too. Rob rang this morning to confirm that I'm working on the next book (*The Sixty Minute Mother*). Perfect timing, and good to know he feels I'm not on the scrap heap yet! (Just for that, I'll forgive him for getting me out of the shower—twice. The first time accidentally, the second deliberately—'just for fun!')

WEDNESDAY 14 APRIL

Dreadful night's sleep. Bad start with chemo today. Sleep and plenty of water to drink seems essential, in order to cope.

Early evening

Chemo was fine again. However, a two-hour wait for my blood results to be processed and checked held things up a bit. The nurses are so calm and organized. Nothing ruffles them. They're used to all the waiting, and know that very little hurries anything. Began to feel very sick as I stirred the cheese sauce for tea tonight. It got gradually worse, so I handed the sauce over to R's mum and went horizontal for a bit!

Started reading Hilary McDowell's *Some Day I'm Going to Fly*.[11]

I'm frustrated at what this school holiday has meant for the children. They have been stuck at home most of the time, whereas usually I would have the car and take them out at least once or twice. I'm angry that nobody has thought about what my illness means for them. Maybe I should just ask someone to include them in a swimming trip or outing, but I shouldn't have to ask. R says that people just don't think. Would I be any better? It seems that this illness disrupts so much. It's hard not to feel resentful. Do you mind me grumbling, Lord?

And now I've just read in Hilary McDowell's book:

Given back to God, any negatives can be transformed into the positive which he had originally intended for the person concerned. In my experience he fulfils his potential for our lives, not necessarily by removing the difficulties, but by climbing inside them with us and transforming the situation from within. (p. 3)

Lord, save me from self-pity. Inward-lookingness doesn't lift my chin straight up to you; complaint for complaint's sake, indifference, slow nibbling anger that accuses others of weaknesses that are entirely human and understandable, intolerance and impatience.

The prefix 'in-' is there a lot. So much of all that is apparent *in* me. Sorry, Lord. Help me watch the slow build-up—the 'nibbling anger'.

Self-pity and moaning are nearly as bad side-effects as nausea… and doubtless more destructive.

Took the plunge today. I went into town and had my hair cut short. Lois came with me and had a trim, just to keep me company. It was heart-breaking watching all my beautiful fair hair fall on the floor around my feet. I felt like asking if I could take it home. I cried, too—just for a few seconds (am doing an awful lot of that lately). Then the understanding hairdresser made me a cup of tea and gently carried on, with Lois hanging on to my hand, until it was very short (my hair, not my hand).

Afterwards, we targeted Boots for some red hair dye (we thought we may as well get some fun out of adversity!) so now I have short, spiky, bright auburn hair and the bathroom wallpaper has a few interesting ginger splashes! I look about ten years younger!

On the even more glamorous side of things, I am getting a bit, um, constipated, courtesy of the drugs. The ward sister has given me some nice brown shiny capsules, affectionately known as anti-bungs, to help. But they don't seem to know what their role is!

10.15pm

I'm getting into a slight panic. Still can't 'go'! Have had three lots of the shiny capsules since yesterday and enough fibre to start a sisal works!

THURSDAY 15 APRIL, 12.10AM

Well, here I am in floods of tears, desperate with constipation. I'm sure I am probably making it worse with anxiety. What a wonderfully dignified thing to have to write here! But it's part of it, isn't it? R is downstairs working and I'm up here in a real fix! Well, I wouldn't expect him to share the experience; he can't *do* anything! Nothing will budge… but it's got to. If it wasn't so awful it would be terribly funny. I would never have believed something so basic (in more ways than one) could be so humiliating and lonely. I think this is the first time I've really felt I just want the cancer and its associates to go away. Stop, I want to get off. I want my beautiful hair back. I don't want to put on weight with the steroids or go black and blue with chemo. I don't want any of it. *Please God, help me*!

1.40am

I give in to your tender sense of humour, Lord. Thank you that you've just taught me that I can even pray about *that* and you'll hear, and understand... and act! Thank you! That you understand even the loneliness of *that* is amazing. I think that little episode (actually it was more than a little episode; it was a long-running, tension-building, cliff-hanging, hysterical, dramatic saga in about four hundred episodes!) was almost a catalyst for the frustration that has built up over the last few days, as I've begun to deal with the effect of the drugs and the impact this will have on my life. Help me to be real with you, Lord. Help me to voice the frustrations and miseries as well as rejoice in your provision. Because if I don't, I'll bury them and become bitter. If I can't be real on these pages with you, knowing your acceptance, there'll be no outlet. Thank you for your incredible love for me, your gentle understanding. I'm going to drift off to sleep now, listening to the beautiful choral music you gave me right at the beginning of all this. Please give me your peace as I sleep. Forgive my self-sufficiency. Forgive me my 'brave face' when it should be an honest one. Keep talking to me, Lord. I want to listen.

8am

Lord, as I awoke I was reminded of the words, 'Weeping may endure for a night, but joy comes in the morning (Psalm 30:5). I wanted to add to that, 'A lesson can be learnt overnight; don't let me forget it in the morning!' But joy is here too. And peace. Acceptance of my need for dependence on you. The sky is blue. I love my boys—and my girl, of course—and can hear them talking about goals and R saying to Benj: 'The only way Man U will ever win...' Life. It's wonderful.

I look a fright with red, spiky hair like a chicken's bottom. I feel a bit sick, but nothing bad, just like mild morning sickness. Benj and I had a lovely chat early this morning (about football). And I read another great chunk of *Charlie and the Great Glass Elevator* to him—it was great not to cough my way through it. He pats me on the back when I finish!

3.55pm

Nausea all this morning, but manageable. I'm a bit spaced out. Needed a sleep this afternoon. The chemo is kicking in. An odd, poisoned feeling. As Liza says, they *are* basically poisoning me, hoping that the cancer cells will be on the receiving end. Still a bit constipated. It's quite a struggle! Perseverance is the watchword (or the 'wait' word).

FRIDAY 16 APRIL

Sometimes I feel under pressure to get straight in my mind how I feel about this cancer. It's something akin to making a public statement in a time of crisis on the White House lawn—as if deciding how I feel about it once and for all will give me some kind of security. But that would mean getting off the roller coaster of emotion and illness, and it's impossible to do that. There is almost an unseen process of change going on under the surface—more to do with my attitude to any life there may be ahead, but mostly about how reckless I was to take it all for granted before.

MONDAY 19 APRIL

Another nightmare last night. I dreamed we were at our old house in Home Park Avenue. It was in its original Edwardian state (brown paint and dust) and I was lifted up the stairs on a brush rack, then wheeled hurriedly, as if in an emergency, to the back bedroom on an ancient trolley, flat on my back. It was such a bleak and hopeless scenario. Like the last bad dream, it seemed short, but the fear was very real. Something to do with a sense of helplessness, I would imagine.

TUESDAY 20 APRIL

Absolutely bucketing down with rain. R took Benj to school, as he doesn't want me catching cold while my blood cells are low. He's looking after me like a clucking mother hen! The bruising on my arm from chemo is a beautiful shade of blue mauve and my arm is tender. The result of having to dig for veins again (and there isn't even any gold in them!)

Read the information booklets about chemo and cancer again last night (well, it beats going out clubbing). I felt I should buy a more comprehensive book, so I looked at the suggested reading and discovered one entitled *Cancer and Beauty*. Bit of a contradiction in terms, I think! Especially if my puffy face and chicken-bottom hair are anything to go by. I still can't locate a Christian cancer charity. Interesting, that. Is cancer even taboo for Christians? Should it be? Does that mean death is taboo, too? I always thought it was something we were meant to look forward to! I wonder if this is just more evidence of the secularization of the Christian community. We even adopt the world's view on illness and death. But Father God, you are bigger than all that!

FRIDAY 23 APRIL

Woke feeling really rough. Headache and nausea. Took two pain-killers with my tea, then promptly brought up both. Dozed for an hour then woke and was very sick with bright yellow bile. Yuk. Two pneumatic drills going in the street outside. Their timing is perfect! It's like that Japanese TV programme called *Endurance*!

Pain in my head is now curling over my forehead and hammering on my eyelids. I'm staying in bed.

Evening

Horrible day. Every 45 minutes or so all day I was sick with the same horrible yellow bile. Rang the ward at 5pm. It was too late for them to help, so they suggested I call a GP out. She came very promptly and gave me a large shot in my backside, which did the trick! Well timed (and aimed!) as I couldn't keep water down and needed to take the drugs tonight. She thinks the sickness might continue tomorrow and said to phone the ward if it does. I think maybe it's been bad because I overdid it yesterday on very little sleep. Whenever I feel quite well I will go for it, overdo it, and regret it later. Thank you for your presence at the worst moments today, Lord.

SATURDAY 24 APRIL

Thankfully much better this morning. Took anti-sick drugs and weak tea. They stayed down! Have started Rob Buckman's *What You Really Need to Know about Cancer*[12] (not quite *Gone with the Wind*, but hey…). It's an incredibly thorough, practical book. No scaremongering, lots of optimism. Just what I need.

WEDNESDAY 28 APRIL

R awake a lot during the night. So both of us awake and talking at 5am. Just as well that we seem to take turns to have weak and gibbering patches. The weight is piling on already. Felt such a blob that I treated myself to a facial and a manicure today. That's a first. And probably a last, considering the price. But it was an experience! Enjoyed the St Andrew's ladies' Bible study this morning. I especially enjoyed meeting Margaret, who lives along the road from us. We have never met before!

FRIDAY 30 APRIL

Beautiful flowers from Mum and Dad for my birthday (in advance). House is looking like the Chelsea Flower Show! I keep expecting Alan Titchmarsh to pop up between blooms! Off for our break in Wiltshire tomorrow. We're going to find honeymoon country. The children are groaning already. Have had to promise to find clothes and sports shops for them!

SATURDAY I MAY

Stopped at the Mall at Bristol, and IKEA. Whom should we meet at IKEA but Rob and Di. Very disappointed that they recognized me with short, red, chicken-bottom hair, an extra ten pounds in weight and wearing an Ermintrude the cow T-shirt reading 'Moo!'

MONDAY 3 MAY

Somebody's 39th birthday. Can't think whose. Loads of pressies had arrived in a huge box from the office crowd on Friday, so we brought them all away with us to open here in the Travel Inn. Lots of little fun bits and pieces. They gave us a lot of giggles. Benj bought me a garden gnome called Albert. He's great. At last, someone apart from myself to talk to while I hang out the washing! Bound to get more intelligent conversation out of him than me. Lois bought me a bright pink 'Supermodel' T-shirt! Am not thinking about whether this will be my last birthday. Pointless. After all, I didn't think about whether my first was my first, did I?

TUESDAY 4 MAY

We enjoyed a lovely weekend away. Found the cottage in Coln St Aldwyn's where we had our honeymoon, while the children got very bored at all our romancing and sighing. ('Yuk! They're our *parents*!') There are even more flowers everywhere here at home. The lounge smells absolutely gorgeous—heady with scent. At least if my sense of taste is going, my sense of smell isn't! But still no sign of Alan Titchmarsh. Pity. I could do with his help in the back garden.

Clinic today to see Dr P. and have my blood checked. (Will they be able to tell it's just turned 39?) Must ask questions. I keep thinking about the possibilities of secondary cancers. Especially to my brain. I can't think of anything worse. I also want to find out how strict I have to be in the 7–14 days after chemo, where infection is concerned. Do I have to be hidden away from all humanity for a week following chemo? The children are just as likely to bring infection home from school.

WEDNESDAY 5 MAY

How much I am appreciating the Bible study with the St Andrew's ladies. Today Margaret brought the most beautiful little posies of lily of the valley for three of us… and I was a lucky one! They are from her garden and just exquisite.

SATURDAY 8 MAY

Pains in my back today have been difficult. Just digging pains. Went up for a sleep this afternoon, but still so tired later.

Tonight was awful. R and I lost it with each other. I had been dragging myself around the kitchen trying to get the meal. He found me in tears on the floor by the freezer, as I had been unable to fix the freezer drawer and my tiredness and frustration had made me cry. Cramp stops me from squatting now, so I have to sit on the floor and stick my legs out to get to the freezer. Then I have trouble getting up again. Just makes me feel more of an invalid! Then I burnt a naan bread and R yelled at me: 'Why don't you leave it to me? Sit down!' Benj and Lo sat silently at the table. I just sat and cried. Benj said later that he felt like crying too, as it seemed so unfair and he couldn't understand why his dad had shouted at me. We talked about it all and were soon laughing again, but it was an awful time. We're both so tense and stressed with trying to cope. It's so much worse for R as he can't actually do anything to help with the illness. At least I can let my veins be filled up with poison.

Rob P. explained to me that he had felt similarly helpless when Di was ill. Having been a senior partner in a law practice and controlling this and that, it was very hard to find that he could not control the illness she was facing. At work he was able to just say the word, but at home he was powerless to help. It's just the same for R.

I came up for a bath later and while it was running had a good howl. Another cancer patients' tip:

• Running bath water is good for muffling crying. (And it also stops you crying for too long—just until the bath's full!)

I indulged in a good dose of self-pity. Feeling tired and trying not to look at the fat body I now have to live with after being so slim.

We also feel bereft of support. Sadly it's just not enough to say, as some people have, 'If you need help, let us know.' Because you just don't let them know! I guess it's partly that I look well, so people think we don't need help. I've just got to start asking and being more honest about the fact that it *is* tough at times.

SUNDAY 9 MAY

Got up at 3am this morning. Couldn't sleep. As I feel more debilitated by the chemo, so my defences are down. I feel weaker, and more susceptible to fear. I have to remember that it is healthy to confess and confront my fears and sorrows. Jesus did. Didn't he say, 'I am deeply grieved, even to death'? But last night it seemed to be about more than that. I sat at the kitchen table, aware of that fear but also aware of how much my sin separates me from God. I couldn't seem to find any of the verses I usually rely on for comfort. It was a 'dark night' in more ways than one. Right at the end of the night I came across, almost by accident: 'Surely I will deliver you for a good purpose' (Jeremiah 15:11). But the darkness almost obscured it. I was hanging on by a thread. It was as if I came face to face with the selfishness and sin my life contains. Especially the way in which I might use my illness, even unconsciously, as an excuse to turn a blind eye to sin.

Lord, I'm trying to distinguish between self-pity and your teaching. Help me. I need to remember that my faith is based on fact, not feelings, but at the same time I acknowledge that my feelings can often be an indicator that things aren't right between us.

My morning readings included Revelation 2:8–11: 'I am the first and the last, who died and came to life again.' My Bible notes[13] say: 'This is always the manner in which the Lord seeks to comfort his people in times of distress. He reminds us that all things are under his control and that his overcoming life is ours for the taking.'

Later

Psalm 84 (Baca and the valley of tears) was mentioned in the sermon at church this morning. I was able to spend some time thinking about that, remembering what I had read before in James Jones' book about the springs and autumn pools to be found in the valley.

Tonight I had a first look at James 5:14. The 'Is any of you sick?' verses about going to the elders for healing just don't seem to apply to me. I guess my experience of their use has been so often to see people hurt, confused and damaged in their faith as a result. Correct me if I'm wrong, Lord. Maybe they are for later?

What a muddle of meditations today! Sometimes I feel bombarded by so many words. Other times I am scrabbling around for a crumb of comfort or instruction. Like tuning a radio, Lord, I need your Holy Spirit to distinguish and discern. I don't want to miss anything you might be saying—or read significance into words that contain none.

MONDAY 10 MAY, MORNING

The digging pain in my neck and shoulders, my back and legs continues. It makes me feel as if the cancer is going everywhere, but it's more likely to be the steroids having a party. I feel very isolated and it's hard to stay positive. I constantly feel as if I'm living on a different planet from everyone else. I feel I daren't admit when I'm tired because it just puts more pressure on R. I just wish the church would organize some help, for R's sake, if not for mine. He's carrying so much extra without complaint. But I must remember those words inspired by Hilary McDowell: '… slow nibbling anger that accuses others of weaknesses that are entirely human…' It's easy to blame others. They just don't think. I'm just as unthinking.

7pm

The children have been wonderful to have around this evening. They cheered me up so much when they got home from school with their accounts of their respective days. Almost as if they are trying to outdo one another with things to make me laugh and gasp.

Have started reading David Watson's *Fear No Evil*. I first read it years ago. Doubtless it will mean more this time round!

10pm

At the end of this day of turmoil it's as if I'm finally at rest. The Good News Bible translation of part of Psalm 16 says:

> *You, Lord are all I have,*
> *and you give me all I need;*
> *my future is in your hands…*

I am always aware of the Lord's presence;
he is near, and nothing can shake me.
And so I am thankful and glad,
and I feel completely secure,
because you protect me from the power of death...
and you will not abandon me to the world of the dead.
You will show me the path that leads to life;
your presence fills me with joy
and brings me pleasure for ever.

Father, I need to keep this perspective—to lie down to sleep with it, and rise with it in the morning.

TUESDAY 11 MAY, 6.30AM

Have finished *Fear No Evil* already. I could not put it down. There is so much in it with which I can identify. I must keep it by me. Like David Watson, I find it hard to believe that my 'job' on earth is done. The children aren't grown and independent, for one thing. This is key, as I always put them first, especially where work is concerned, wanting to be at home for them. It would be ironically sad to have that taken away at the very time (the early teenage years) when they probably need me most. I can't imagine R being too keen on having two teenagers to bring up alone! After all, my prognosis is not that bad... is it?

I've also been wondering about the significance of the Jeremiah reading which flickered like a tiny candle in the darkness of that black night a few days ago. 'Surely I will deliver you for a good purpose.' It doesn't mean things will remain the same for ever where the prognosis or God's promises are concerned. They may be 'for now'. It may all need looking at again in the light of the possibility of the cancer not responding to treatment or returning. *But* God's timing is perfect. I cannot bargain or argue with him over how he chooses to do things. This precious dialogue continues. But that doesn't mean there'll never be any fear.

WEDNESDAY 12 MAY

Chemo today. Disturbed sleep last night. Really following on from what I was thinking about yesterday. Letting myself go down the 'What's it going to be like for the kids if I die' route in my imagination. I'm bound to feel some fear, and it must be faced squarely. At the same time I absolutely must plan for good positive things the other side of this cancer, or the negative side will start to take control. Maybe I should plan to revamp the kitchen, or the study! Even if we don't get round to it until we're a hundred, at least it will be something creative to do. Something to build on and hope for in this life. That's important. I spent a lot of time praying for other people in the middle of the night too, trying to offset the self-pity and fear. It's all too easy to concentrate on our own situation. I don't want other people to think we're forgetting their lives and concerns. Couldn't bear to become completely inward-looking.

Evening

Still feeling quite low. Also, I'm spending what seems like long hours on the loo again… waiting! Sitting there, I often feel like looking beyond the bath for a number 7 bus. Or taking in my cross-stitch. David Watson used to listen to worship tapes on his Walkman in a similar situation! I've got heartburn, look about six months pregnant and am very uncomfortable. The extra weight is really getting me down (and it's hard to get up). But while I'm on steroids there's nothing I can do about it.

FRIDAY 14 MAY

Amanda continues to send the most beautiful cards. They make such a difference. Must write to her today and also send Fiona an update. I seem to spend an enormous amount of time writing letters with a pen. I can't face the PC. It's as if I'm reluctant to get up there and start writing in case I find I can't do it after such a long break. I'm concerned that the inspiration won't come and the ability will be lost.

Isaiah 3:1—4:1… It bothers me that so much of this includes references to baldness being a judgment upon women!

Evening

Dreadful build-up of stress tonight, culminating in a scene with Lois at supper-time. She sat in the breakfast-room, motionless, watching TV while I struggled with meal-time preparations. Then I accidentally smashed a full bottle of pasta sauce all over the tiled floor. Benj came to help but Lo carried on watching television. I exploded, partly because she hadn't turned over for *Blue Peter* as normal but was watching some dreadful soap. She retaliated by accusing me of emotional blackmail because I'm ill and emphasized the point by pushing her dinner, and most of ours, off the table and on to the floor. Benj was covered in most of the contents of the water jug and half of his meal. But his reaction was a cool as a cucumber. He just muttered 'Women!' under his breath and then a huge grin spread across his face as he helped me clear up. This is real life, living with the stress of cancer, folks!

I did go up to Lois and we talked it over and had a cuddle. But I'm still trying to work out whether I have been using emotional blackmail, or whether at that moment I was genuinely feeling too ill and tired to get the meal and she should have helped. I shouldn't have lost it quite so badly. I do tend to 'martyr' on and then blow a fuse. If I nipped things in the bud earlier, we'd all be better off. R says Lois must take some responsibility for getting the meal.

Time for some nice relaxation in the bath, I think, and some 'whooshing music' (my relaxation CD).

Cancer patients' tip:

• Invest in large quantities of the most expensive bath oil or bubbles you can afford, and scented candles. They're a great de-stresser.

Later

R has told me about the wife of David, a solicitor he knows through work. She is in her early 40s and has cancer (breast, I think) with about a month to live. They have two children just a couple of years older than ours. Felt very upset, but it's got me praying for them.

SUNDAY 16 MAY

Good night's sleep. That helps to minimize the moments of feeling down. Dreamt vividly about Highmoor Hall, the beautiful retreat centre we visited on the bike ride last year. Maybe I feel I need a visit! R and I were again discussing the apparent absence of a Christian cancer support group. Is it because Christians have a tendency to focus on healing and not on you, Lord? We are no good at remembering that you are bigger and more powerful than every tumour and aggressive cancer put together and that your purpose can often be greater than physical healing. I do wonder what seeds you are sowing for the future, for the other side of this experience for all of us. My heart is much more turned towards sharing your love and care with other people in a similar situation—to helping them find the 'treasures in the darkness' that I am finding. I guess that experiencing your support for myself makes me naturally want to encourage others to find it too. Thank you for covering the magnitude of niggling thoughts, aches, pains and weariness of the last few days with your love.

Today's reading was 2 Corinthians 4:16–18: 'Therefore we do not lose heart. Though outwardly we are wasting away, yet inwardly we are being renewed day by day. For our light and momentary troubles are achieving for us an eternal glory that far outweighs them all. So we fix our eyes not on what is seen, but on what is unseen. For what is seen is temporary, but what is unseen is eternal.' Thank you, Lord.

PS. The trouble is, I'm not wasting away on the outside; I'm fattening up! Richard will be able to sell me by the pound to cannibals for their Christmas lunch!

MONDAY 17 MAY

Liza came round yesterday afternoon and did some ironing. R had mentioned to her that I hadn't really seen anyone and that the novelty of 'the person with cancer' was obviously wearing off. My conclusion is that people have their own lives and just don't have time to remember that I might need a pile of ironing doing or benefit from a phone call. Let's face it, how much do I remember other people?

Read the wrong page in my Bible reading notes by accident again today, but it's obviously a good accident. Psalm 73:23–28: 'Yet I am always with you; you hold me by my right hand. You guide me with your counsel, and afterwards you will take me into glory. Whom have I in heaven but you? And earth has nothing I desire besides you. My flesh and my heart may fail, but God is the strength of my heart and my portion for ever.'

TUESDAY 18 MAY, EVENING

Benj made me laugh tonight. We were having a discussion about various churches and sects. He said that until recently he had thought that the Mormons were the same as the Normans of 1066. At least he can laugh at his own mistakes; it will stand him in good stead. He offered to feed me grapes, Roman slave style, as I lay on the sofa tonight. 'Yes,' I said, 'and after that go and iron my toga!'

Lois doesn't seem to be holding my 'emotional blackmail' against me. I playfully asked her if she'd like to eat her meal from the floor tonight and she gave me a little grin and said she didn't think it would help the flavour. So we kept it on the table instead.

WEDNESDAY 19 MAY

I need to find ways of getting over the tiredness 'hump' that hits me in the early evening, so that I am able to have a decent conversation with R when he gets in. It can't be much fun for him having a horizontal, snoring wife to *not* welcome him. Even if I am in the same room and reclining on the kitchen table! The days of sitting and doing *The Times* crossword as he eats his meal are well and truly in the past. I don't think I could even distinguish Across from Down. (One across, 10, 4: 'Husband finds on kitchen table'.)

THURSDAY 20 MAY

Well, the inevitable has started. I've lost several handfuls of hair today. When running my fingers through it, about seven or eight hairs came out with them. And, strangely, it's falling out very quickly from somewhere more delicate! It will be interesting to see whether it takes days or weeks. (What do I mean, interesting… this is traumatic!) I wonder how many hairs there'll be on my pillow in the morning? Probably more of mine than R's now. This is where I start vacuuming the bed. I'd better get the hats out and put them on the hat stand, ready.

FRIDAY 21 MAY

Counted 22 hairs on my pillow this morning. R had ten on his!

9.05pm

Hair has been steadily moulting into my fingers all day. It's better that it does that; otherwise I'll keep picking hairs off the kitchen floor, and that isn't very hygienic! I now have several noticeable bald patches. It really is awful. But it's unavoidable and there's no point fretting too much. I just hadn't realized how white my head was underneath! Please, Lord, could I hang on to at least some of my eyelashes?

SUNDAY 23 MAY

R's mum is coming to stay tonight to help out. Steve W., my friend and colleague from the office in Cardiff, is coming to see me on Tuesday, so the social whirl is hotting up! Have still got to work out how to meet his train. Looking forward to seeing him and having some contact with the world of work and Cardiff!

11.45pm

The wife of R's work acquaintance, David, died at the beginning of this week. It turns out she had lymphoma and was undiagnosed for ages. R's mum found out today, as the family live near R's Auntie Grace in Callington. Auntie Grace first mentioned her when she discovered I had lymphoma, and R realized he knew David. R's mum obviously thought I knew, at least, that it was lymphoma. I've just asked R if he'd known what kind of cancer it was, and he admitted that he had, but that it was too close for comfort and he couldn't face telling me. Panic at a 'same scenario' for us and prayer for them followed each other in quick succession.

MONDAY 24 MAY

Woke early. First thoughts for David and his children. The funeral is at 11am today. Can't help feeling that those two children should only have to worry about whether or not they've done their homework this morning, not about what their mum's funeral is going to be like.

On a trivial note, by comparison, my hair is so thin that I need a headscarf in order to go out without feeling cold. So I'll put down 'First Official Scarf Day' as 24 May 1999.

Later

I've just been up to the children's rooms and burst into tears. I prayed very fervently, 'Please don't let me die yet.' I want to see the children through to adulthood. I can't imagine what Benj would do without his mum. Lois' schoolbooks are already full of half-finished work; what will she do if I suddenly disappear?! (Knowing her, rise to the occasion and get it all done on time!) I know I just feel worse today because of David's wife's funeral.

A stinging pain has been hitting me in the chest every thirty seconds or so. I can remember making a note of these little pains in the months before the diagnosis, wondering what they were. I feel very fragile. Jacqui will be here soon. About the best person to see, feeling like this.

TUESDAY 25 MAY

Well. I don't look very beautiful this morning. Definitely won't make the hair shampoo ads—but I'm still worth it! Dear Jacqui is giving me a lift to meet Steve at the station.

Mum sent the headscarves today. They are so beautifully made. Tiny stitches sewn with much love.

Later

Lovely to see Steve, if only for a shorter time than we thought—his train was delayed. We had lunch at the China House, an idyllically situated pub across the water from the Barbican, and caught up on all the news. It all seemed a bit unreal telling him everything about all this. A far cry from thinking up silly titles for bits of the *Parentalk* course. They used to get sillier and more unrealistic the more we suggested. Pity the cancer talk wasn't the same.

R said Shelley prayed beautifully for me at Pray 7 (the early morning prayer meeting at church) today. She mentioned how impressed she was with how I was facing up to the illness. She should see me on the bad days!

THURSDAY 27 MAY

Second cycle of chemo starts today. First tablets taken last night. Bible study yesterday gave me the opportunity to talk a little bit about being ill. We studied Psalm 46 and were asked which words first came into our heads when we thought about 'protection'. Everybody else chose words like 'armour', 'shield' and 'covering'. I didn't get any of those. What came vividly into my head was being in the palm of God's hand. It's where we are in relation to God that protection is found, as well as—or even more than—what defences we put around ourselves. Hence the disciples in the storm. They didn't need to ask for protection because they had Jesus with them. But of course they didn't understand that. Neither do I. But it's a perfect illustration—that Jesus is in the storm with me.

Evening

Chemo fine, although poor Nurse Michelle had problems getting the cannula in again. My veins really are a pain. I feel sorry for the nurses when it's difficult to find a vein. The needle finally went in after four attempts. My arm will be black and blue... but it's my arm's fault; it ought to be more co-operative! Nurse Shirley reminded me to see the 'appliance lady' just to try wigs, in case I decide to wear one. I am still so fascinated by the idea of the 'appliance lady' that I've decided I definitely will! Shirley will make the all-important hotline (or hairline) call! It's very touching how other people seem as unhappy about my hair going as I am. Shirley felt so sad for me and the first thing Jonathan said was, 'Oh, all your lovely hair!' Let's hope when it does come back it comes back the same, or people will be asking for a refund!

SATURDAY 29 MAY

Prayed especially for all the riders on the weekend cycle ride for *Care for the Family*, for Rob and Jonathan and all those joining them. It feels odd not to be with them again. I've been feeling a bit far away from everything. There's so little I can do workwise. It feels increasingly isolating. Lord, I know you can use me in lots of ways, probably especially when I feel weak and left out of things. Can you show me that I *do* matter?

Later

Thank you, Lord, that you reminded me that I am 'precious and honoured in your sight' and that you love me. I clearly had the sense that I was sitting on your knee and you were holding me and gently explaining that I have to trust you for *now*. Then you were standing just ahead of me, but beside me, on the end of a beautiful red carpet, the kind used for VIPs at special occasions. Some of it we were standing on; the rest was hidden out of sight behind you in a roll. You had your hand on top of it behind you, ready to unroll it as needed. You seemed to be saying, 'What more can I do to reassure you now? I cannot roll the future out before you like a carpet. You have to trust me for each small thing, for each step along it.' Lord, please comfort me and uphold me as I try to do that.

R wisely reminded me that I wouldn't be 'normal' if I didn't have patches of frustration and disorientation. I wasn't aware that he had ever considered me normal!

TUESDAY 1 JUNE

The drugs have made me feel very 'seedy' for most of today. It's an odd feeling, almost 'oily'. I was trying to explain it to a friend on the phone, much to her amusement. The feeling reminds me of when I make ciabatta and have to add the olive oil to the dough. There's an odd, creepy sensation inside, coupled with a sick, sluggish feeling. Great! Cramp also keeps grabbing my feet and fingers—especially when I try to hold something small. My fingertips are beginning to go numb and tingly too, so I wonder how long writing will be possible.

WEDNESDAY 2 JUNE, MORNING

I've just received a 'Cyclist's Survival Pack' from Pete, Andrew and Lisa in the *Care for the Family* office. They're so mad; I love them to bits! They were thoughtful enough to know how I might be feeling about missing the bike ride. The pack contains a banana (obviously—Pete wouldn't forget that![14]), a Lucozade drink, a Tracker energy bar and a map of the route!

Feel fat and plodding. Baldness, weight and pink skin mean I really do look like Mr Blobby in a headscarf! And I'm just as unfunny! Taking this thing one day at a time is very hard. It's so difficult not knowing how I'm going to be, and how to plan for things. Makes me feel much more closed in.

9.55pm

Very dull chemo day today. Nurses very busy and nobody else willing to chat or have a giggle.

I haven't got another chemo session now for nearly three weeks—I just have to continue popping pills for a week or so. Nurse Michelle got the needle in at the second attempt today, which she thinks is awful enough, but it's a big improvement! Off to town to have my wig fitted tomorrow. Evidently it's done at the hairdresser's behind Sainsbury's. Perhaps they sponsor them. Maybe each wig has a label attached, reading, 'It's clean, it's fresh… this wig is sponsored by Sainsbury's.' After seeing the Tesco-sponsored stained-glass window in Ely Cathedral, nothing would surprise me! I feel an article coming on…

FRIDAY 4 JUNE

Busy day yesterday! Wig fitting was hilarious! The initial 'consultation' took place in a tiny, rather seedy barber's shop. It is being taken over by the hairdresser from Liskeard in Cornwall who arranges the wig fittings for the hospital wig service. When I walked in, the front salon was full of men waiting for their haircuts. I felt as if, at any moment, I was going to hear one of the assistants ask, 'A little something for the weekend, sir?' But it didn't happen within my earshot!

Had quite an uncomfortable few minutes while I explained what I had come for. It was the kind of experience that would make anybody who was unable to see the funny side, or who was having a difficult day, dissolve in tears. Maybe the directors of the 'appliances' service should come and experience this for themselves. It's certainly something I wouldn't want to repeat. I was then ushered into a tiny cubicle fitted with pine 'saloon' doors. A dear lady called Trish (why are all hairdressers over a certain age called Trish?) then attempted to convince me that one of the numerous styles of wig might compensate for losing my beautiful, long, fair hair. She was very sweet, but to convince me she would need training with the United Nations arbitration specialists. We tried a short Shirley Bassey style in a fetching rust; 'Suzie' in strawberry blonde; 'Irene' in a silvery grey (unnerving to see what I'll look like in 30 years' time; the wig was obviously based on an aged Nyree Dawn Porter in *The Forsyte Saga*… that dates me too!) Nothing was really me, and I kept feeling as if I was really choosing something to help me complete a KGB assignment in stylish disguise. There should have been a suitcase around somewhere for me to stuff into a left-luggage locker on Plymouth station. Actually there *was* a suitcase but that was where Trish kept producing the wigs from.

We decided to order the style of one in the colour of another. (Well, I like to be different.) But I'm not convinced. It's very obvious that it *is* a wig. If I wanted anything more sophisticated, I would have to pay a couple of hundred pounds, and it's just not worth it. Trish will let me know when the wig arrives and then give me a final fitting (to show me how to pull the drawstrings that keep it on my head!) Really, she couldn't have been more kind and helpful, but the whole arrangement is bizarre beyond words.

After the trauma of that little episode, I treated myself to some very expensive skin cream in Dingles. The psychology behind this is that, as my hair's dropped out, I ought to keep an eye on my skin as well. It might cave in. The beauty consultant told me with some enthusiasm about the 'Look Good, Feel Better' group at Derriford Hospital Macmillan Centre. (A pleasant change to meet a 'consultant' who aims to make you look beautiful, rather than just saving your life!) Evidently, a bunch of cancer patients get together and are given make-up and skin-care demos and loads of free goodies by various cosmetic house consultants. She says that a good time is generally had by all, and that although you don't actually talk about cancer unless you want to, each of you knows that the others are in the same boat. Maybe I'll give them a ring. I'm beginning to feel as if I'm getting to the 'Look, I'm a freak' stage. Maybe it would be good to meet some others who feel the same way.

The 'cartoon' illustration of me that will accompany my *Home and Family* column arrived in the post yesterday. Of course, it doesn't look like me any more; I'll have to make light-hearted reference to that in the next column! There I sit at the PC with long, fair, cartoon hair! But Richard and the children have been drawn wonderfully. They look just like themselves!

I might cut the last few bits of this annoying wispy hair off. Or get someone to do it for me. It's really irritating. And it would be better just to be completely Yul Brynner-ish. I really could go to a fancy-dress party as a roll-on deodorant now. Although I'm not sure that you can get roll-ons in 'Super Economy Extra Large' size.

My fingertips are definitely numb and tingly, so it's all beginning to happen. They feel a bit like they do when I put my very cold hands into hot water, or when I've been typing too much.

Maybe part of the point of all this lies in my reading this morning: 'Praise be to the God and Father of our Lord Jesus Christ, the Father of all compassion and the God of all comfort, who comforts us in all our troubles, so that we can comfort those in any trouble with the comfort we ourselves have received from God' (2 Corinthians 1:3–4).

Evening

Wanting to have some flowers in front of the mirror in the lounge, I bought some white stocks in Safeway this morning. They are stunningly beautiful, especially in the evening light, and their heady scent fills the room. Then tonight, in the bathroom, I lit several candles to enjoy while I had a bath. They too produce such beautiful sight and scent. I can't help thinking that if there are such wonderful sights and smells for our senses on earth, how much more beautiful heaven must be. Aside from the bright light of God's glory, there must be subtleties of glowing light in which to bask.

THURSDAY 10 JUNE

Pains in my legs during the night kept me awake. Steroid withdrawal, I would imagine. It was quite difficult to walk about when I first got up and I was having to hold on to the wall for balance. I need a Zimmer frame. The weight is piling on and my face is very puffy. The expensive skin-cream can't do much about that!

Evening

Sally took me to the cinema tonight to see *Notting Hill*. It was very much like *Four Weddings and a Funeral*—funny, disposable, not needing too much brainpower. Rhys Ifans was hysterically funny as the lodger. He made the film, really. Life's a bit unreal at the moment, so a film like that, however much a fairytale, is even more so.

Quite fun to experience the new multiplex cinema. It was like being on the set of *Star Wars*. I wouldn't have been surprised if Darth Vader had walked out of the gents. I've been plagued by a dreadful headache all day, so the neon flashing lights in the cinema didn't help that much.

But I suppose they wouldn't bother Darth.

SUNDAY 13 JUNE, EVENING

I feel guilty that I got a bit impatient with Mum on the phone tonight. She is trying to be encouraging and look on the positive side, but I am concerned that she's not facing the implications or possibilities of this illness head on. She keeps saying, 'You'll beat it!' and things which imply that it is all down to me. I was trying to explain that cancer is indiscriminate and doesn't only make a mess of people who let it. Positive attitudes do help you live with it, but they don't stop you from dying from it. Plenty of people who have had terrific attitudes to the cancer they are suffering from have still died. Mum doesn't seem to understand my need to face this head on and not depend on a kind of false optimism. And yet I have to allow her to have the freedom to do what helps her. Very difficult!

It reminded me of something John Diamond wrote about his parents:

For the first couple of weeks we didn't have a single conversation that didn't have them minimizing the threat, the difficulty of the cure, the length of time it would take for me to get better. It was understandable enough, of course. What was happening seemed unlikely enough to me; how much more unlikely it would seem to those two who, inasmuch as they considered the matter at all, had assumed absolutely, and for so long, that they would predecease me… The problem I had was their non-acknowledgment of what was going on… It was just, he said, that he was scared for me and didn't want to show it.[15]

Of course Mum and Dad are scared—for all of us. But if only they would just say that, instead of indulging in 'chin up and you'll get better' tactics. I'm trying to say that tactfully, but I'm not sure that I'm succeeding.

MONDAY 14 JUNE

Got up at 4.30am because I couldn't sleep. As I looked along the landing at the house, I was suddenly overcome with the most incredible sadness at the idea of dying and leaving everything. Not pain or fear, just sadness.

As I got back into bed, R sleepily put his arm around me. The sadness wrapped itself round me too, as I drifted back to sleep. I was thinking just how much the children will need me over the next few years. Yet a few hours previously I had been feeling quite content about what might be ahead, whatever it was. Almost feeling impatient to get to heaven. Like David Watson, I feel caught between this world, which I know, and the next, which I long to know—a foot in each camp. But unlike him I'm not yet at the stage where I don't mind which foot I land on. I still want to land here.

There is always this disconcerting roller coaster of feelings. I never know when I'm going to tip over the edge and plummet, and it's so often just after I reach a contented straight or an ecstatic high.

TUESDAY 15 JUNE

Off to Cardiff this morning! The plan is to spend a couple of days trying to bash out some of the details of some work with Lisa. We need to think about how much progress we can make while I'm still well enough. We also need to meet with Rob to discuss work on Rob's *Sixty Minute Mother* stuff. I feel a bit apprehensive. I'm sure they'll all see a big change in me. And I'm also concerned as to how I'll cope physically. However, I am staying over at the Travel Inn for two nights—and Lisa, bless her, has promised to be my personal chauffeur for the duration!

WEDNESDAY 16 JUNE, MORNING

It was so lovely to get back into the office and to see everyone. They had even given 'my desk' a dust and set it up for me with an in-tray, a vase of beautiful flowers and a welcome card! Steve and Jill W. took me out for a meal last night, which was incredibly generous of them, although Steve got a parking ticket in the process! I felt very guilty about that. But, as Jill said, maybe he shouldn't park on double yellow lines! The big surprise of yesterday was discovering that the other Jill W. is coming to join in the discussions on the book tomorrow. She's going to help out with some interviews.

Thank you, Lord, for keeping me going physically and for the privilege of doing all this.

Evening

A full and busy day—just how I like it! And my energy held out! I was aware of all the love and care for me. I will be concentrating solely on the *Sixty Minute Mother* for the next three weeks or so, which will be great. There is a lot to do, so I will just have to learn to pace myself and work when I can.

Went to 'TGI Fridays' in Cardiff tonight for a meal with Lisa, Linz from the office and Pete, my bike ride co-driver. Great fun. Tomorrow I'll go to the office and have coffee and join in the prayer time and then make my way home around lunch-time. I can't believe the way you've kept me going, Lord. I should be exhausted!

THURSDAY 17 JUNE, LUNCH-TIME

I'm sitting in a café in Cardiff, having a coffee, as I've just missed a train to Bristol!

I was asked to lead the staff prayers today, and to share something of my situation with them all. It was difficult to focus on just a few verses that have meant a lot, but in the end I chose the Valley of Baca psalm, and shared something of God's goodness to me.

It was hard leaving everyone. Lots of tears and hugs all round. Feel as if I'm almost plummeting now. Coming down the roller coaster at top speed, having reached the very highest point. They love me and care for me so much here. I could do with taking some of that back to Plymouth in a paper bag.

Linz encouraged me to include a 'Dear Well Person' perspective in anything I write eventually. She too has found (suffering with ME) that she is treated differently and experiences similar frustrations. She also reminded me of the conversation in *The Lion, the Witch and the Wardrobe* where the children and Mr and Mrs Beaver are discussing Aslan. The children ask, 'Is he safe?' and the Beavers reply, ''Course he isn't safe. But he's good.'[16]

I almost feel a real passion to get writing now. Maybe this will help me to write something for Rob's book on my cancer and how it affects motherhood. He is concerned that I do that, but I don't know how. I don't think it's something that I will be able to write and re-write until it's near perfect. If I do get anything down it will be almost like thinking out loud. Done in one burst and then left. Technical perfection will have to be neglected. It will be too painful to write otherwise. I can't help thinking that there's too much to do for you, Lord, to die yet.

FRIDAY 18 JUNE

Arrived home to find dear Granny (R's mum) holding the fort, as planned, and a beautiful basket of flowers from everyone at Hodders, who know me through *Care for the Family*. How incredibly lovely of them. It is quite the most beautiful basket of flowers I have ever seen. The most amazing thing is that it would be easy to believe that whoever sent them had known the colour scheme of our lounge. The flowers are all creams, yellows and rusts. They look perfect on the mantelpiece. I keep wandering in to look at them in all their splendour and smell them.

SATURDAY 19 JUNE

Went to a house-warming party given by some work friends of R's tonight. It was full of well-dressed, slim women… with hair. I just don't feel as if I belong to that world any more. Again, it's like being part of another culture, with me very much an outsider in my scarf and 'fat' clothes. I felt like yelling, 'Excuse me, but I looked slim and elegant like you just a few months ago—don't take it for granted!' None of them gave my situation a second thought, of course. They probably thought I was the fat lady who would sing later. Well, I didn't sing later—I cried.

Lord, you know I couldn't help feeling, 'They are all healthy and fit, except me…' but of course you have a different perspective on all of this that I have to learn to share. It will be a very long time before I am 'back to normal', whatever 'normal' is… if ever. It's a very hard thing to accept, but I know you understand that difficulty. It's just a burst of 'well-person envy'. But it's the first time it has hit me, and it left me feeling self-pitying and low.

I instantly thought, 'Do these fit, healthy people know how well off they are?' Yet did I a few months ago? And are they really better off, anyway?

SUNDAY 20 JUNE

I was reading David Spiegel's book *Living Beyond Limits*[17] again this morning. It's comforting to read what he says about facing cancer head on: 'I have become convinced through twenty years of clinical work and research that the best way to face the threat of serious illness is to look it right in the eye, to face the worst rather than to simply hope for the best.' I think that's what I'm trying to tell Mum.

I guess yesterday's 'after party' feelings are natural and something to face, handle and get through. Lots of these up and down emotions and situations need to be treated like mundane paperwork. Picked up out of the in-tray, given my full attention until they're understood, and re-filed quickly. Either in the out-tray or into the bin. I like the quote from Euripides: 'This is courage; to bear unflinchingly what heaven sends' (although I'm not sure our ideas of heaven would be the same). Sorry, Lord. There's been a bit too much flinching lately and not so much courage.

TUESDAY 22 JUNE

Clinic today… and back on the drugs.

WEDNESDAY 23 JUNE

Brothers Chris and Geoff both phoned today. Chris told me some more about his MS. He also mentioned that he had lit a candle for me in St Antoine Abbey, in the village where he lives in France. Amazing for my agnostic brother. But I notice he has moved there from his previous atheist position. He said that somebody had done the same for him on the day of Saint Somebody who was the patron saint of lost things and it was the day that his sight came back. 'I think that was more than coincidence!' he said. Amazing.

I told him briefly what a different perspective this illness has given me on my faith. It seemed like the simplest introduction to something I could never explain in entirety! Incredibly, it's something we've never really talked about much before. Very precious. I never thought I'd have such a conversation with my special and cynical brother!

He has still not told Mum and Dad that he is ill. They knew about his sight problems when they happened, but not about the final diagnosis. He is wary of burdening Mum, because I am ill too. But also because he knows the reaction he will get and feels he can't handle telling them at the moment. I understand that. But it's worrying that there is a certain amount of deception going on. No matter how much of it is meant for their protection, it can't be right. Geoff and I talked about it too, but decided it must nevertheless be Chris's decision.

THURSDAY 24 JUNE

Benjamin's class assembly this morning. The children sang, 'Think of a world', which I heard so many times while I was teaching. I sang it for the first time at Rockland St Peter in Norfolk, on teaching practice. I could almost smell that little school this morning, singing it again. I thought of some of the children I had taught over the years, and our own children's class assemblies. Then I looked at Benjamin's dear, eager face in the front row. It was all I could do not to cry. I had to blink back the tears and work hard at holding myself together.

SUNDAY 27 JUNE

I think that a lot of my frustration and sense of uselessness is due to my desperate longing to get back to normal. The key thing is remembering that for me, unfortunately, for the next few months this *is* normal.

Have just found the following in Christine Leonard's book[18] and marvelled at the way you answer my mutterings and frustrations, Lord: 'And I smiled to think God's greatness flowed around our incomplete-ness; round our restlessness, his rest.' It's from one of Elizabeth Barrett Browning's poems, 'Rime of the Duchess May'. I guess that's part of how I feel, too; I'm restless and want to speed everything up, yet I can't. I have to rest in you.

7.45PM

Even after finding those words, I am feeling tearful. Anguished, almost. Can't settle to anything. You seem so far away, Lord. I need your comfort so much. But I know that 'you have kept count of my tossings, put my tears in your bottle. Are they not on your record?' (Psalm 56:8).

Later

After a lot of tears and searching for reassurance, an answer. I began to read from Christine Leonard's book again. Lord, it is as if you are answering me. I've underlined these words that speak so clearly.

I hear your longing... I'm wet with your tears... I know the time is long and that hope of any improvement seems a bitter mockery to you... But you do not say, 'Where is your God?'—rather, 'When shall I come and behold the face of God?' ... When your anguish, your anger flows through your words, your groans and tears, I receive them as your sacrifice, more precious than your praise in happier times. But the symphony of your life will not howl in a minor key for ever... As truly as I love you, you will come again with glad shouts and thanksgiving, leading my people deeper in their rejoicing, because you have not only splashed about in my gentle streams but plunged under the thunder of my waterfalls... Know that, though all my waves swept over you, I have not—and never will—let you drown. And now, can you hear as the deep places in me call out to the deep places in you? Those who identify with my sufferings will experience to the full the unimaginable joy of my resurrection. (pp. 89–90)

Thank you, Lord. For hearing my cry... and answering me.

> *If I stoop*
> *Into a dark, tremendous sea of cloud,*
> *It is but for a time; I press God's lamp*
> *Close to my breast; its splendour, soon or late,*
> *Will pierce the gloom: I shall emerge one day.*[19]

MONDAY 28 JUNE

And this morning? It's like coming in from a storm. Checking on dried-off clothes the morning after. That wonderful sense of being warm after being cold—and knowing you are safe.

And again Christine Leonard quotes Robert Browning:

If I forget
Yet God remembers! If these hands of mine
Cease from their clinging, yet the hands divine
Hold me so firmly that I cannot fall;
And sometimes if I am too tired to call
For Him to help me, then He reads my prayer
Unspoken in my heart and lifts my care.

I dare not fear, since certainly I know
That I am in God's keeping, shielded so
From all else that would harm, and in the hour
Of stern temptation, strengthened by His power.
I tread no path in life to Him unknown;
I lift no burden, bear no pain alone.
My soul a calm, sure hiding place has found;
The everlasting arms my life surround.

TUESDAY 29 JUNE

Macmillan Cancer Relief has started a brilliant ad campaign. I've seen a couple of ads in the paper and on station platforms. The key phrase, 'Living with Cancer', is an attempt to change the perspective on how cancer interrupts lives. There's a lot of emphasis on carrying on as normally as possible, especially in family relationships. They are brilliant ads and could really change people's perception of cancer as a killer disease. I read yesterday in the newspaper that the dictionary definition of cancer is being changed; that it is no longer going to include the phrase 'usually leads to death'.

Evening

Went to the 'Look Good, Feel Better' group this afternoon. About ten of us (most of the others are in their 60s) sat around a long table for a skin-care and make-up demo. Because I was the youngest and the one who least cared about making an idiot of herself (I mean, after all, look at me, I'm already Mrs Blobby; why should I care?) I was the guinea-pig! The model, in their nice words. Nice to know I'm a model something. I was cleansed, toned, moisturized and made up, and was in the enviable position of not having to do anything for myself, which enabled me to watch the sometimes hilarious efforts of the other ladies as they tried to copy what the beauty therapist had demonstrated on me.

There was one darling, Millie, in her 70s, one of a trio who hadn't worn make-up for years. She drew lipstick across her face by accident. And her mascara was everywhere but on her eyes. She laughed so much with the rest of us that all her eye make-up ran, anyway! The laughter alone must have been therapeutic. It was amazing how much better all of us looked at the end, just for a bit of TLC and make-up.

The groups are run by a charity formed and supported by the major cosmetic houses. It's great to know that an industry which at first glance is about fripperies and false image can make such a positive difference to women's lives in this way. We all came away with more than a hundred pounds' worth of good-quality cosmetics and skin-care stuff in a box donated by the cosmetic houses! Can't imagine what Millie will do with all that! She had enough trouble getting the tops off the bottles!

Feeling good about how you look is important. It's not vanity but self-esteem. Getting the balance is important, I guess.

WEDNESDAY 30 JUNE

Trish, the wig lady, is coming to the house this morning to deliver and fit my wig. I'm so excited. Only Hitchcock could portray the suspense.

Evening

What a hilarious evening! The wig fits. And how. I couldn't believe that this dear lady was sincere in expecting me to go out in it. 'There, it's just like the hair you lost!' she assured me. Well, she didn't see the hair I lost and I'm quite sure the hair I lost didn't have a parting like that! Maybe it's just that she eats, sleeps and breathes wigs. Anyway, I thanked her profusely and smiled sweetly at her supposition that I could wear it to meet Benj from school, and wouldn't he be pleased? He wouldn't recognize me for a start. If he did, he'd never, *ever* forgive me. And anyway, there's no way I'd be seen outside in it. I look as if I'm either a transvestite or about to rob a bank! What it is that creates that effect, I can't say. Perhaps the synthetic appearance of the hair against my skin? The memorable parting? The way it swings around my cheekbones like a final curtain at the opera?

It was consigned to its box until the children came home. Then I put it on to demonstrate, wondering if maybe I was being hypersensitive. 'I've seen plenty of other women in lovely, short wigs which look marvellous on them,' I thought. 'Doubtless it's just me.'

It wasn't. As soon as the two of them saw me they burst out laughing and chuckled on and off all the way through *Blue Peter*.

I've accepted my entitlement to an NHS wig. I am very grateful for it and it will serve a purpose—just not the purpose intended. I'll put it on to give us all a good laugh at frequent intervals.

FRIDAY 2 JULY

My goddaughter, Judith, has come to stay. Now we're in for some fun. (Daren't show her the wig!) Judith is one of my most favourite and much-loved people. She will be a complete tonic for all of us.

SATURDAY 3 JULY

R and I had a good chat this morning. We talked about our position at the moment and about trying to make the most of our time together. R made the first black joke of my illness. He hasn't been able to do that as I have, but today he did. 'Live for the moment and make the most of life by all means,' he said. 'But don't forget: I might have your funeral to pay for, yet!' A turning point, I think!

Took Benj and his big bunch of buddies to Quasar this afternoon as part of his tenth birthday celebrations. I sat outside and read while Judith, Lois, Benj and his friends—and R—darted about inside, 'shooting' one another. I don't really know what I think about the ethics of Quasar, but they all seem to enjoy it! Especially R. He's the biggest ten-year-old! Today Benj rolled out first, exclaiming, 'You should have seen Dad, Mum! He was just like James Bond!' No sooner had he said this than Richard came through the door of the Quasar suite hobbling and wincing—he had hurt his leg! Quite badly, in fact, and although I laughed I shouldn't have, because he's still finding it hard to walk now! Let's hope a night's rest does the trick.

SUNDAY 4 JULY

Benjamin is ten today. R and I spent the morning in casualty where R had his leg X-rayed! Nothing is broken except his pride, but it's been strapped up (his leg, not his pride—that's still aching). Judith stayed at home with the children and they all 'accidentally' missed church. How's that for a goddaughter! Benj seems to have enjoyed a quiet day. Tennis finals on the TV and his favourite food. Something of a relief after his dad's heroics at Quasar yesterday!

TUESDAY 13 JULY

Sad article in *The Times* this morning. One of the contenders for Preacher of the Year is interviewed. She's had cancer on and off for 15 years and says that it has 'seriously undermined' her faith. She often asks God, 'What on earth do you think you're playing at?'

Maybe I'll feel like that after 15 years. Who am I to judge? The article referred to 'the problem of cancer for Christians', which this woman is now looking into as part of a research project. Maybe it's easy for me to say this at this point in time, and I'm being unfair: but not appreciating that God may have a different perspective on illness is something I quite honestly cannot understand. I wonder what her faith was built on? On the fragility of an image of God as one who will provide life that goes the way 'I' want it to go? Or a God who lets us go our own way, whether it's the best way for us or not? Doesn't a large part of faith involve trying to see things from God's perspective?

But, Lord, I guess it's easy to think that every journey is the same as my own. Doubtless there are things I struggle with which she would consider trivial. I pray that you'll be in her search for answers. I have a feeling that she won't find the kind of answers she hopes for, but maybe along the way she'll find you, as you long to be found.

Evening

Saw the doctor at clinic today. One less drug to carry home today, as I shouldn't need the allopurinol (anti-gout) now that the cancer cells should be drained of most of the stuff that causes it. Another chemo cycle starts tomorrow. On and on we go. Cycling uphill, too. The doctor is going to try to arrange a scan for about six weeks' time, so that we can see how it's all going. Still a long way off, but I'm already thinking, 'What if…' Remind me that you know all the 'what ifs', Lord.

WEDNESDAY 14 JULY

I seem to have stopped thinking through the whole dying scenario, which I suppose means I've faced it and dealt with it as much as I can at this point. It's funny how there seem to be cyclical stages not just to chemo but to living with the cancer. Almost like an ongoing relationship. Wouldn't mind a divorce from this one.

SUNDAY 18 JULY

Lovely day out yesterday at Chagford and Drewsteignton. R and I drove there on our own, as both the children were out in different places for a few hours. We really enjoyed the drive and had lunch at the Drewe Arms. Yet as soon as I got back I felt low and angry. I think it was the prospect of being shut in and restricted again after a bit of freedom!

Evening

Found church difficult this morning. The service started off with a 'turn to someone you don't know and tell them you love them' kind of thing. I just couldn't cope; it made me cry for a few seconds. I felt I couldn't be honest about how I was and most of the people around me either didn't know I was ill or will have forgotten. Sometimes I like it that way, but not this morning. There are a few individuals within the church who have been, and continue to be, great. But nothing has been organized to help us practically and sometimes we really struggle. I find this 'expressing of love' in the middle of the service difficult when it isn't accompanied by practical action. I must be careful not to let myself become bitter and cross about this, and I must remember to *do* something about it myself when I can.

MONDAY 19 JULY

Woke up feeling a bit brighter. Lord, I'm sorry about how I felt yesterday. Self-pity and sour grapes make a lethal cocktail of moaning, don't they? Please help me guard against them both.

TUESDAY 20 JULY

R had a lovely letter from David, whose wife died of lymphoma in April. It's a moving, simply expressed letter, obviously written by someone who knows dark times. He is offering space for R to talk to him, which I think would help both of them.

My nightly relaxing bath with scented bath oil and candles is a great de-stresser. I said to R tonight, 'You know that line that says, "It ain't over until the fat lady sings?" Well in this house it's, "It ain't over until the fat lady has had her bath."' Splash!

WEDNESDAY 28 JULY

There seems to be a kind of plodding through no-man's land in this situation. You just keep on keeping on, feeling progressively more tired.

It's a bit like getting very behind in a cross-country race and watching other faster, fitter people disappear into the distance. Everyone else is getting on with their lives and leaving me behind. They don't even come back with a wheelbarrow for me any more! People forget very quickly. I can go for days without hearing from anyone. I sometimes feel lonely and isolated, almost as if I'm living in some kind of invisible parallel world. I can understand why BACUP use the phrase 'Who can ever understand?' for their booklet on communication and cancer. Only people who've been there can understand. And I know only one or two. I hope that's not self-pity, but stating fact.

THURSDAY 29 JULY

Have borrowed the car today whilst feeling that I really shouldn't be driving. My reactions are much slower than they were and my fingertips so numb at times that I can hardly feel the steering-wheel. Maybe I should give up driving. But I wanted to bring the children to the beach, so here we are and I've spoilt them and bought them body-boards, which they are now flapping about with in the sea.

Evening

I think I really messed up the day by wanting everything to be perfect. I got cross with Benj when he wouldn't make the most of the sea and the beach. As normal, they didn't want to stay for very long and I felt that I'd made incredible efforts for nothing. I kept thinking, 'This might be the last time I take them to the beach', and that seemed to colour everything. To top it all, it seems the sun has hit me. I've got a dreadful headache now and don't feel great!

FRIDAY 30 JULY

Had the most awful night. Whether it was the sun, chemo or exhaustion, I was almost delirious with headache and sickness for half the night, with funny hallucinations. I was regularly sick, and not really knowing where I was for part of it. It's now 8.30am and I feel weak and not at all with it. Am just sipping water, trying to stay hydrated. Can't keep down anti-sicks, of course. I think it's a case of lying perfectly still until it's all over.

Later

Have just got up to the loo and caught sight of myself in the mirror. My face and head are almost yellow. I look drained and ill and, if I'm honest, almost not human. A strange thing to say, but I can no longer recognize myself in the mirror, such is the change in my appearance. Waxy skin and bulging eyes. I just looked at the mirror and said, 'Where are you, Wend?' and big tears plopped on to my cheeks. No wonder I feel asexual half the time. There seems nothing left of the me I knew before. I've been inflated like a reluctant balloon. Even now I'm joking about it, but I don't feel like laughing. I want myself back.

SATURDAY 31 JULY

R didn't come to bed at all last night. (Doesn't have a thing about nauseous yellow balloons, obviously.) He must have slept in the study. No point in him sleeping here when I'm heaving myself in and out of bed all night to be sick, anyway. Feeling slightly more with it this morning. There are things we need in town. Hopefully by this afternoon I might be strong enough to walk about and we can all go in.

Evening

Did go into town for a while, with the children and R alongside in case I didn't make it. I decided to go without my hat as it was so hot. It meant going bald for the first time! Reactions ranged from fair to disastrous. Those who looked and kept on looking were the funniest! One guy actually stopped, turned on his heels and looked again! A shop assistant in the bookshop, with whom I've had long conversations about books before, obviously didn't recognize me and was decidedly frosty. Had me down as an anarchic, lesbian, feminist terrorist, I expect. Sorry, that's being unkind and stereotypical. She could have thought I was a roll-on deodorant. I bet she doesn't get many of those asking for books. ('Excuse me, have you got *Armpits I Have Known and Other Stories* by B.O.

Strong?') But at least I can now understand the prejudiced attitude other people have to endure. It got the kids and me talking about prejudice in general, anyway.

TUESDAY 3 AUGUST

Spent half of yesterday doing housework very slowly and the other half doing a jigsaw. (Oh, what a life of leisure!) Have got into jigsaws again—R's ploy to make me rest! It's sometimes hard even to handle the tiny pieces with fuzzy fingers, but better than sewing. I can't hold the needle for cross-stitch.

FRIDAY 6 AUGUST

The children have been away, staying with their cousins in Truro so that they actually get to 'do' things during this holiday. Wonderful of Hilary to take on another two! I've missed them terribly, but the best thing has been not having to constantly worry that they're not able to do the kind of activities they usually do in the holidays because of me. They've had a great time beaching and bowling and going to the cinema.

Had another very strange dream in the early hours of the morning. It was unbelievably vivid and coloured with rich, golden honey colours. I seemed to be at some kind of Christian retreat, having a wonderful time talking and listening to various people. I felt so well, and it was obvious that I didn't have cancer. I also had hair. It was just marvellous being part of such a friendly crowd and having in-depth conversations. Everything seemed rich and warm. It was so vivid. When I woke up I felt tearful with disappointment because it wasn't real. It made me feel lonely. Lord, what was that for? When I feel lonely it seems such a cruel thing to have to endure. Yet its vividness made me feel it was from you. But how? What was it about? Was it heaven? Sometimes my dreams are so mixed up. I can't believe it's just the drugs.

SUNDAY 8 AUGUST

Yesterday afternoon we went to the Moscow State Circus! I've never, *ever* been to a circus and I enjoyed it so much! More than the children, that's for sure. Maybe it's just the current heightened enjoyment of the simple things in life. The clowns weren't at all funny, which made them funnier, somehow. But the acrobats and trapeze artists were amazing.

I've struggled a bit over the last few weeks, Lord. Although I've prayed, I've written little down. The mental confusion makes it worse. Sometimes I can't think straight and I get easily disturbed emotionally. Keep me safe, Lord.

MONDAY 9 AUGUST

The traffic is building up for the eclipse on Wednesday—slowly trailing into Cornwall.

Have just stuck the rest of my most recent cards into my scrapbook. Amanda has sent 18, to date. What a commitment she's shown to me in that simple act.

Helen Rollason, the sports presenter, died of cancer today. I remember her broadcast a few weeks ago when I thought she looked bloated, ill and very drugged—as if she was determined to struggle on. She was 43.

Sometimes I feel really well at the end of my breaks from chemo (like today) and can't believe I'm not getting better, and other days I feel tired and ill.

I found three photos of me this morning, which illustrate a lot. The first is me at my cousin's wedding two summers ago, with gleaming hair and skin, looking fit and well. The second is me at breakfast on Alice's wedding day in September last year. I had recently got over the worst of the virus that had bothered me since the bike ride. I still look ill. The last photo is of R and me in February, just before I went to the GP. My skin is pale, my hair is lank and my eyes are sore. I am leaning on R's shoulder, clutching his hand, looking very thin and tired, although smiling. We had no idea then how ill I was. Both of us were fed up with my always being tired. The contrast between the first photo and the last via the second is amazing. Why didn't we notice? I must have become ill so gradually that it wasn't apparent.

Evening

I felt quite upset by the media coverage of Helen Rollason's death. She kept going long enough to see her daughter through her GCSE exams, but didn't make it for the results, which are due later this week. And there she was, pictured with characteristic chemo coiffeur: very short, cropped hair with a straight front hairline. The news report called cancer a 'killer disease'. I wish they wouldn't. It must make Macmillan Cancer Relief groan with frustration after all they are trying to do to change the image. Yes, it does kill—but not always.

WEDNESDAY 11 AUGUST

I've got chemo today but it's eclipse day so we'll be going up to Plymouth Hoe first (with thousands of others, no doubt) to witness it all if we can. What a historic year for the children to live through. The end of a century and a millennium, with a total eclipse to get the ball rolling (or the moon rolling).

Evening

We went up to the Hoe, along with thousands of other people, hoping for one of the best eclipse sights in the country. But from the news tonight it looks as if Edinburgh and London had clearer views! A large screen was erected to relay the BBC coverage taken from an RAF plane. And that's really where we got our image of the eclipse from! There was too much cloud to see anything *au naturel*, although we did experience the gathering darkness until it was pitch black. It was a wonderful sight to see all the flash cameras and torchlights across the water. Very moving moments. I stood with tears in my eyes as I watched the sun being obscured, thinking of the God who created it—its perfect sphere and brilliant power. I don't think anybody there was unmoved. Unfortunately, the smelly hotdog stall next to us was unmoved, too.

Tonight a Radio 4 presenter made the point that the way the eclipse had uniquely united millions of people looking skywards was rather like a giant Mexican wave across the world. People were looking thoughtfully heavenwards, many for the first time in their lives.

Later

I'm now paying for all that walking and not enough time to drink before chemo. Although chemo went well and was quick, as hardly anyone was in, I was obviously exhausted and dehydrated and as a result have been constantly sick all evening! Must lie flat. Can't write any more.

THURSDAY 12 AUGUST

In the end I rang the hospital late last night, as I knew I wouldn't keep the chemo drugs down. A nurse suggested I delay taking them until this morning to avoid wasting a dose. The sickness has stopped now and I feel I should be able to keep the drugs down, so I will try. Am feeling pretty weak.

SATURDAY 14 AUGUST

The appointment for my interim scan arrived this morning. It's for Thursday 26 August. Hopefully that means the results should be back for the clinic on the following Tuesday.

SUNDAY 15 AUGUST

Lord, the mist of the last few weeks is disappearing. I feel as if I can hear you again now. The morning's Bible notes sum up how things are—based on Matthew 11:25–30: 'Come to me all you who are weary': 'When in harness with Jesus we are built up and affirmed; our lives discover meaning and purpose, and the struggles of life develop character rather than despair.' I guess I'd got 'out of harness' more through physical weakness than deliberate intent. When the weakness hits, it becomes harder and takes more effort to keep you in focus.

And I read Romans 5:3–5: 'Not only so, but we also rejoice in our sufferings, because we know that suffering produces perseverance; perseverance, character; and character, hope. And hope does not disappoint us, because God has poured out his love into our hearts by the Holy Spirit, whom he had given us.' Hope does not disappoint us. Thank you for reminding me of that assurance, Lord.

MONDAY 16 AUGUST

Mum and Dad have arrived to stay. I don't think I shocked them too much with my appearance!

I have been reading through Fiona's *Rainbows through the Rain*[20] again and came across Shirley Vickers' poems. I can identify so much with them, I guess because she wrote them during chemo.

TUESDAY 17 AUGUST

As Mum and Dad are staying, I was able to go to a church house group get-together with R. Enjoyed chatting to two older friends about their respective travels. Had no idea that one of them, Peter, had travelled all over the world as a young man and is still travelling! He had recently come back from a trip to New Zealand and he had the most beautiful book of photographs with him, which I marvelled at from the point of view of your creativity, Lord. It was for me as if the revelation of your creativity and the might and wonder you display through it supported my own trust in you at that moment. One of those special unspeakable experiences of the knowledge of God—a tiny glimpse of you.

Peter was talking about flying in a storm, and mentioned that once a plane is up in a storm, it can be impossible to fly either above or below it; the pilot has to fly straight through the middle. I thought, 'Just like this illness.' You can't fly above or below it, opt for an ejector seat to bail out or look for an airfield to touch down on, away from it. You have to fly straight through the middle.

FRIDAY 20 AUGUST

We're in Bath! One of my favourite cities. We left the children with Mum and Dad and travelled here yesterday, arranging B&B at the last minute. Bath is beautiful in the evening sun—restful and gleaming. A good contrast to my meditations on the storm.

Reading *The Message* today, I was struck by Eugene Peterson's paraphrase of part of James: 'Anyone who meets a testing challenge head on [like the storm?] and manages to stick it out is fortunate. For such persons, loyally in love with God, the reward is life and more life.' On goes this dialogue of reassurance and blessing. I do love you especially for that, Lord. Your words are like a huge, sheltering umbrella.

SATURDAY 21 AUGUST

Yesterday was a really busy, interesting day. We did the whole tourist bit: open-top bus tour, the Georgian house, and the Roman Baths tonight, by torchlight. That was certainly something to experience. Never would have imagined I would enjoy the Roman Baths so much. It's years since I did the tour, and never by torchlight. More social history than old stones. The lives of the people for whom they were a focal point almost breathe through what's left behind.

There was one very moving inscription on one of the surviving tombstones. It was in memory of a baby girl who lived to just one year and nine months. She had been born into slavery but adopted by a Roman family who had obviously loved her dearly and were heartbroken at their loss. I seem to remember that the Romans got their attitude to adoption right, giving their adopted sons and daughters identical rights and privileges (and obviously, in this case, love) to their own children. We don't know if this Roman family had any more children. But the heartbreak they felt at losing this little girl is almost carved into the inscription.

And, of course, Paul used that illustration of adoption to show how you love us, Father. Reading those words really brought that home to me. Born into slavery, adopted into love. But unlike that little child, I cannot be snatched from your hand.

Evening

I felt very ill at midday today. Think I must have overdone it, but desperate to make the most of Bath. Came home to a lovely, tidy house; good old Mum. She must have worked like a Trojan. (Or a Roman!)

MONDAY 23 AUGUST

A friend has offered us the use of a flat overlooking Cardiff Bay next weekend. Two weekends away so close together seems excessive, but we might not get another opportunity, and it will take our mind off the scan results due the following Tuesday!

TUESDAY 24 AUGUST

Took the kids to Superbowl today with two friends. Not sure that I should be driving! While the kids dashed around in the Quasar centre I sat outside to wait for them, reading and jotting down notes. James Bond was missing this time. Must be off on a mission.

The music at Superbowl is always very loud and intrusive, but today I found I listened more than usual. They played 'All my loving' by the Beatles first of all. I loved it as a child, and as I listened I could almost smell the bungalow where we lived at the time, and see the maze of corridors between rooms, and Mum at the kitchen sink, washing up for the umpteenth time. Then they played Diana Ross's 'I'm still waiting', 'Dancing queen' by Abba, and others that I danced the night away to at parties as a teenager. It was as if my childhood and teenage years were being paraded before me. I realized how many memories music carries with it. Smells and sensations return with the memories. The whole experience evoked strong emotions at a time when I was trying to keep a sense of perspective and hold on to the knowledge that this life isn't all there is. But, of course, it's hard to do that when this life is all we know.

WEDNESDAY 25 AUGUST

Sally took Benj and Lois out to an adventure park today with her boys. I was so grateful. If only someone else could have been as thoughtful earlier in the holiday. The children, although they never say as much, must resent my lack of energy! Benjamin had a lot to tell me when he got home. Mainly about a little boy he'd met there. He had noticed him because he had no hair, 'like you, Mum'. We concluded that possibly he had leukaemia. He also had some bad sores around his mouth, but a lot more energy than me, it seems! We discussed how much harder it must be for a child to cope with the side-effects of chemo. Benj has such gentleness and compassion on his face as he concluded: 'I really liked him, Mum. He was enjoying himself so much. He seemed so happy, as if he wanted to make the most of every little thing.'

The children are probably learning far more from their experience of this illness than I'll ever know.

10.30pm

Feel very lightheaded, quaky and not at all well. Rang the ward to ask their advice and they suggested I go in tomorrow, after my scan, to be checked over, so that I can go off for the weekend with an easy mind. As long as they let me go!

THURSDAY 26 AUGUST

The 'interim' scan went ahead as normal. Not too much waiting around, and it was lovely to have Margaret's company (my friend from the St Andrew's Bible study group). It was an odd sensation, leaving the room after the scan, knowing that the radiographer was looking at the tumour sites and interpreting them before I could see them myself. Rather like an invasion of privacy. I felt like saying, 'Hey, let me see my insides first; they are *my* tumours, after all!' (Margaret thought I should have said that, just to enjoy their reaction!)

The doctor checked me over on Birch Ward. She says my white cells are right down, which means I'm just neutrapaenic (blood counts low), but not dangerously so. She thinks it's possible I overdid it in Bath and that maybe I've had a virus over the last few days. She says we can go to Cardiff on condition that I really must rest, as I'm not doing enough of it.

SATURDAY 28 AUGUST

I'm sitting in the lounge of this beautiful flat overlooking Cardiff Bay. It's 8am. I've read 1 Timothy 4:6–16: 'Rather train yourself to be godly… Godliness has value for all things holding promise for both the present life and the life to come' (v. 7). And godliness doesn't depend on health, beauty or freedom, thankfully.

MONDAY 30 AUGUST

It is so beautiful here, sitting on the balcony. We could happily stay another week. But of course we have to go back tonight for scan results tomorrow and to start the next round of chemo on Wednesday. The children and R have hired bikes and are buzzing up and down Cardiff Bay on them. I've been watching them from here. Benj would like a new bike. He finally got round to learning to ride this summer on Lois's old small-wheeler, but he really needs a bigger one of his own. The determination and speed with which he mastered the skill deserves some kind of reward. Maybe an early Christmas present?

TUESDAY 31 AUGUST

Home now and off to get the scan results later. I had a burst of silent 'angry, angry' in the car on the way home from Cardiff last night. Still two months of chemo to go, more than two stone overweight, looking awful. A burst of 'well person envy' again after our lovely weekend away. But it does worry me how deeply I feel such things at times. It's as if all the emotion is buried away and just surfaces every so often for an airing. Maybe that's the best way.

Oddly, at the moment I don't care what the scan results are. It's as if I'm past caring. If they're good, they're good; if they're not, they're not.

Last night in the car, crying silently in the dark just seemed to sum up how I felt. R and the children didn't know I was crying and the tears just cascaded down my face. It's not that I'm not trusting you, Lord. I'm just so tired that I feel as if events are carrying me along. But maybe it's you carrying me along. I'm not sure I'd get far otherwise.

So much time has been taken away from me by this illness. But what's a year or so in eternity? It's just hard to keep that perspective right now. There's still a seemingly relentless haul ahead. I know it's going to get worse before it gets better, especially the toxicity of the drugs. I fell over in WHSmith in Cardiff yesterday. I lost my balance because of the effect of the chemo. I felt so silly.

If the scan results are promising, everyone will be expecting me to throw a party, and I just don't feel that way. Because it's not over yet, and I'm feeling so worn down by it all that it's as if I just don't want to know. I remembered some words from one of Rob's books last night: 'Just occasionally... I can hide.'[21] When I was a little girl I used to hide behind Dad's chair when the Daleks came on the scene in *Doctor Who*. Lord, I'd just like to do that now for a bit, please—hide away until the nasty things have gone.

Evening

Well, more than one nasty thing has gone. The tumour below my diaphragm has gone, as have the ones in my neck and one little crowd in my chest. There are three left around my aorta and trachea, but they have reduced in size a bit.

Dr P. was intending to carry on with the chemo from tomorrow, but once he heard about my bad balance, fingers and weight, he wondered if the Vincristine was getting too toxic and if we should try radiotherapy instead. We came home, having been told that he would discuss it with the radiotherapy doctor to decide whether or not the tumours were small enough to zap.

I was jumping with joy at the thought of no more chemo, but almost as soon as we got home Nurse Shirley rang us to tell us that I still have to go in for chemo tomorrow as tumours are too large to rely on radiotherapy alone and they need to risk more chemo.

The prospect of two more cycles is daunting. It means I won't finish until at least Christmas. At least Granny is here to help and has done the ironing and cleaned a lot. I'm so grateful, as I'm so tired.

Tonight, it sounds silly, but I felt too tired to lift my knife and fork to eat and just lay with my head in my arms on the table. I now understand why people refuse to have any more chemo and give up on it.

Somebody phoned tonight and said: 'Wendy's cancer must be on the back foot by now, isn't it?' R was frustrated at the assumption, having just witnessed me almost crawling around the place. He spent a few minutes calmly putting the person on the end of the phone right! Of course it's not their fault. They simply don't understand. Can't write any more.

—— *Part Three* ——

GOD KNOWS

WEDNESDAY 1 SEPTEMBER

We're now six months into this fun game. Another gold star on the chart, please!

I need to rest this morning before chemo. Dr P. explained that if you do too much beforehand, the chemo has worse effects. That explains a lot of the sickness episodes, anyway.

Evening

Well it seems that the three remaining tumours are about 2cm. Too big for radiotherapy at this point. Hence today's chemo. The nurse had trouble finding the vein again. My arm didn't want any more, either. It obviously didn't hear the revised verdict. Dr P. should have explained it to my arm, too.

THURSDAY 2 SEPTEMBER

Rob phoned last night to see what the results were, but everybody else apart from the two mums has obviously forgotten. I think the novelty is wearing off.

My left arm where the chemo went in is extremely painful this morning. The nurse did have a struggle. It took three attempts in each arm in the end. It felt as if the needle had gone completely in the wrong place at one point. I have taken two pain-killers to no avail.

FRIDAY 3 SEPTEMBER

Looking forward to our third weekend away in almost as few weeks. We go to stay with our friends Greg and Rach at their lovely farmhouse tomorrow. Have packed my pain-killers (not because of Greg and Rach, you understand...). I can identify this morning with Elisabeth Elliot's words: 'There is fellowship among those who suffer; for they live in a world separated from the rest of us.'[22] The subculture idea again. This society is for the young, reasonably beautiful, fit and able. You don't fit in if you're not in at least two of those categories. At the moment I feel as if I fit into none. Help me to remember how that feels when I'm well again, Lord.

SUNDAY 5 SEPTEMBER

We're at Greg and Rach's lovely farmhouse. We all enjoyed a great meal out last night at the Drewe Arms again (fast becoming our favourite!) and came back here to watch England beat Luxembourg 6–0, much to Benj's delight. It is so peaceful here. Beautiful countryside and nothing but cows mooing for accompaniment. Greg and Rach have a table-tennis table in their games room, of which the children are very envious. 'Mum, we could have a games room and put the snooker table in there too…'

MONDAY 6 SEPTEMBER

Feel low this morning. Tired after the weekend, although I enjoyed it so much. And of course the children go back to school tomorrow and I always miss them dreadfully the first few days. I never was a mum who couldn't wait for school to start.

Poem by Amy Carmichael that I read today:

When stormy winds against us break,
Stablish and reinforce our will.
O hear us for thine own name's sake;
Hold us in strength and hold us till

Still as the faithful mountains stand,
Through the long silent years of stress,
So would we wait at thy right hand
In quietness and steadfastness.

But not of us this strength, O Lord,
And not of us this constancy.
Our trust is thine eternal word,
Thy presence our security.

WEDNESDAY 8 SEPTEMBER

Dreadful night, with pain in my arm where the chemo went in last week. Tried to cool it down with a wet flannel as it was burning up so much. My arm was so hot that the flannel was dry in no time at all! Phlebitis? Off to hospital today, anyway, so they'll check it. So tired.

Later

Now sitting here in floods of tears. Have just spotted the mess Lois has left in the bathroom and the other things that need doing. How can I get it done? I'm so tired and in so much pain with this arm, and my temperature is up. Lord, where is some help? Help me get the right perspective on this. Feel my tears. They have to be a prayer this morning. I can't find the words. I know you're there but it's as if I have to swim through this storm of tears to reach you. I haven't the energy.

Later still

Cried myself to sleep. Must have been exhausted. Woken by the post arriving very late. It brought a letter from Mum, dear Amanda's card as usual, and a letter from Fiona. So lots of encouragement just when I needed it. Sat on the edge of the bed with the opened letters and just started singing 'Faithful one' to remind myself of your faithfulness in all this blackness. And then remembered and sang a verse from 'O love that wilt not let me go'.

> *O joy that seekest me through pain,*
> *I cannot close my heart to thee.*
> *I trace the rainbow through the rain*
> *And feel the promise is not vain*
> *That morn shall tearless be.*

This morning, Lord, I could not reach you through the darkness and tears, but your joy found me instead. It is true what Hilary McDowell said: you climb inside the pain with us; there is hope.

'Our circumstances are not the window through which we under-

112

stand his love but rather we must view our circumstances through his love.' Don't know where that comes from, but it means a lot today. 'For the Lord will not cast off for ever, but though he cause grief, yet he will have compassion according to the multitude of his mercies. For he doth not afflict willingly nor grieve the children of men' (Lamentations 3:31–33; much lovelier in the King James Version).

MONDAY 13 SEPTEMBER

Lovely to see Jacqui again today. I value her so much. And, being a hospice nurse, she doesn't flinch when I want to talk about the nitty-gritty. Not that we only talk about the nasty stuff. We have quite a hoot as well! We can really talk about *you*, Lord, can't we? I look forward to it so much.

Jill W. e-mailed to say how many people from Mothers' Union circles are asking about me now that my column shares news of my illness. How kind people are and what an encouragement that kindness is.

TUESDAY 14 SEPTEMBER

This morning my reading from Elisabeth Elliot's book contained John 11:4: 'When he heard this, Jesus said, "This sickness will not end in death. No, it is for God's glory so that God's son may be glorified through it."' Interesting or what?

And I read Romans 4 today from THE MESSAGE: 'Abraham entered into what God was doing for him and that was the turning-point. That is why the fulfilment of God's promise depends entirely on trusting God and his way and simply embracing him and what he does.' It reminds me of something I read on payer which says, 'Prayer is not telling God what you want but opening yourself up to what he wants in you.'

Evening

Interesting. A couple of months ago I came across an old Revised Standard Version 'giveaway' Gospel of John lying face down with all the old papers on the conservatory floor. When I picked it up and turned it over, my thumb was marking John 11:4: 'But when Jesus heard it, he said, "This illness is not unto death; it is for the glory of God, so that the Son of God may be glorified by means of it".' At the time, I almost didn't dare take it as meaning anything. Yet today I have read those same verses twice. Once in Elisabeth Elliot's book this morning and once tonight in Ron Mehl's *Surprise Endings*.[23] Is this wishful thinking, God's reassurance, or just another verse? I'm sure there must have been times when Christians have held on to these verses and then died, and left others, with whom they have shared the verses, heartbroken with disappointment that the words did not prove prophetic. We have to be so careful about our application of God's word. It's so easy to use verses like fortune cookies. And yet, if this is God's consistent reassurance, am I pushing it away?

WEDNESDAY 15 SEPTEMBER

Elisabeth Elliot uses the analogy of a seed again this morning: 'Suffering is necessary; suffering is the key to existence', and, 'When all seems lifeless, all that is beautiful withdrawn and shrouded, the invisible, miracle-working power of God has not come to a halt. He operates silently and secretly in the seed and in us.'

Lunch-time

The Bible study this morning was difficult. We were, coincidentally, beginning the theme of suffering. For me, there was again almost that sense of two 'cultures' alongside one another—of those who've been through it and those who haven't. It smacks almost of spiritual pride, but isn't meant to.

I found it difficult to keep quiet where my perspective was concerned. The perspective of most others was that suffering was to be avoided. Only a few could understand when I said that I felt it was almost to be welcomed because of the treasures within. One of the group was obviously quite irritated by what I was saying. (Did I really sound that pompous and pious?) She also misunderstood someone else who was, in agreement, desperately struggling to describe her similar experience of God. I think I have to remember that this reaction is often simply a difference of experience, nothing more or less. It would be so easy to think that because I've suffered I've arrived. It's also easy for other people to try to put me on a pedestal as some kind of spiritual 'super-saint'—with a very long fall from the pedestal if my faith even wobbles, or if I feel like blowing a large raspberry. I can think of another situation where this is happening to someone who has been coping with chronic pain for some time. And it worries me for her sake. Thankfully, it's not likely to happen to me. I haven't quite got the spiritual super-saint characteristics!

Lord, you are teaching me that as much as I want to share the wonder of you in all of this, there is a danger in the very act of doing that, which I hadn't anticipated: a danger of being misunderstood, or thought arrogant or bumptious; of building barriers instead of breaking them down; of creating defensiveness instead of meeting vulnerability with compassion.

Lord, give me wisdom and humility in knowing when and what and how to share. I want to draw people to you through this experience, not exercise some kind of spiritual exclusivity. And thank you for the 'fellowship of suffering' between those who have experienced that unspoken, inexplicable closeness of you in such times. It's beyond understanding.

3.20pm

I've been lying on the bed here for almost two hours, dozing after the Bible study. (Gosh, it comes to something when even a Bible study makes you feel tired.) I guess it was all the conversation and the emotional stress of dealing with issues that are very real. I'm grateful, Lord, that you so quickly taught me where I have to tread carefully in this whole area of sharing my experience. I would hate to hurt anyone, and I do not have the monopoly on an understanding of suffering, neither do I want to give that impression. There are others whose suffering is a million times greater (if it can be measured) and all the 'answers', when there are any, lie with you. What a responsibility you have given me, Lord. Make me worthy of it, and give me the right words and attitude.

Tonight R saw David, whose wife died of this illness. He thinks their time together helped them both. He has said very little about it. Perhaps it's for him to keep.

THURSDAY 16 SEPTEMBER

Very painful legs in the night. I presume it's steroid withdrawal again. Makes it very difficult to get going this morning. I can hardly walk from bedroom to bathroom (I need that Zimmer frame again).

I love the little slogan in my Bible notes this morning: 'A gossip is someone with a well-developed sense of rumour!' Rather more seriously, Elisabeth Elliot writes, 'Those who... fling soul and body down in joyful abandonment to whatever choice the Father may make for them rest in the confidence that God will make no errors in timing, or anything else.' Doesn't stop me feeling impatient to get on with things, though!

Evening

Have struggled terribly with tiredness today. Found it difficult to cook the tea and get the washing organized. Fell over halfway up the garden path again! My balance is getting really bad. I really could do with some help with the cleaning, cooking and ironing just occasionally. I just don't like to ask, which is my own problem! Friends have occasionally done a pile of ironing, but we really need more than that now. I guess I must stop smiling. As I suggested to Jill, I need to develop a pathetic persona in church to get help with the ironing!

SATURDAY 18 SEPTEMBER

R has bought Benjamin's (bargain) bike... and one for himself! (James Bond on a bike?) Benj is like a dog with two tails... and a bike! It's so lovely watching him whizz about on it with a huge grin on his face. He said goodnight to the bike tonight. I'm amazed he didn't drag it up the stairs to bed with him and tuck it in.

MONDAY 20 SEPTEMBER

It's 9.40am and I'm tired already. It's been an 'I-must-do-it' thing for me to keep walking Benj halfway to school each day. He could do it on his own but he enjoys the company and we have a good chat. I've only missed a couple of days all the time I've been ill. But it gets harder and harder. It's really only a short walk, but because I find I walk there at Benj's fast pace, I have to walk very slowly back! I've only done a couple of very simple jobs this morning and yet I collapsed on the bed, light-headed and aching. All I want to do is sleep, which is ridiculous as I've just had a very good night. Lord, please help me cope with the frustration of this terrible tiredness. There seems to be no rhyme to it (although I think I know the reason!) and it's making me very cross with myself. Let me know when I must give in, give up and stop.

WEDNESDAY 22 SEPTEMBER

The horrendously expensive vitamins and 'nutritious drink' I ordered from a recommended nutritionist have just arrived. I have just had my first taste of the so-called nutritious drink. It looks like pale green silage mixed with liquid cement and doesn't taste much better. If I have to go through a glass of this every day to retain my health and fitness, heaven looks even more attractive!

It's a fact: spiders are scarier than cancer. I spent last night with a very large spider lurking under the bed. I spotted it as I walked into the bedroom and it spotted me too and raced beneath the bed. It was so large I thought at a distance that it was a false eyelash. (Whose? I haven't needed to replace mine!) But I've never seen an eyelash run—flutter, yes; run, no. I could only move the bed a little to the right or left so the spider stayed happily underneath (still pretending to be an eyelash). It's there now as far as I know. Unless, of course, it ran across my face during the night to escape.

TUESDAY 28 SEPTEMBER

Lisa came down from the office yesterday, not to catch the spider for me, although I'm sure she would have done, but to chat over the work projects we're planning. It was *so* lovely to see her. She brought a beautiful big bunch of white lilies for me. She always remembers they are my favourite! But of course after all that excitement, I was shattered in the evening!

Saw Dr P. at clinic today. Despite the fact that I have caught Benj's cold, chemo goes ahead tomorrow. I will have another cycle after this, and then probably some radiotherapy to get rid of any remains. I feel a bit apprehensive about that. I know it's not as bad as chemo but it's yet another round of treatment.

I'm also not looking forward to the laborious round of re-staging tests, especially the much-loved (I jest) bone marrow biopsy. Ho hum.

I feel like a good holiday at this point. So did the spider. He has not reappeared.

WEDNESDAY 29 SEPTEMBER

Chemo today. Two little lines in my Bible reading notes this morning defused my worrying: 'Faith is… a relationship of trust in God… not a measurable substance.' What's ahead is difficult. All I *can* do is trust you, Lord. You've got me this far and you know what lies ahead. 'No one who trusts God with his heart and soul will ever regret it.'

Evening

Very sick after chemo. My own fault. I shouldn't have walked down to pick up Benj's inhaler prescription before I went to the hospital. I was exhausted before I started, and being tired always makes the toxicity worse. I got home from the hospital and tried to get the kids' tea organized early so that something was there for them to eat. I thought a hot bath would help with the shivering, so I ran one. But I started being sick in the bath! I was busy making the sick-bowl feel wanted all evening until about 10pm. I've not settled enough to doze a bit. Haven't taken any drugs, as I know I won't keep them down and they'll be wasted. I'm sure I'll be OK tomorrow and will start them then.

Thank you that you're with me through it all, Lord. Sometimes I feel as if you're sitting on the end of the bed looking concerned. I think you'd hold the sick-bowl if you could. I guess figuratively you do. I do love you.

As it is, Benj often comes and holds the bowl for me, even empties it. Such compassion in a ten-year old boy. And he's still saying goodnight to his bike.

THURSDAY 30 SEPTEMBER

Have come back to bed after putting the washing in the machine. Benj took himself to school and will meet his friend on the way. It's quiet and peaceful now and I can take the chance to rest after last night. Just hoping I can keep the drugs down. Feel a bit isolated. The problem is, I guess, everyone carries on with their lives and unless I yell for help they don't know I need it. I'm not much good at yelling. I feel like a little child. I need to trust in you, Lord, rather than my own abilities. I know your power is made perfect in weakness. In my disappointment with so much, I need to keep my eyes on what you want out of it all—now or in the future. Help me be patient and trust in you. Let me remember that the phrase 'God knows' is a positive, hopeful statement rather than a despairing one.

SATURDAY 2 OCTOBER

Thursday morning's isolation was followed by a buzz of activity yesterday! Mum rang, then Kate, and Liza called and took me into town for just the short time I could manage for a coffee and back to hers for lunch. Arrived home to find a bunch of flowers on the doorstep and offers to drive me to the hospital from my Wednesday Bible study group. As a finale, Kathryn phoned to check dates for going out to lunch next week. Wow! Thank you, Lord. You know how to mobilize the troops!

SUNDAY 3 OCTOBER

So, after all that generosity and thoughtfulness in people yesterday, why did I feel so weepy? It's roller coaster syndrome again! Lord, you had assured me clearly of your love, yet by late morning I felt so tired and as if everything was getting on top of me. Moving around is so difficult when I'm tired.

Some days I feel as if I've no right to ask for help, or to complain. Maybe it's that my cancer is not seen as a serious one, or that I don't appear ill. And it's true that when I feel well I almost wonder what all the fuss is about. Yet other days I feel like yelling, 'Hey, I've got cancer; help me!' (And I said I was not good at yelling. Maybe I should try it.)

This morning my Bible reading notes begin by asking: 'How peaceful and contented a person are you?' Usually... fine. Now... not. Well, let's read on and see what you're saying, Lord...

Psalm 131:2: 'But I have stilled and quietened my soul; like a weaned child with its mother, like a weaned child is my soul within me.' Well, of course. Only the other day, Lord, I was telling you that I felt helpless like a child, and now you are telling me to be still, to stop fretting, that this is how you want me to be: like a child in its mother's arms. It's an image I know so well—the quiet after the storm. It's as if I need to go through periods of struggle to appreciate the need to be still and rest in your arms.

The notes continue: 'The psalmist knew striving and turmoil in the past, but has finally come to rest contentedly in God's motherly arms, secure in the knowledge that all life's present circumstances and future hopes are under his omnipotent control.' It's so much like the times when the children have cuddled into me, crying, and I have rocked them to and fro, saying 'I know, I know...'

Father, I am sitting in your lap again with my head against your chest, but keep lifting my head to look into your face to tell you things. The things I tell you are sometimes gasped with desperation, sometimes yelled with frustration. Often they are things I feel I can tell only you. And you look down at me and say repeatedly, 'I know.' And you gently push my head back against you with your hand, as if to say: 'Rest. Stay for a while. Because I know.'

And the notes continue: 'But all those who seek God himself as their hope will be surprised to discover his parental plans for them achieve much more than they could ever ask or think.'

I have the sudden, wonderful realization as I look back over my notes of months past that this dialogue with you is real and practical and intimate. I ask and you answer; I mention and you remember; I moan and you listen; I cry and you mop the tears. Yet through it all there is a constant to-ing and fro-ing of words and sharing of feeling and love. You *are in* my situation. The King of heaven converses with me. I matter to him.

In the silence as I write, the overwhelming reality of that almost caresses me with its truth. Father, you *know*.

MONDAY 4 OCTOBER

A beautiful, blue-sky, sunny morning. I'm looking out of the window at the clouds drifting across the sky. They look as if they are a foretaste of heaven encouraging me to 'look up'. Although I am rather glad that heaven will not be just clouds carrying me around the sky with a harp.

I can remember reading J.I. Packer's introduction to David Watson's *Fear No Evil*, about how Christians tend not to think about heaven, or death, or dying. 'All stress among Christians is laid on present knowledge and enjoyment of God, and the old awareness that only one who is ready to die can live to God's praise has been generally forgotten... There is something here that we need to relearn.'

WEDNESDAY 6 OCTOBER

Not much sleep last night. And this morning, lots of cancer stuff in the post. Lymphoma Association News, a bottle of dye to drink before my scan. Sometimes it seems there can't be a moment without something that reminds me I'm ill!

Evening

Chemo took ages today. I went in at 12.20pm and came out at 3.35. Everything took time. But, as I'm always saying, it's why we're called patients.

There is a definite culture of the very ill. It's almost like an exclusive club. There are agreed entry rules (serious illness), a dress code (in my case, at least, a head covering) and an accepted code of behaviour (stoicism and making light of the awful). Although not everybody manages that, the most popular members have turned it into a fine art. The medical staff, although they rush around the clubhouse, cannot 'enjoy' full membership. They have only an impression of what membership really means, but more idea than those on the outside. Therefore, they are welcomed as honorary members.

The main aims of this club are to stay alive and retain dignity. It's an unusual club in that most of us are desperate to have our membership cancelled, and certainly don't want it renewed at a later date. Yet for a lot of us, that's a distinct possibility.

Sometimes it seems that in joining this club, a member has forfeited the right to belong to any other. It's almost impossible to be a fully paid-up member of the 'normal life' club. It should be possible, but unfortunately the membership criteria clash. For the most part, it is very difficult to belong to the 'normal life' club and just happen to have cancer.

THURSDAY 7 OCTOBER

Care for the Family awayday today. I wish I could be there; I'd love to see everyone. But I'm not sure they'd love to see me. I've decided my face resembles the Pilsbury Dough boy, complete with currant eyes.

Later

Jonathan and Steve have just phoned from the car on the way to the awayday! I felt quite weepy talking to them and knowing I wouldn't be sharing today with them. It was such a lovely thought, to ring.

SUNDAY 10 OCTOBER

Dreadful night. Feeling very bloated and uncomfortable, with bad backache. The night was filled with black, difficult dreams.

Evening

Back pain continued all through church. Hadn't a clue what it was. Tried a hot bath, but nothing worked. Perhaps it's just a bunged-up, drugged-up, mangled and confused body! Gosh, I'm looking forward to my new one in heaven. But I can wait.

I think the drugs have become about as toxic as they can be. I am dreadfully tired, wobbly on my feet, uncomfortable and forgetful, and I feel pretty sick. To top it all, I have a heavy period. I thought these were supposed to be stopping, early menopause being one of the delights I'll face as a result of chemo.

MONDAY 11 OCTOBER

Pains in my legs during the night. Oh, I do go on! I'm fed up with writing about it all! But I just feel it's important to include the difficult details—to write about all this as it really is. I do feel like occasionally writing an alternative diary entry: 'Breakfast was champagne and smoked salmon, after which we spent an hour in the garden reading the papers. Then off for a three-hour walk across the moors and down to that nice little pub for lunch. Dancing till the early hours tonight after cleaning the house from top to bottom this afternoon.' But was I ever able to do all that?

Now I'm going to name-drop. This morning I received a lovely hand-written card from James Jones (Bishop of Liverpool) in response to my letter. I had written to say how much his book had helped me in the early stages of this illness. I was quite blown away by the way he responded so quickly and personally, and with a fountain-pen! Now there's a rare item!

Evening

Felt very tired today. (What's new?) Have slept on and off for most of the day, only getting up to load washing in and out and hang it on the line. I fell over again in the garden. It seems to be something to do with leaning up and back to hang the washing on the line. It's difficult. But at least the washing's all dry now. (And so am I—but I wasn't earlier, as not only did I fall over but I fell into that big puddle where the path needs re-doing!) It just needs ironing (so do I)—all four loads of it!

Feel very light-headed and neutrapaenic. I just want to feel better.

The children are lovely at the moment—particularly precious.

TUESDAY 12 OCTOBER

Where are you, Lord? Well, I know you're still there, but I can't find you. I had a difficult night last night. Not much sleep. In it all, I felt distraught because I couldn't seem to find you when I was praying. When I went to bed, I felt so ill and isolated and asked for your comfort, yet it wasn't there. When I awoke I asked again, but nothing. It was like waiting in a dark, empty room, with not a speck of light. Sometimes that's hard to understand. But I guess you are asking me to trust you even when you don't speak or don't seem to have your face turned towards me, as well as when we're deep in what can only be described as long-distance conversation—my precious dialogue with you. But the darkness is hard, without even a match to lighten it. I felt very alone, distressed by lack of sleep and a bad headache. Nothing in the heavens changes. Lord, please help me find you again.

It's the next scan tomorrow. Have dutifully drunk my dye.

WEDNESDAY 13 OCTOBER

It's a beautiful day again. The clouds have tinges of pink in between the blue, grey and white. Probably means it's going to rain, but it's still beautiful. There's a message there somewhere.

Later

Scan was on time. Feel like an old hand at it now. But I didn't feel well when I got home afterwards. Felt terribly, terribly cold and could not get warm. Very odd. Eventually I covered myself up with layers and layers and got some sleep. I awoke feeling a lot better. It's as if my whole system is terribly confused.

MONDAY 18 OCTOBER

Thank you, Lord! Our prayers for some practical help are answered. We are almost overrun with meals. Four people have cooked meals for us, and one dear friend has offered to come and do some housework on Monday mornings for a few weeks starting today! Thank you, Lord!

SATURDAY 23 OCTOBER

I suppose there will be quiet periods in my dialogue with you, just as there are in any relationship. As long as I know I have done nothing to halt it, or to block up my ears, and that you are still there, I can totter on—'totter' being the operative word at present! My balance is dreadful.

SUNDAY 24 OCTOBER, 9.30PM

I thought my hair was here to stay this time, after the last load of chemo, but it is falling out again. The tiny quarter-inch that had grown, making me look like an Action Man doll, is falling out fast. Better set my hopes on being a Barbie with my wig on instead, then. (Never!)

WEDNESDAY 27 OCTOBER

Lois's 13th birthday. Can't believe it's 13 years ago that I rang R from the hospital to suggest that he joined me, as my labour had started. By the time he arrived, complete, as 'the book' suggested, with the Scrabble under his arm, I was well into close contractions. The midwife looked at the Scrabble and said, 'You certainly won't be needing that, Mr Bray!' One of my favourite photographs is the one of R holding a tiny, minutes-old Lois. The word 'proud' is just not big enough to describe the expression on his face!

The evening she was born, I can remember looking out of the window and seeing one very bright star in the sky. I could almost audibly hear you say that it was the mark of her birth and was a sign of your blessing.

THURSDAY 28 OCTOBER

If all the giggling and talking at 4am was anything to go by, Lois and friends had a good time at her sleepover last night! All four of them decided it would be fun to walk round the block in their pyjamas this morning at about 10am. I reminded Lois later that she does have to live here all year round!

I have my initial consultation about radiotherapy this morning.

Later

On the way to the oncology department, Benj said, 'Mum, will you have all your radiotherapy in the ornithology department?' He was very amused when I pointed out his mistake. It made us feel like comparing various waiting patients to different species: 'Oh, there's Mr Sparrow and that's Miss Parrot.' I guess I must be the bald eagle.

We were kept waiting for an age and a half before seeing the radiotherapy doctor. When my blood was taken, the poor nurse had three attempts in alternate arms and then had to give up and take it from my hand instead. The worst thing was being dumped in a room after an hour-and-a-quarter's wait, not knowing what we'd been dumped there for! It was eventually to see the doctor, but as the room was empty we didn't know and weren't told. It just made me feel more tense. For some reason, the radiotherapy doctor reminds me of Rowan Atkinson. Bit worrying, as Benj said, being given radiotherapy designed by Mr Bean. And if I tell my brother Chris, he'll worry terribly that yet another comedian is looking after me!

FRIDAY 29 OCTOBER

Liz has written from *Woman Alive* magazine to say she is pleased with my article about supporting a friend with cancer. Hopefully it will be of some practical help to a few people.

SATURDAY 30 OCTOBER

I think part of my problem is facing another round of treatment when I'm only just recovering from the chemo. Everything just seems to go on and on. I'm my own worst enemy where other people are concerned because everyone just expects me always to be smiling and bubbly, and I am OK most of the time. However, sometimes I just feel like kicking everyone in sight! Frustration, I guess.

SUNDAY 31 OCTOBER

Am very weepy. What is the matter with me? Tonight I felt that a nice, hot, soapy bath might help, so I filled up the bath, then wondered why the bubbles hadn't done much. It turned out the boiler has broken down! It was the last straw and I just sat and cried! My weight is really getting me down, too. I don't even want to make light of it (!) any more by joking. I have two pairs of leggings and one skirt that I can fit into. Everything else is acres too small. It will take me months to lose all this. I know it doesn't matter really but it is important to my self-esteem. I know that those who say, 'The important thing is getting well' are absolutely right, but somehow it doesn't help. Lord, please help me—either to lose the weight or to change my attitude. Preferably both.

I can understand why it's often said that the end of cancer treatment can be the worst time. Who knows why? Sometimes I have just had *enough*! After it's all over, what next? If I've made it, I face months of dieting to regain my clothes-wearing ability, an early menopause, months of growing my hair back to look as if I'm not a radical feminist, HRT and the ever-present shadow of the reappearance of tumours. And they call it 'getting back to normal'. You don't even get a prize. Cheerful, aren't I?

Lord, you know that tonight I got really angry with you about all this for the first time. I was in the bathroom, with lots of little things going wrong, crowded in with all the thoughts of what lies ahead and just yelled, in your direction, 'I've had it!' I stropped and moaned and carried on for a bit until I'd given you an earful. I don't think you minded. At least I was talking. But I minded. I sat there feeling totally and utterly alone and very, very low. I'm sorry. Help me remember that going forward and 'keeping going' involves putting one step in front of another. I only have to make one step at a time.

Radiotherapy 'measuring up' tomorrow. It's just the next step.

MONDAY 1 NOVEMBER, EVENING

Much better experience of oncology this morning. I was seen practically as soon as I got there. The radiotherapy team were friendly and helpful. They spent the time drawing lots of pretty lines on me as I lay there on the 'simulator'. Most lines were rubbed off before I left, leaving a tiny, tiny tattoo mark. They'll use this mark as a 'registration' each time they line up the machinery. They explained everything brilliantly. I feel much more reassured. Somebody must be praying. It wasn't me much today. I feel exhausted and badly in need of a lot of TLC.

THURSDAY 4 NOVEMBER

Alison has organized the Bible study group wonderfully to give me lifts to and from the hospital for radiotherapy! They look after me as if I'm royalty.

FRIDAY 5 NOVEMBER

Lord, I feel so tired and low. I know I've let you down so much with this attitude. But you still sit by me and I still rest in your lap. It's just that sometimes there isn't anything to say. Everything seems such an effort at the moment. I wish there was someone to talk to who has been through this who could explain to me why it's happening.

SATURDAY 6 NOVEMBER

Very low again today. Did virtually nothing all day. I sat in the bath and howled (ran taps as usual so the kids wouldn't hear). Turned to Shirley Vickers' poem 'Black hole' in Fiona's *Rainbows through the Rain* (p. 24). It sums up how I feel. But why?

SUNDAY 7 NOVEMBER

R needed to work all day today so the children and I went to church on our own. We did things our way all day and enjoyed each other's company. Benj sat with me and I helped him with his sewing from school. (Sewing, poor lad, not exactly what most ten-year-old-boys would choose to do!) Then he did some of his school project on the Second World War, which is coming along very well. He said, 'I enjoy sitting here and chatting with you like this while I do my writing.' Ordinary things. It's what's so precious when life is threatened. Radiotherapy begins tomorrow. The next step.

MONDAY 8 NOVEMBER

Radiotherapy was fine. It took all of ten minutes and was a bit like a ride at Alton Towers but without the scariness. I have to lie on a hard table below a large, round, metal and glass canopy. Green and red flashing lights, beams, hums and buzzes follow. Once that bit is done, it gets very exciting as the large canopy is spun around until it is lined up underneath the table. At the same time the bed moves up into the air to make room for it, so that it can zap from the back too. As soon as it's in place, all the buzzes, hums and beams start again. Once I'd been lowered down to earth, I felt as if I wanted to ask, 'Can I go on the big wheel now?' Another 'go' tomorrow. Just a very slight, warm sensation in the depth of my chest. But that's likely to be excitement, or heartburn!

THURSDAY 10 NOVEMBER

Almost wept in oncology today. In front of me while I was waiting sat an older couple, perhaps in their early 60s. It was obviously the wife who was waiting for treatment. At one point, she turned her face to one side to struggle out of her jacket. She did not notice that her husband was trying to reach across to help her. In the end, he saw it would be easier for her to do it herself. But his expression filled my eyes with tears. His face was a mixture of the most tender love, care and compassion—and complete helplessness. I wanted to go to him and tell him that he *was* helping just by showing her that much love. Goodness knows what her prognosis is, but they both looked desperate. It was as if they were openly facing the fear of separation in public. I had to put my head back in an attempt to blink the tears back under my hat. I couldn't bear the idea of anyone thinking I was crying for me.

This kind of 'compassion' weepiness has happened a lot lately. It alarmed me so much this morning that I called into the Macmillan Centre on my way back to the bus to ask them what I can do about it. It's OK weeping when I'm on my own, but weeping about things in public is more difficult. I was reassured that it's perfectly normal and that sometimes there needs to be a release of emotions at the end of a long period of treatment because of the tendency to 'hold yourself together' throughout the treatment. I thought I hadn't always been brilliant at holding myself together! It was suggested that I needed a bit of TLC and to do something for myself. 'How and when?' I wanted to ask!

There must be something special about these tears because they do seem to come from the depths and are very different from tears of frustration or self-pity. I wonder, in a sense, if they are God-given because they really only happen in circumstances where in some way I am identifying with the suffering of others. That sounds very deep, but I think it might just be a natural (or supernatural) way to transfer grief from a potentially selfish situation to a useful one.

MONDAY 15 NOVEMBER

Two pieces of exciting junk mail in the post this morning. One was trying to sell me a racehorse, the other a catalogue of ladies' clothes (sent out unsolicited from a dubiously named 'fashion house'), which I couldn't believe anybody expected me to wear. Maybe there's a supposition that your dress sense goes with cancer treatment as well as your hair. Don't think there's any significance in the racehorse.

Benj has got asthma quite badly so he will stay at home today.

I'm still weepy and irritable. Is it hormones, or roller coaster syndrome? Sometimes I feel as if I've been kidnapped by one (a roller coaster, not a hormone… although I'm sure I'll experience that soon, too). I'm up one minute and down the next.

I read Psalm 121 this morning. It is a beautiful psalm of blessing and protection: 'The Lord watches over you—the Lord is your shade at your right hand [very apt with radiotherapy beams blasting away!] … The Lord will keep you from all harm—he will watch over your life…' Lord, these are beautiful words of assurance and love from you. But why do I feel so flat and find them so hard to grasp at the moment? What's happened? I still trust you implicitly for everything that's going on, but it's as if my focus has moved. I am no longer focusing on life itself but on 'normal' life as I see it. I am desperate to get back to normal life, normal weight, and normal hair. I'm taking my eyes off you too often, I guess. And I must also remember that faith is not based on feelings.

TUESDAY 16 NOVEMBER

Benjamin is still not well, but the bonus is that he was able to watch me being zapped in the radiotherapy department today. There are two friendly, young radiographers on duty this week who have taken a shine to him and let him stand at the control point and watch everything on the TV monitor. He is most amused by all this!

It was lovely to get a card from Amanda this morning—though I could do without references to her new ball gown (size 10, no doubt!) for a ball in Bath next weekend, and to how she is waiting for her new Aga to be installed. Not envious really. Just blew a large raspberry. Will have to tell her!

I read Numbers 9:15—10:10. The accompanying Bible notes contain these words: 'God's presence and guidance bring with them certain expectations and responsibilities; above all, that we live lives in response to that presence and the direction it brings.' Lord you do beautifully and patiently remind me what is more important than balls in Bath, new dresses and Agas. But I also know you understand the 'womany' bit in me (as R lovingly calls it). You would not have made me with the few positive, creative bits of me if that were not the case. I almost felt in reading this that you were saying, 'Yes, I know all that, but remember what a privilege you have to share what I have done and am doing in you through the situation you are in now.' It's a question of not missing opportunities with you (for learning and relationship) and for you (in witness and service), isn't it, Lord? I'm sorry that I'm letting you down so much and shifting my gaze too much to the worldly. Maybe I'm doing it because that's the most apparent evidence of 'normality' and getting well. Give me patience to accept that seeking you first will mean all these things will be added. Not necessarily a ball in Bath and an Aga, but the things which you know are the very best for me and which will glorify you.

8.50pm

The roller coaster has kidnapped me again. In floods of tears in the bath tonight. (Oh, the many and varied connotations of 'bath'!) Can't bear the sight of myself at the moment. Vanity, or what? I wasn't just bathing in water, but in oodles of self-pity. I am not a very fast learner.

The trouble is that when I look at myself in the mirror I have to search hard for any physical similarity to what I was like before. I am still so puffy around the face from chemo. Still I stare at this puffy-faced creature and it stares back at me. And I think, 'Where are you, Wend? I can't find you!' I feel a permanent scruff. I find myself dreaming of my favourite clothes—my suits, my little black dress, my tight jeans, my beaded 1920s evening dress and the elegant evening shoes I bought last year. I would flatten them now. It should be the time to wear them soon, with all the Christmas and millennium parties coming up. I'll have to wear wellies. (The potential for wearing wellies and a ball gown gets more real.) I'm also terribly fed up with everyone saying, 'It doesn't matter', because it *does* matter!

WEDNESDAY 17 NOVEMBER

Not quite so gloomy this morning. Maybe I have to accept that at the moment the bath is a safe place for limited self-pity and tears, rather than somewhere to prepare to slip into a size 10 dress and elegant shoes. Like a safety valve. At least I'm not moaning all over everyone else then.

My coughing kept me awake a lot of the night.

Breathing became difficult in the middle of the Bible study this morning. It became quite laboured as time went on and Mandy wisely insisted on getting me to a doctor. I've got a chest infection and a urinary tract infection. Great! The GP has given me huge doses of antibiotics. I am sitting up in bed and dear Benj has just given me some lessons on how to cope when you get really breathless: 'Think of something nice, or pretend you're walking somewhere you like going,' he said. I was just about to imagine a lovely bit of one of the Dartmoor walks we do, when Benj said, 'Imagine you're going round John Lewis at Cribbs Causeway.' Am I that transparent? But I have to say, it works! I'd spent several hundred pounds in my head by the time the breathing got easier! I haven't experienced laboured breathing like this since I had pneumonia seven years ago. My poor old immune system can't cope, I guess. I've been told to stay in bed except when I go to radiotherapy. It shouldn't stop radiotherapy unless it gets really bad.

Thank you, Lord, for Mandy's generosity in running me around everywhere today, to the doctor and chemist to get me sorted. Thank you for her love and kindness.

THURSDAY 18 NOVEMBER

Breathing not quite so difficult today. But it was good to collapse into bed again after radiotherapy.

SATURDAY 20 NOVEMBER

Poor R is having to do so many more extra jobs because I'm like this. He must be so fed up with it all. Thank you for the way he never moans at me for being ill... even if sometimes he looks as if he wants to!

I received a letter today from my very first infant teacher and Sunday school teacher. She heard that I was ill and has written reminding me that I wrote to her at a very difficult time in her life to assure her that God had a very definite plan for her, even though she could not see it at the time. I must have been all of 18 or 19! She said she had kept the letter and wanted to return the message! How wonderful that the encouragement I tried to give has been returned to me. And imagine keeping my letter for more than 20 years! (Must have been written on parchment with a quill!)

SUNDAY 21 NOVEMBER

Bright blue sky again this morning, but icy cold. Have just spent half an hour jotting down what I might want to include alongside bits of this diary if I decided it was right to share it by having it published. I've had so much encouragement to do so; maybe I should think about it seriously. But I'd have to include all the grotty self-pitying bits, or it wouldn't be honest. I also don't know how I feel about books I've read which have chronicled people's illnesses. Even Christian books can be enormously self-focusing and indulge in a bit of super-saint promotion. I couldn't bear to do that. I'd have to do a warts-and-all-thing.

Please confirm that it's the right thing to think about, Lord. I'm not sure I feel right about it. Would people really *want* to know about all this? Only if it turns their eyes to you, to your goodness and faithfulness, your humour, creativity and wisdom in the way you have sustained me. Otherwise, no thank you.

I read Psalm 138 this morning: 'When I called, you answered me; you made me bold and stout-hearted... Though I walk in the midst of trouble, you preserve my life; you stretch out your hand against the anger of my foes, with your right hand you save me... The Lord will fulfil his purpose for me; your love, O Lord, endures for ever—do not abandon the works of your hands' (vv. 3, 7, 8).

The notes add, 'The whole experience has changed the psalmist's life irrevocably. Through it all, the psalmist knew without a doubt that the Lord's purposes for him were being fulfilled and God would not abandon him like some half-finished work. God's love and faithfulness would never end.'

Why am I such a whinger? Drown my self-pity in verses like that, Lord. You are always there and my sin is that sometimes I refuse to even acknowledge you when you are there, let alone lift my head to look into your face. You are saying, 'Hang on in there, don't forget I am here to be your strength and there is a purpose in all this.' Thank you, Lord. And maybe I shouldn't abandon this prayer diary like a half-finished work either, but do something with it.

MONDAY 22 NOVEMBER

Radiotherapy took ages today. A very bossy radiotherapist sent me off on a wild goose chase to see a doctor when I didn't need to! Arrived home to find that two dear friends had done my housework between them! Felt very loved and cared for.

Jill has written encouraging me to have a go at writing up this prayer diary. Is that a yes?

WEDNESDAY 24 NOVEMBER

Still coughing—and how! Got so hot walking Benj halfway to school and back that my head was wet through when I took my hat off!

My Bible reading notes this morning follow up my thoughts about the difficulty of sharing my experience of being ill. The notes suggest that we must have great respect for the history and baggage of other Christians. 'Cultivate your relationship with God,' it says, 'but don't impose it on others.'

Is that a no? Would I be imposing, or sharing?

ADVENT SUNDAY 28 NOVEMBER

I can now start Delia Smith's readings for Advent, which I always enjoy. They get me feeling Christmassy in the right way!

My Bible reading notes today included Psalm 130:5: 'My soul is waiting for the Lord; I count on his word.' This was the verse I finished my just-published *Home and Family* magazine column with, so readers who read that in the last couple of days and who read Delia this morning will have it underlined![24]

Evening

Psalm 139: 'O Lord, you have searched me and you know me.' Those words are very much in my thoughts, as I know there is nothing you don't know, Lord. You know the depths of my heart and the outposts of my imagination. You know all my fears and weakness. 'All the days ordained for me were written in your book before one of them came to be.' So how can I *not* trust you for the future?

In my Bible notes this morning, I read, 'The greater our trust, the more we'll know the security of his acceptance, his listening ear, his faithful presence, his total understanding of what has made us the way we are and his desire that we might be all that he intended us to be.'

MONDAY 29 NOVEMBER

Ian C. visited me today and shared the verses from Psalm 37:3–7 in the belief that you had 'illuminated' them for me.

> *Trust in the Lord and do good;*
> *dwell in the land and enjoy safe pasture.*
> *Delight yourself in the Lord…*
> *trust in him and he will do this:*
> *He will make your righteousness shine like the dawn,*
> *the justice of your cause like the noonday sun.*
> *Be still before the Lord and wait patiently for him.*

Having found out today that I won't know the outcome of all this treatment until February, I certainly need to learn to 'wait patiently', Lord!

The radiotherapy carries on working for several weeks after it has finished and I have to wait for the whole batch of re-staging tests to be done before they'll know the picture for sure. So as my next clinic appointment is on 20 January, we'll be into February before the tests are done.

TUESDAY 30 NOVEMBER

Took Benj to the doctor this morning and saw our own GP—a rare privilege. He seemed genuinely pleased to see me (alive, she adds!) Benj perked up considerably once it was established that he could take away a whole bag of medicines and have the rest of the week off school to clear his asthma!

SATURDAY 4 DECEMBER

Yesterday was the last day of radiotherapy. R brought home some smoked salmon and champagne last night, to celebrate the end of the treatment. What a wonderful husband! We also took a couple of photos of me with my 'fuzzy' hairstyle.

MONDAY 6 DECEMBER, 6.50PM

R and I went to Exeter for Christmas shopping. It followed the usual pattern of our 'day off' trips together—more or less unmitigated mini-disaster from start to finish: dreadful traffic getting to Exeter; nowhere to park, so R had to drop me off and park miles out; we couldn't get into the cathedral because there was a carol service on; my pub lunch was almost inedible and we couldn't find most of the things we wanted to buy as gifts. But we had a day together!

The journey home was traumatic. Two ambulances, a fire engine and several police cars passed us as we left Exeter and I felt sure that we would soon come upon a road accident. I am so fragile at the moment that the slightest sadness means tears. R assured me that there were lots of roads in the direction we were travelling and it was unlikely that the accident was on our stretch of the A38. But, of course, it was. We got close to the service station just before the lanes split for Torquay and Exeter and saw the air ambulance lifting off. That was the trigger. The tension of wondering and waiting for several miles collapsed and tears rolled down my cheeks. As we neared the scene, we had to drive through the service station forecourt to avoid the concertina of cars from which passengers had been released. There were emergency vehicles everywhere. It had obviously been a horrendous accident.

What can I do with this fragility?

THURSDAY 9 DECEMBER

My Bible notes this morning read, 'Each person is given something to do that shows who God is.' What's my 'something to do', Lord? Maybe that's yes to the diary? It certainly shows the wonder of who you are. Trouble is, it shows the unwonder of me, too.

WEDNESDAY 15 DECEMBER

Christmas is fast approaching. It seems as if there is so much pressure to have a good time this year, with the millennium hype. Will we forget the wonder of your birth amidst the fuss, Lord?

FRIDAY 17 DECEMBER

Saw Benj's school Christmas concert for the second time with R last night. It's an ordeal for Benj, who can't bear doing it—especially as he has to stand next to... a girl! But it's the last time we'll see one of our children in such a performance, because Benj will be at secondary school next year. It was quite hard for me not to get weepy singing 'White Christmas'. But I couldn't embarrass poor old Benj like that!

I've got an appointment for my bone marrow biopsy on Monday. A little pre-Christmas cheer! At least I'll get it out of the way before Christmas.

SATURDAY 18 DECEMBER

I feel a bit coldy. I know my immune system is still low. Must be careful to avoid germs. The mind boggles. Germs don't really identify themselves so that you *can* avoid them.

I love the quote by C.S. Lewis in my Bible notes this morning—very apt in this millennium season: 'All that is not eternal is eternally out of date!' We need this impressed on us in a time of materialism, consumerism, up-to-the-millennium fashion and flashing lights.

Tidied up our bedroom today and took away the 'in-siege' supplies of kettle, teabags and other items that I've never used; it gave me a good feeling, and made me thankful that I have never been as ill, or for as long, in that room as I thought I'd be. Maybe in the spring, or earlier, if all is well, we can move back upstairs! I can remember very clearly the tears and anguish of leaving our pretty room on the top floor.

SUNDAY 19 DECEMBER

I read Psalm 142 today. Three strong statements of faith amidst a desperate cry to the Lord from the psalmist: 'It is you who know my way… You are my refuge, my portion', and the notes say quite rightly, 'We will find ourselves with a stronger grasp of his greatness and an increased depth of understanding because of what we learned in our times of darkness.'

Evening

I'm already worried about the bone marrow biopsy tomorrow. A reading tonight, out of context, but I believe your way of reassuring me, Lord: Exodus 14:13–14: 'Do not be afraid. Stand firm and you will see the deliverance the Lord will bring you today… The Lord will fight for you; you need only to be still.' OK, Lord. I'll try to keep still… but have you ever had a bone marrow biopsy?

MONDAY 20 DECEMBER

Well, it's over. The least said about that the better. Seemed worse than last time. Probably because I'm better and my nerves are sharper, and of course I knew the procedure. When I remember that a broad needle is driven through the bone to get at the marrow it's easier to understand why it's so agonizing! Let's just hope I never have to have another! My back was a bit sore afterwards, but I still went Christmas food shopping with Mandy! It was like a trolley dash for 10,000 people in unison! Ooh! I do love Christmas!

THURSDAY 23 DECEMBER

The tree is up and the house is decorated. Wasn't going to bother with so much ivy this year. But Diane reported that Benj had told her that his favourite thing about Christmas was 'when Mum decorates the house up beautifully with greenery'. So I've gone just as mad as usual!

Had to prop the poor Christmas tree up even more than last year. It's fallen over once already and Lois and I had to do a rescue job in fits of giggles. The angel even lost her wings (I know how she feels). But it does all look beautiful. This house definitely lends itself to being decorated for Christmas.

CHRISTMAS EVE, 10PM

I've been busy all day, preparing for tomorrow. Poor R is driving through dreadful rain and flooding in Cornwall to get to his regular Christmas Eve get-together with old school friends. The children and I have had a lovely evening together wrapping presents and finishing things off. Their excitement is infectious. I listened to 'Nine Lessons and Carols' from King's College, Cambridge this afternoon, as usual. Like Delia Smith, I peel my vegetables to it. This year I was a bit behind, and was only just starting the sprouts at the chorister began 'Once in royal...' Usually I'm at least on the carrots. Oh, these little securities of life! It's funny how every year I can find something different in the service. This year, understandably, it's the idea of light transforming the valley of death.

CHRISTMAS MORNING

Happy birthday, Jesus.

The children didn't wake this morning until after we did! We were chatting away in bed, hoping to wake them up. In the end R got up and was trying, in a very funny way, to be very noisy to hurry them. What reversal of roles!

My reading this morning from Isaiah 9:1–7 included the words that stood out for me in yesterday's radio broadcast from King's College:

'on... those living in the land of the shadow of death a light has dawned.'

SUNDAY, BOXING DAY

A quiet, relaxed and happy day yesterday. Probably just what we needed. R bought me the most beautiful pearl necklace and earrings to match—his lovely way of trying to help me feel glamorous. Benj and R are both enjoying using the new video camera to film us. We thought we should get some film of us all. Especially me—just in case—and the children so enjoy watching the early video films we made of them as babies and toddlers. Having seen myself on film, I don't think I'll be getting any Oscars.

Have noticed some odd, digging pains in my back and under my arm. Daren't think about them.

NEW YEAR'S EVE

Telephoned the NHS Direct advice line this morning to ask about these pains. They are across my right breast particularly, and under it, then right through to my back and in my armpit. They are very like the tumour pains I had at a similar time last year, not knowing what they were. I put those down to PMT, so it's very possible that these are also hormonal. If they are, they are painful.

Early hours of 2000

We were intending to go up to the Hoe to see 2000 in, but decided to spend some time with Chris and Kate early on in the evening and then come home for a late meal. The trouble was that I was feeling so rough with the pain and a temperature, and still not letting on much about it to anybody, that I was not exactly a bundle of laughs doing the cooking! But we enjoyed a delicious meal, opened some champagne and watched the Dome celebrations on the TV. R and I haven't done our usual thing of hoping next year will be better than this one, because we always do and it never is. We're going to call its bluff this time!

NEW YEAR'S DAY

Well, I've made it into the new millennium! But how much further?!

The pain is worse today. I finally rang the ward, as I was convinced that this pain was something to do with the cancer. They told me I have 24-hour cover there anyway, so I could have rung much earlier! The doctor who examined me was concerned and explained that I couldn't have a scan until Tuesday but that it was unlikely that tumours would return quite so quickly. Then she examined me and found a red rash I hadn't noticed. I have shingles!

I'd heard it was painful! I've never been so pleased to have an illness in my life! I've got some anti-viral tablets and just have to be anti-social for a bit to keep chickenpox away from those who might be vulnerable. Evidently, the chickenpox virus lies dormant in the nervous system until it is reactivated when you are low or stressed. Compromised immune system problems again!

SUNDAY 2 JANUARY

Feel quite rough now with this and am staying in bed today to nurse a high temperature. Flu-like symptoms—but I don't mind them at all. They're a wonderful relief!

Amused by your sense of humour, Lord, which had me reading in Leviticus about infectious skin diseases this morning. I feel as if you are teasing me for not trusting you!

TUESDAY 4 JANUARY

Spent a long time in the bath this morning, thinking about various outcomes of the final scan due at the end of January. Started off thinking about a good outcome and then even went as far in the other direction as to be thinking about the strain it would put on Jacqui to have to nurse me in the hospice! But what struck me more than anything about my contemplation of death was how ill-prepared I am for it, in terms of what my life is. How much I do that I shouldn't do and how much I don't do that I should do. As simple as that. How little I really do in my life for Jesus. I might kid myself that I do my work for him, or care about others for him, but I really do it mostly for me. Lord, I mostly make and follow my plans loosely alongside yours, don't I? The words in my head that I've almost sung the last few mornings are from Stainer's *Crucifixion*. It's an old hymn, but the words are everything:

> *All for Jesus, all for Jesus,*
> *This our song shall ever be;*
> *For we have no hope, or saviour,*
> *If we have not hope in thee.*

Rob once asked what 'hope' meant to me. In the inarticulate and drugged-up state that I was in at the time he phoned, I tried very hard to explain that every single pathway of hope, however you follow it, always leads to God. I think those words illustrate that. Everything else is pointless because the only end it leads to is a dead end—in more ways than one!

David Watson said: 'Who else apart from Christ and his resurrection (the evidence for this being overwhelmingly powerful) can give us any solid hope for the future?' Hebrews 6:19 says: 'This certain hope of being saved is a strong and trustworthy anchor for our souls, connecting us with God himself behind the sacred curtain of heaven where Christ has gone ahead.'

Lord, I know I have failed you, disappointed you, and I'm sure I will repeatedly do so, even though I don't want to. You are the only hope I have. My heart's desire is to do what pleases you, even if the world despises it. Help me break through this snare of self-centredness and to do 'all for Jesus'. Build the desire, the will to live like that daily. Otherwise how will I meet you in heaven other than with my head hung low?

THURSDAY 6 JANUARY

Oswald Chambers' words in my reading this morning should set my attitude for getting back to work. 'There are not three stages to spiritual life—worship, waiting and work. Some of us go in jumps like spiritual frogs, we jump from worship to waiting, and from waiting to work. God's idea is that the three should go together.'[25]

FRIDAY 7 JANUARY

Lung function test today. And guess what, I got it wrong again. Did what I thought was the right kind of breath in and out of the Heath Robinson machinery only to have my knuckles rapped. 'That wasn't very good!' I was told. 'You can do much better that… have another go!' Have you ever felt inadequate just for breathing? I thought I had to do a little breath in but it was supposed to be a short breath. Is there a difference? Obviously so. After about 45 minutes of puffing and blowing, I was finally released. It is the most amazing experience. Something you do so naturally on a day-to-day basis suddenly becomes akin to a lung marathon. And they wouldn't even tell me if the results were any better than last time (or worse). Just the echogram (with the jelly stuff on a topless me and the guy with no sense of humour) and the CT scan to go, and that's the full set of tests done again. You really should be able to collect stickers on a card.

SATURDAY 8 JANUARY

Went into town with Lois to buy her a school coat and me another pair of warm pyjamas. Glamour. One or two sizes bigger than they need to be, but I'm feeling fat today. Would rather have bought the beautiful, shoestring-strapped, bias-cut, bronzey crêpe evening dress we saw in the sale in Debenhams. This time last year it would have fitted me beauti-fully, but I don't think I'd even get my left thigh into it now. I'll have to make do with grey fleece pyjamas. Don't have quite the same glamour factor, somehow. I could wear them with my pearls?

SUNDAY 9 JANUARY

Got very angry last night. The bathwater ran cold again once I got into it. I was so tired, it made me mad. It was really a catalyst for all the hidden anger about my weight and my hair. I'm treated differently by those who don't know me—aggressively and abruptly. My hair gives the impression that I'm hard and aggressive, I suppose. The difference in the way I'm looked at as I walk along the road or ask for something in a shop is amazing. Prejudice, quite simply. It wouldn't matter so much if it reflected my personality, or if I had chosen to adopt a trendy, spiky hairstyle, but it's just not me. I feel like making a badge which says, 'I did not choose this hairstyle; it chose me.' How can I possibly go to R's office dinner next Saturday like this? I literally haven't got anything to wear. My evening dresses are both size 10. Maybe I should wear the fleece pyjamas!

Actually I don't even feel like laughing. R is wonderful about it—tenderly sympathetic. But, as he said, there are no easy answers. I've just got to wait for all the pounds to come off. It's going to be hard work and a long wait.

It's funny how your emphasis shifts. Six months ago I was concerned with staying alive. Now I want to stay alive *and* get my figure back. Greedy? Yes, greedy, impatient and ungrateful.

But, Father, I know you understand all these angry and hurt feelings. You know that although all this doesn't matter in the big scheme of things, it matters to me at this moment. It matters to my self-esteem, my sense of femininity and who I am, my creative side and to the way I measure my health. You see all those things differently, and you see my heart. But you also see the sadness in it. You know I'm not ungrateful, or dismissing the gift of life that I am able to hang on to, at least for the moment. You recognize the disappointment, and I don't think you're angry with that. You understand. But I still need to be shown the way you see things so that my perspective is balanced. At the moment I feel like a petulant child. And not for the first time. As the poster says, 'Give me patience, Lord—but hurry!'

THURSDAY 13 JANUARY, EVENING

Have had the most horrible day. Went to Laura Ashley's sale to try to find something to wear for the dinner on Saturday. Nothing fitted and the sight of myself in the mirror just made me feel depressed. Then I shrank R's beloved red jumper accidentally, which seemed to begin a run of a dozen other things to wallop my self-esteem and make me feel useless.

Lord, maybe this is all to rattle my trust in you before my scan tomorrow?

FRIDAY 14 JANUARY

Have got this odd feeling about the scan. I want to live and get well, but it's as if I've lost interest. Why is this happening? I have done so many things as an act of faith that I'll be OK. I've bought 'Thank you' cards to send to everyone who's helped me over the past nine months, and a new Filofax; got myself back in the flow of work officially, and tomorrow I'll move our bedroom back upstairs. I can't believe there's any cancer left because I feel so well. Is this attitude misguided?

Later

Scan all over and done with very quickly, with not too long to wait. Verdict on Thursday.

SUNDAY 16 JANUARY

Really enjoyed the 'do' last night. One poor guy at our table, who didn't realize I had been ill, asked me what the haircut was in aid of! I did feel sorry for him. He was so apologetic about putting his foot in it.

We are back in our top floor bedroom. It took me ages to change everything around yesterday, so that R's mum could sleep downstairs while babysitting. It's wonderful to see the 'higher' view across the Sound again.

Psalm 146 this morning: 'The Maker of heaven and earth, the sea, and everything in them...' Very apt with this breathtaking view.

THURSDAY 20 JANUARY

V-Day (Verdict Day at the hospital).

I rang the hospital yesterday, just to make sure that the scan report and, more importantly, the scan pictures will be there today for Dr P. The last couple of times, they haven't been there, and he's then revised his opinion of the situation—and we've been worse off as a result. I don't want that happening today!

Please be with us today, Lord. I'm sure the results will be good. I've arranged to ring Steve afterwards so that they can cheer for me at the *Care for the Family* awayday today.

Matthew 5:35–43 is my reading today: Jairus' daughter. My Bible reading notes say, 'To this family he [Jesus] wanted to bring back wholeness and life… Miracles could happen in our family too.' Yes please, Lord.

Lord, we're in your hands. I trust you completely. I can do nothing else. You have been beside us all the way these past nine months. You won't desert us now.

Evening

Not good news. We didn't see Dr P., but saw Dr C., one of his partners, instead. He asked me how I was, and said the bone marrow and lung function tests were fine. But he ignored the scan until he finally asked, 'Have you got any other questions about your treatment?' To this I replied, 'Yes—I want to know my scan results!'

He hadn't realized I'd had a scan and was just about to book one. I told him that I had rung the ward previously to make sure the pictures, as well as the report, were available. He left the room to read the report on the computer but had no pictures. When he told us that, I really snapped at him. I explained that we had been in this situation twice before, and that it was awful to have the opinion later revised once Dr P. had seen the pictures rather than just the report. He was apologetic (as I was for snapping) about the disorganization—and then he dropped the bombshell.

According to the report, the three stubborn lymph nodes in my chest are still visible. He explained that this means they are either still inflamed because of radiotherapy or that the cancer is still active. I was stunned. I had been so sure I would be in full remission. Everything seemed to point to the final radiotherapy clearing things up completely.

I now have to go in for a stem cell harvest. It means a big dose of chemo, staying in hospital at least overnight. This is new and different chemo and will knock my bone marrow down to zero, just when it is healthy. My blood cell counts drop as a result and I have to give myself growth factor injections every day for a week or so, to promote the production of stem cells. These will then be harvested through a Hickman Line (a tube into a large vein) in my chest, and frozen. If I have intensive chemo and stem cell support because the cancer is still active, they are then ready for use. He said it was a precaution, but I read between the lines… and his face. Stem cell support is usually last-line treatment for removing the cancer completely.[26]

We left, stunned, and went straight to the Macmillan Centre, where we got some info on stem cell support. We'd always planned to go to the 'Who'd Have Thought It' for lunch to celebrate. We still went, but our hearts were sinking. Telling Steve in Cardiff on the phone was a nightmare. I was in floods of tears when I put the phone down. We both feel very, very fragile. It's such a shock.

Diane came with flowers tonight and I hugged her hard and cried. 'It's OK,' she said. 'You're allowed to cry.' With those words, Diane freed me from the trap which causes the pressure to be brave.

A nurse rang from the ward to arrange dates. I'll go in on 31 January and stay overnight. The nurse's words had a slightly different emphasis: 'Well, it *could* be inflammation from the radiotherapy.'

After the harvest of stem cells, there'll be a wait until the end of February and another scan. If there's obvious growth in the nodes they'll know the cells are cancerous and will do the stem cell support. It's arduous, risky treatment, involving weeks in isolation in hospital. If they're still the same size, we hold our breath for another month and scan again, and so on, until about Easter, when we should know for sure if it's inflammation or active cancer. At the moment, it seems probable that it's still active cancer.

Nevertheless, I cannot believe that you have let us down, Lord. You know what you are doing. I can still do nothing but trust you and will hold on to you. You will be glorified through this.

You have never said things would be OK by now. That's been our supposition and hope, both from what we've been told at the hospital and from how well I've been feeling. You know better. It's just not over yet. There must be more to be pulled out of this for you. And when I feel bright I can grasp that.

It's your plans that matter, not mine.

10.25pm

I feel very fragile. Bewildered. Yet I cannot shut you out, Lord. Please give me your reassurance. Where can I find it? You may not be able to give me reassurance of life or health. But please give me reassurance of your protection and care, especially for R and my babies. There seems to be nothing around me but a deafening, blank silence. Yet I know you will let me hear your voice through that, if I will only listen hard enough. R is taking tomorrow off work, as he does not want to leave me when I still feel fragile—as he does.

11.30pm

I didn't have to listen for long. As I was reading my set Bible readings in Deuteronomy, I came across the verses that I first read right at the beginning of all this from Rebecca Manley Pippert's book: 'Do not be faint-hearted or afraid; do not be terrified or give way to panic before them. For the Lord your God is the one who goes with you to fight for you against your enemies to give you victory' (Deuteronomy 20:3b–4). You remain the same, Lord, with the same words. Your constancy is our security. Thank you, Lord. Whatever form that victory will take, I can do nothing but trust you.

FRIDAY 21 JANUARY, MORNING

Shock and fear have subsided this morning. They seemed to slip away as I lay down last night. I thought I wouldn't sleep and asked R if he minded me keeping the light on to read. But within a few minutes my eyes were closed and I slept not too badly. Even in the middle of the night, the worst time for imagination and fear to go into partnership, I was fine. Yes, I thought long and hard, but not in a negative way. For that I'm grateful, Lord. Thank you for your protection.

My main concern right now is for R and the children, and that I will have the physical and emotional reserves to cope with what lies ahead. But, of course, it is when I'm at my weakest that you step in.

Even Rob's editorial in the new *Care for the Family* magazine this morning reminds me again that 'Don't be afraid' verses appear 365 times in the Bible. Lord, help me deal with the frustration of not being able to get back to normal, with my anxieties for R and the children and with my concerns that I will not be able to cope.

Evening

Telling people is the worst thing—to hear them so upset when they were expecting good news.

Lord, I want to hear people saying: 'Whoopee, look at what God is doing in all this!' I want to live, too. Remind me that you *know* about all the things that worry me: you *know* about R and his job and how he feels he can't cope with both its stresses and my illness. You *know* about my ability to cope; you *know* the reserves I have left, and how you can make them stretch. And, most of all, you *know* whether these lymph nodes are enlarged because of inflammation or cancer. If you *know* and have it in your control, then I can let it go.

It's hard to believe that a couple of days ago I was fretting about being overweight. How fickle I am. I wonder if this is partly what it's all about. Lord, let my realization that you know everything dispel my fear.

David Watson wrote in *Fear No Evil*:

When we are quite sure that God loves us and have his perfect love within our hearts, all fears about pain, sickness and death must vanish. There is no room for them. As soon as we lose that conscious awareness of his love, even when in our minds we may still know it to be true, those fears may return to haunt and disturb… But one way or another, we need to find God's love and stay resting in it. Nothing is more important than that. (pp. 62–63)

The fears do return to haunt and disturb. It's as if I've lost my balance on a much-loved and trusted bicycle: I've fallen off and wonder how it happened—and it hurts. But somehow I have to get up, rub the bruises and jump back on the bike. That takes courage, Lord. Please help.

SATURDAY 22 JANUARY

R is so fragile; it's breaking my heart. He almost looks crumpled with the strain of it all, as if in some way the news we've had has dehydrated him, made him screw himself up into a tiny ball. What can I do to help him? His agony is worse than mine in many ways.

There were a few difficult moments yesterday. In the middle of town, I was struck by the futility of 'buying' things and by the rush and bustle of the crowds. Then last night, when I was cooking, R said, 'The trouble is, I would hate it if you weren't around; it would be awful.' We held each other and I tried to reassure him and myself by saying, 'I still can't believe I won't be here. I still have so much to do.' I still have to see my babies grow to adulthood, and support R and see him working at something he's happy with. There's loads of work ahead, people to care for… I can't finish on earth now. We love each other so much and have been through so much together that it would seem terribly cruel to leave him without me.

Lord, I was reading back through my prayer diaries yesterday and came across the part where you clearly showed me that you could only unroll one bit of the carpet at a time for me to walk ahead. The carpet was firmly under your control and you were with me, standing on it, but you did not roll it very far ahead. That's hard, Lord, because I want to know.

But all that matters is that you know. Help me to grasp that there is a freedom and peace in that.

SUNDAY 23 JANUARY

It was the 18th birthday party of Sarah, R's niece, last night. It was difficult to enter into the spirit of things, but we tried hard. It is an utterly beautiful, sunny Sunday morning. Deep blue sky and sunshine, with a band of gorgeous cloud hovering above Plymouth Sound.

Lunch-time

Ian's sermon this morning was very apt for us, although of course he doesn't know our news. It was based on Elijah and the widow of Zarephath. He made the point that Elijah had to see God's plans through to the end where she was concerned, so that she would come to faith in God.

Then Ian said, 'So often we say, "This is my plan"—but Jesus didn't have a Filofax.' That's exactly what I've been doing. I planned when I would be well; I planned the getting back to normal at a certain date. Lord, I've had no patience, but your plan is continuing. You haven't finished yet. I even bought a new Filofax a while ago, ready for the next bit of 'my plan'! There's nothing wrong with wanting to get on with things, Lord, I know, but it has to be according to *your* plan.

We sang 'Great is thy faithfulness', which was one of our wedding hymns. 'Strength for today and bright hope for tomorrow' is all we can ask for, because your faithfulness *is* great.

Evening

Chris, our surgeon friend, came and talked with us tonight and prayed powerfully. We talked for a long time about faith. And it set me thinking again, in the middle of the night, about what faith really is. It's true what David Watson said about the constant running battle between faith and fear in this situation.

There also needs to be an understanding of what role faith has alongside the medical world. It is not something to be divorced from the decisions being taken by the doctors and the care being given by the nurses. We must pray for and trust in their wisdom, respect their experience and expertise. We mustn't see faith as being in a different world from science. But we have to remember that God is bigger than both.

I agree with David Watson:

Science is undoubtedly a wonderful part of God's creation. At the same time God is bigger than science, and we should not reject various aspects of his nature or working that lie outside our current scientific knowledge… What is needed is not a rejection of science in favour of faith, but a widening of our worldview. We need an alternative worldview which embraces humbly all that science can offer yet appreciates that there is more to come. It is like seeing the world with an extra dimension which in no way denies the other dimensions but presents another perspective. This is what Jesus meant by the Kingdom of God. (*Fear No Evil*, pp. 76, 79)

And one rule of that Kingdom is to trust, whether I understand or not. In all these decisions about stem cells and chemo, I have to hold on to that perspective.

MONDAY 24 JANUARY

Chatted with Amanda on the phone today. It was good to be able to be real with her about the fear of pain and procedure. I've always been quite unfussed by facing such things before, but the two bone marrow biopsies have given me a real fear of such things. I'm wondering really if I am transferring the pushed-down fear of the whole situation to the treatment.

Lord, take away the fear. Please begin to build up my physical and emotional reserves for next week. I depend on you utterly. I haven't got anything else. Lord, I love my husband, my Lois and Benjamin—please don't take me away from them so early. And yet I know that your will, even if I don't understand it, must be done. I am so glad that your ability to understand what I mean when I struggle in prayer does not depend on my ability to make myself understood. The Holy Spirit knows what I am trying to pray and presents that prayer to you for me.

TUESDAY 25 JANUARY

Missed writing this first thing as I went straight into town. My heart was just full of trusting you as I walked down the hill. Yet last night I was feeling so vulnerable about everything. It really is a roller coaster ride.

Had an incredibly generous financial gift from a dear friend today, for me to spend 'frivolously'! Such love and generosity towards me is almost heartbreaking.

Then dear Benj tonight was in floods of tears, worried about me. We haven't told him the full implications of everything, but he has a vivid enough imagination. I find his pain so hard to bear. He doesn't seem to want to leave my side for long, and needs the ultimate reassurance, which I can't give him. He held the sides of my face and, looking up into my eyes, said, 'I love you, Mummy!' He rarely calls me Mummy now. It's usually Mum. Just evidence of his insecurity in all this, I guess. All I could say was, 'And I love you too, my darling!' If only my survival depended on how much we love each other in this family, there would be no question of it. They'd be putting up with me until I was 307!

Lord, if only I knew the outcome of all this, it would be easier. But, of course, that would take away the necessity to trust you. It seems at the moment from various people's reactions that I am expected to die from this illness. But I somehow can't get my head around it. I still feel as if it's happening to someone else. I feel that I simply cannot leave these three. They need me. I can't imagine the practical chaos that will result, apart from the heartache. R is always working so hard and is here so rarely that he simply does not know how things work with the children —what they do when they get in from school, their habits and routines. I will have to leave long lists.

But, Lord, I really *do* have to learn to let go of the children into your hands. I know you do a better job than me in caring for them, but they need to know that too. I was trying to explain to Benj that you love him a billion times more than I do. But to him that would mean that you will let me be OK. He would only think, 'God, if you love me, you'll let me keep my mum.' He has no ability to understand anything else more complex. Please protect his faith and his heart, Lord, through all that lies ahead.

Lois I can't fathom. She hardly mentions anything to do with me being ill. It's as if she's pushing it all away. In the end, it could be that she will struggle the most because of her inability to face what's really happening, Lord, please protect all three of them.

WEDNESDAY 26 JANUARY

'Then he climbed into the boat with them' (Mark 6:51). Jesus didn't just say, 'Don't be afraid'; he got into the situation with them. Remind me that you are 'in the boat' with me always, Lord.

SATURDAY 29 JANUARY

Interestingly, our friend Chris sent us a card, which arrived today, and which echoes those very words. He reminded us that Jesus is in the boat, so we need not fear. I have never been one for boats. I have always hated the 'tipping' sensation, and vast expanses of water around me make me feel insecure. So I need Jesus to walk across it towards me. R said this morning that he did not understand the significance or point of that part of the account, that he did not understand the supernatural side of it. But I do. When necessary, God will go beyond the bounds of the things we understand to rescue us and give us the reassurance we need, because he loves us so much. If I know nothing else, it is that I am loved very much. So he will be there, in the boat.

Today I will clean the house carefully in preparation for leaving it for hospital on Monday.

I do not know what lies ahead. As yet there is no 'happy ending'. I have to wait some time for that. The prognosis from the world's point of view is not great at this moment. The statistics say that stem cell support works 'for some people'. But God is not included in those statistics. He has his own.

He numbers not only my days, but the hairs on my head (of which I have a fair number growing now… but not for long, the new stronger chemo will knock them out again very soon).

I can only trust him. And listen to him. And learn patience. And in all that discover not the Why but the What. What he is saying, what I must do in response. What I am to be for him. My Saviour. My wonderful, longsuffering (of me), forgiving God.

Peter Graystone echoes my thoughts:

When I reach out my hand to the one who called himself the Way, I am reaching for the security of him who already knows and has charted each of life's bewildering paths. I may do so with utter confidence, because he holds the map, and therefore I will trust him. He may make me confused; make my spirit weary; fill me with apprehension with what the future holds. But he holds the map, and therefore I will trust him.

He may lead me to question all the things I used to be sure of; he may give me every indication of his plan for me, then lead me abruptly to a closed door. He may put me through events whose significance will be a mystery until the very day I reach heaven. But he holds the map and therefore I will trust him. I have no idea what the road is like beyond the next turning.[27]

But (I add), I will trust him. I will trust him because he asks me to, and he never asks the impossible. Six weeks in hospital, half in isolation, await me. Separation from the children and arduous, difficult treatment that 'might' work, lie ahead.

That's as far as we know. God knows more. All things are possible with him. He gives nothing away. When I ask for a sign, he asks for my trust. When I want to look ahead, he asks me to look at him. I am learning to live with the uncertainty, because God is certain. 'Remember,' I tell myself, 'it is in where we are that our protection is found.'

We may not know what the future holds, but we know who holds the future. And he holds us. All four of us remain 'in the palm of God's hand'.

✣

UPDATE, JUNE 2002

I wonder how I would have felt, had I been told as I tapped out the words for the original introduction to this book, that two years later I would not only be alive and reasonably well, but tapping out the words to an update.

I imagined then that a thousand or so copies would be spun out from the printers, and I hoped that the words I'd written and their story of God's faithfulness would encourage those who dared to believe that he could be found in its pages and speak into their lives. I wrote then that I hoped 'an awful lot of good would come out of it'. It seems that many have dared to believe, and that he has spoken into lives. 'An awful lot of good' has come out of it.

I have begun friendships by e-mail and letter with dozens of readers since publication of *In the Palm of God's Hand*, shared its words with hundreds more at speaking engagements, and recently seen it win 'Best Biography' at the Christian Book Awards 2002. It has sometimes seemed as if God was rubbing his hands in glee and saying, 'Well, what lot of good shall we see come out of it today, then?'

Almost from the day the book was published, one question has been asked by readers: 'What happened next?' So, this new edition will attempt to answer that question. I have added a selection of diary entries relating to the 'crunch' time around the stem cell transplant of summer 2000, and have brought the story up to date.

What lies beyond is still very much 'in the palm of God's hand'.

The story continues...

I went into hospital on 31 January to begin the clever process of stem cell growth and harvest. The word 'harvest' would only conjure up visions of the Wurzels. I was tempted to waltz into the ward singing, 'I've got a brand new combine harvester'.

It turned out that the stem cell combine harvester resembled a candy floss machine, designed to spin the stem cells from my blood at an incredible rate through a centrifuge system. But before that could happen I had to spend several days on high-dose chemo, being very sick, to knock out all my blood cells. Then, bizarrely, I began injecting myself with a growth hormone to grow dozens of new baby cells—stem cells.

So many grew that the pressure of the cells rushing around in my bone marrow made my pelvis ache. But this was a good sign. The candy floss contraption did the rest, spinning them off from my veins and via a tube into plastic bags of what looked like Tabasco sauce. The Tabasco sauce, I realized, would one day save my life.

I was told that I would have to wait for some time before the transplant, while the cancer was monitored. The medical team did not want to go ahead with it until they were absolutely sure of the status of the cancer. They needed maximum detail for optimum results. So, once the stem cells had been collected, we spent three clear months watching and waiting.

As February progressed and gave way to March, scans and consultations continued. The first scan was to doublecheck that the mass was definitely cancerous, the second and third to check its size and position in order to plan the chemotherapy programme that would accompany the stem cell transplant. There was a small outside chance that the mass would reduce or disappear on its own—or, we hoped, with God's healing.

These were difficult waiting days, a roller coaster ride of highs and lows, swinging from utterly trusting God to states of fragility and fear. I knew I was facing last-post treatment. The implications for us as a family were grim. The church leadership at Mutley Baptist organized a day of prayer, the elders prayed again for me, and friends and family across the world were also praying. I could not lose hope in the God I had grown to love more than ever. I longed to see him remove that final mass of cancer. More than that, I longed for him alone, and knew he could be trusted.

On Sunday morning, 19 March, I read, and wrote in my diary, a line by Oswald Chambers: 'Faith never knows where it is being led, but it loves and knows the one who is leading.' Those words perfectly summed up my feelings. They didn't mean that times of struggle and fear would completely subside, but that those times were lived out under the gaze and protection of a great, powerful, loving and infinitely trustworthy Father. The times ahead were still in his hands.

At the end of March, Richard and I left the children to stay with their cousins in Truro, and went to the Isles of Scilly. This was our much-delayed birthday trip, a gift from Richard's mum and sister. It was wonderful. The weather was as warm as June, the sand was white, the sea a glorious azure blue. It was my first trip to the Scillies—and I fell in love. We took several hours of video film (including an interesting thirty minutes of the bottom of the boat!) and those tapes were an enormous delight to me when I watched them while in isolation a few months later.

The Abbey Gardens on Tresco were full of periwinkles—the symbol of the Lymphoma Association because of their use in chemotherapy drugs. They were a reminder to me that God had things 'in hand', that he could be creative in the midst of darkness. I promised myself that one day I'd go back, next time to stay in the Island Hotel on Tresco, closer to that shell-white sand, to write. It remains a dream!

Finally, at the end of May, I was told that the mass had not gone away, and that the transplant team knew it as intimately as they could. The stem cell transplant was to go ahead. God had chosen not to work in the way we had hoped. There had been no miracle. He knew that what lay ahead in sickness would be far more valuable than an immediate declaration of health. But it was a tough few weeks. So many people had thought, 'Maybe this time…'.

In the days that followed, my attention was drawn several times to the same verses. My friend Jacqui, comforting me on the phone one night, said, 'Don't forget, nothing can snatch you from his hand.' The next day, my daily reading confirmed those words: John 10:28 and 29 said, 'No one can snatch them from my Father's hand.' And so it went on. I had God's reassurance that nothing had changed, I was still safely held by him, and nothing could remove that security.

On 22 June, after several months of waiting, hoping and praying, I went into hospital for the transplant—or 'stem cell support'—to begin. I had asked if I could wait until 5 July, which would enable me to spend Benjamin's eleventh birthday at home, but was told, 'No'. Once the go-ahead had been given, the doctors didn't want to wait even a week or so, for fear it would be too late. They wouldn't give the cancer a chance to establish a fatal grip. Hearing that made me realize how close to the edge we were living.

The whole process was to develop in several key stages. The first involved poisoning me, once again, to knock out the cells, both good and bad—the bad being the cancer cells. The 'knocked out' cells would then be replaced with my own cold-stored stem cell Tabasco. I would be nursed in barrier isolation for a few weeks' protection from infection, and the waiting game would begin. We would count from Day 0—Zero day, the worst day psychologically and otherwise—to about Day 14 when the new cells would, we hoped, be established.

My 'central line', a tube in more ways than one, was fitted a few days beforehand to enable drugs, blood products, fluid—and, I dreamed, neat gin—to be given directly into a main vein, and for blood to be taken easily for checking, often several times a day. My dear friend Margaret came with me on that first day, and stayed until late to keep me company. The first drug, Carmustine, was put up at 8pm, and I waited for it to give me the characteristic flushed red face and body. By the next morning I looked as if I'd been boiled overnight. Frequent visits to the loo now became important. How much I toddled off in that direction, and how worthwhile it was for me to be there, suddenly became the focus of everyone's attention. Fluid was essential. Measuring in millilitres was vital. The drug had to be flushed through my system as quickly as possible, such was its toxicity.

On Friday 23 June I wrote:

It's good to be next to the window. I can see Dartmoor from here. Have signed my autograph several times over the last twelve hours—not because I'm famous, but because I need to sign the paper towel which covers my bedpans left in the loo so the nurses know what's what—or what's whose! Good for my humility. Lucy (also in for a stem cell transplant) and I are having a contest. I'm taller than her so reckon I can wee the most. Aren't we charming?

The nurses became my best buddies, popping in and out to check temperatures and chemo progress, beginning friendships which would last throughout my stay and beyond. When a copy of 'the book' finally arrived from BRF, they gradually got to hear about it. The *Evening Herald* and *Western Morning News* articles which had covered the book's publication also raised my patient profile somewhat. I suddenly felt glad to be hidden in hospital away from the limelight. But the press interest continued. I gave one interview to Liz Hogarth at the *Baptist Times* on a payphone while 'wired up' to a drip stand! Denise O'Leary, who interviewed me for the *Western Morning News*, was to become a special friend, and poor Martin Freeman, now a colleague on *The Evening Herald* in Plymouth, prepared the first of no less than three interview pieces that he would write about me over the next two years. 'Hasn't he got anything better to do?' I asked.

The initial chemo was awful, almost violent. The diarrhoea and sickness it caused were so extreme that I needed incontinence pads, glamorous net knickers and a constant supply of grey cardboard bowls. Drug after chemo drug was poured into my central line by drip. The most pleasant to receive was also the most lethal. On 27 June, Martin, the senior nurse, gave me the Melphalan, gowning himself up with several layers of apron and overall, rubber gloves and protective clothing. All that to protect Martin—I was having the stuff poured into my body!

I sat happily chatting to him in my nightie, sucking a Calippo ice lolly to keep the temperature of my mouth as low as possible. We hoped that this would help to protect the small cells lining my mouth and throat, and prevent, at least to some degree, the terrible soreness that I was told plagued everyone. I have never been able to look at a Calippo lolly in the same way since!

On Wednesday 28 June, I wrote in my diary:

The stem cells are due back in this morning, but I feel so sick I can hardly face it all.

6pm-ish: My stem cells have been given back. Thank you. A very simple procedure much like a blood transfusion. The Tabasco sauce runs in my veins again and gives me just a faint taste of old sweetcorn—evidently I'll stink of it for days. Margaret and Diane were allowed to sit with me throughout the procedure, which was great (for me, anyway—I think they'd prefer other entertainment!) Hannah (the doctor) supervised. I was, as always, terribly sick, while Diane lovingly rubbed my back. The guy who brought my stem cells up from the deep freeze lab said they had been stored at -197 degrees centigrade. Cold enough to freeze the fingers of a fish! As he lifted them (the stem cells, not the fish fingers) out of their container to be thawed, an eerie cloud of ice smoke drifted out, like something out of Doctor Who!

It was hard to pray with everyone all around as the red current flowed in, so I pray now, Lord, that those baby cells will find their places very quickly, set themselves up for business and start producing new red and white blood cells like happy little haematological entrepreneurs.

Lord—work a miracle.

As I became weaker, the handwriting in my diaries became weaker too. Spidery, uneven script covered the pages—sometimes just a line or two, ending with the words, 'Can't write now.'

THURSDAY MORNING, 29 JUNE (DAY ONE)

Sick quite a lot during the night, but you were so with me! Yesterday, when I was finding it hard, I prayed you'd carry me through the difficult bits. I imagined being carried at waist height, but you gave me a clear picture of being carried high up on your shoulders, higher than I'd imagined, carefree and light, the breeze blowing through my hair (long hair, too!)

The sickness is still a big problem. One sip of tea and I feel terribly nauseous—and I dread the food trolley coming round!

Saying the name of Jesus in my weakest moments has an incredible effect. I feel lifted out of the situation in my senses. I'm still there, but somehow removed—difficult to believe or understand.

And later…

Very weak, sickness continues. Into my barrier room tomorrow.

SATURDAY 1 JULY: INTO BARRIER

The barrier room was a small exclusive side-room with a tiny bathroom, located at one end of the Haematology ward. Access was restricted, and visitors wishing to get within ten feet of me went through a complicated procedure of scrubbing up, 'gowning up' in a large plastic apron and switching on a special extractor fan designed to pull out of my way all the bugs they might have introduced into the air. It was incredibly noisy, and I wrote in my diary within hours of arrival:

One of the worst things here is the constant noise of the air extraction system— it's like living in the midst of a force ten gale.

One side of the room was a huge glass window. Visitors might have felt as if they were watching a whale (me) in a tank, but it was equally funny watching them arrive and go through the motions required to visit me. Especially amusing was every individual battle with the plastic apron dispenser:

It's funny watching those who want to come into the room put their aprons on. How and when they pull the plastic apron dispenser seems to determine what comes out of it—an apron or a ripped bin liner! Liza looked elegantly Edwardian in hers, Richard looks as if he's about to bath a baby, but Jon Bush [our associate pastor at Mutley] looked as if he ought to be selling doughnuts beside a motorway!

That little room, far from being the trap I'd anticipated, became something of a cocoon. I felt so drowsy and sleepy for much of the time, or was so busy being so sick, that I really didn't mind the fact that I wasn't allowed beyond my glass boundary. The only thing I really missed was being able to have a bath. I had a shower next door but, feeling so weak for much of the time, I never stayed under it for long, and had to be careful to protect my central line with a plastic bag when I did.

The two days when I really did feel isolated were the day of Benjamin's party and his birthday. It just didn't seem right for me to be shut away in there and Benj to be at home without me. I shed quite a few tears. Two of the nurses, Becky and Andy, were brilliant, comforting and reassuring me, but nothing really made up for missing his day.

On the day of his football party (Saturday 1 July), heroically organized by Richard, Alice and Jonathan, I wrote:

Had one buttered cream cracker and half a glass of milk—has stayed down so far. As I write this, one excited boy is getting ready for his party.

That was all I could write. Tears followed. Andy might have reassured me, but he was also honest, as he knew I would want him to be, explaining what would happen in the days ahead. In the evening, once I'd been visited by Benj and heard about his day, I wrote about my concerns:

Lord, you know what Andy said about how ill I'm likely to be. I'm bound to get at least one or two infections and I'll have such a sore mouth and throat that I'll need morphine. But you and I know, it needn't be like that. You can prevent infection and terribly sore throats. That doesn't mean you will, but you can. And you know how weak I am right now from the D&V and what it would be like to have those extras on top.

As I have laid low, I have realized that you never wanted sickness like this to be part of our world. Father God, that turns my heart to you. It sets dreams within it for how I want to share your wonderful love and the promise of your kingdom beyond all this. You can make things the best they can be for me through this. What makes it wrong to claim that? Lord, help me through. Protect me.

Monday 3 July continued the theme:

Thank you that I woke feeling a little brighter, that I have eaten one or two mouthfuls of toast and drunk a cup of weak tea. D&V continue; I feel weaker than the tea. The weigh-in says I have lost a stone since I came in. Weight Watchers would be delighted, but it doesn't help much here.

I have to do everything very slowly, but that's fine. I just take each step of the way with you. Lord, please continue to protect me from a sore mouth and

*throat, and infection. Keep people praying that this time will be a great witness
to your cupped hand around me.*

*You made the blood count, you made the stem cells, you can get them settled
and stabilized strongly and quickly—early, even. Keep me leaning towards you
in this weakness, Lord.*

Another nurse, Michelle, had made it her own personal crusade to get
the sickness sorted. She kept an eye on me constantly and was incredibly
tender and encouraging—as well as being good fun. She would not give
up, trying one drug after another. I felt very moved when she came in to
tell me she had stayed awake the previous night, trying to work out some
tactics. Finally we arrived at the last available drug.

*A couple of nasty sickness episodes meant I finally gave in and said yes to the
Nabilone—a synthetic cannabis derivative (I won't live this down). It's the
strongest anti-sick drug they can give me. What a challenge I am!*

*Lisa and Rob both phoned today and both said exactly the right things—
although I was so drugged when I spoke to Rob that I can't remember a word
I said. Doubtless he'll take humorous advantage of that!*

*Had a long chat with the dietician, who didn't seem to understand that I
can't keep anything down—not even water. As soon as she left, I was violently
sick—all that talk of food, I guess!*

Very weak—showering a real effort.

TUESDAY 4 JULY, BENJI'S BIRTHDAY

*7.40 am. Have just phoned Benj to wish him a happy birthday. Feel dreadful
that I wasn't able to do more ahead of time to make his birthday special. Thank
goodness Alice and Jonathan took over his football party on Saturday. They have
been so thoughtful.*

*I may need to be given some blood today, evidently. Makes me feel a bit odd.
But it's necessary, I guess.*

*6.25pm. Have just had my first two units of platelets. Thank you to whoever
gave them in their donor session! Hope you got a chocolate biscuit with your tea
afterwards. Managed to eat a very small jacket potato middle and a choc chip*

biscuit at lunch. Very proud of myself. The Nabilone is helping a bit.

Evening. Right now, as I doze and drift, I feel protected and held in the midst of it all. It's incredible. When I close my eyes I am being wrapped with long lengths of something like swaddling—one for each need—strength, protection, etc. It's probably the drugs that make me drift. But who made the drugs? It's your way of giving me rest and peace and a sure knowledge of your presence and protection.

The boys came to see me late this evening. Benj has had a good day, despite my absence. He's very pleased with his new tennis racquet.

Richard looks exhausted.

I encouraged everyone to pray about the sore mouth, mucusitis and infection. I really didn't think I'd cope with all that on top of the weakness and D&V. I obediently used the mouthwashes provided to try to keep my mouth clean and moist, but most of all kept praying. My Wednesday morning Bible study group focused particularly on that need—they were to see their prayers wonderfully answered.

FRIDAY 7 JULY

Doctors are amazed that I still have no sore mouth, mucusitis or infection. Simon Rule's words were, 'Maybe you'll be one of the lucky ones.' No luck involved here! I know that my heavenly Father is wrapping me in his protection!

Evening. My hair is moulting so badly, I'll have it shaved off tomorrow. Less itchy bed that way.

SATURDAY MORNING, 8 JULY

The doctor says they grew a bug from my blood samples, so I must have had a small infection (they seem determined to get me to have one). 'Probably why you've been feeling so lousy,' he said. But I haven't really. I'm very weak and very sick and always on the loo—but otherwise I can't say I feel ill. I'm just dozy on drugs!

3.45pm. It's the women's Wimbledon Singles final. I keep dozing between points and missing the action, to be woken by the clapping that follows it. Andy has just shaved off my hair. I think it upset him more than it did me—I'm used to it now!

I am very aware of your love and care encircling my little patch here. The big bald patch too.

THURSDAY 13 JULY

Very drowsy sicky day, so Michelle and I are now trying two Nabilone in an attempt to beat it. I'll be really spaced out! Otherwise I'm doing OK. My blood counts are going up really fast, evidently! Good little stem cells. Thank you, Lord!

FRIDAY 14 JULY

Still feel drowsy through the day, but my counts are going up well—so well that Simon thinks I can go home on Wednesday. How about that for early! But must be cautious and not raise my hopes. Simon has a reputation for being optimistic with dates. Everyone thinks I'll be better protected from infection at home with R, the kids and in my own bed. It's only a couple of miles to the hospital if there's an emergency, and I'll keep in close contact with them. Am having a couple of units of blood to give my own a boost and hopefully help the little new cells.

SATURDAY 15 JULY

9.15 am. Becky has just come down and said that my counts are so high that I am technically 'out of barrier'! Which means no more visitors entertaining me by fiddling with aprons—and, joy of joys, I can walk along the corridor and have a BATH!!

After the best bath of my life, I came back to fill in my diary again.

It's 11am. A junior doctor has just come in to tell me that I can go home! I must come back in on Tuesday afternoon to be checked and have my counts done, but until then, HOME HOME HOME!! It's all happened so fast. The counts have shot up so wildly that even the cynical old doctors are wondering a bit about divine intervention. I've been in here only two weeks—it was meant to be up to six!

So, home I went. But it wasn't quite such a happy homecoming. That first Saturday evening I suffered almost violent D&V, which poor Richard had to deal with. We both felt that I had probably been allowed home too soon. I spent the weekend and Monday alternately being sick, staggering down to the loo or sleeping.

On Monday I made an enormous psychological effort to beat it:

MONDAY 17 JULY

Enormous psych-up not to be sick—but still either awake nauseous, being sick, or sleeping. Probably out too soon. Counts might be up, but not very well. D&V on arrival home. Sick all day Sunday.

TUESDAY 18 JULY

Saw Hannah at hospital. My counts are still going up. Told Hannah all about last few days. She said I can always go back into hospital if I want to and feel I can't cope. They just felt I'd probably be better off at home. Psychological benefits outweigh the physical lows.

My friend Corinne wrote a letter, which arrived today. She said she was praying about me and felt God had clearly said, 'Beloved Wendy' and kept telling her how much he loved me. How wonderful!

Over the next days Granny patiently taught me to eat and drink. I started that first morning home with one small triangle of toast and Marmite, and by a week later I could manage a whole slice. We felt like throwing a party.

WEDNESDAY 26 JULY

My counts are going up well, so Harry took my line out yesterday. Managed to eat a very small plate of spaghetti bolognese and it stayed down. Line out, spaghetti down, can't be bad! Have been told to rest, rest, rest.

SUNDAY 30 JULY

Lovely sunny morning. I feel as if I am slowly picking up. It's been lovely lying here listening to Benj chatting in the distance, R typing next door and Alistair Cooke rumbling away on the radio.

Mum and Dad came to stay to take over nursing duty from Granny. My strength returned slowly, but I still felt achingly tired at the slightest exertion. It was often incredibly frustrating.

I decided that I would spend several days just 'waiting on God'. I had to rest, but was feeling more able to read for longer periods, and my handwriting was improving slowly, recovering from the weak and spidery scrawl into which it had disintegrated while in hospital. By amazing 'God-incidence', my daily notes that first day were entitled 'Waiting on God', and the focus was Psalm 27.

8 AUGUST, WAITING ON GOD DAY 1

I am confident of this:
I will see the goodness of the Lord
in the land of the living.
Wait for the Lord.
Be strong and take heart and wait for the Lord.
(Psalm 27:13)

The land of the living greatly appealed to me and I dared to believe that those words would be prophetic. I spent the next few days looking back over my diaries and identifying themes and words which had been significant during my hospital stay.

'Peace' and 'protection' appeared often, but more than anything else I had written about, the knowledge and experience of being carried dominated. Our favourite verses as a family summed that up: 'He tends his flock like a shepherd, he gathers the lambs in his arms and carries them close to his heart; he gently leads those that have young' (Isaiah 40:11).

On 16 August, I went back to the outpatients clinic to be told that the transplant itself had gone as well as could have been hoped—but we wouldn't know the difference it had made to the cancer for some time.

WEDNESDAY 16 AUGUST, CLINIC

Counts good, can do anything now—'within reason,' says Archie, knowing me well. I must be guided by my energy. 'What energy?' I felt like saying. Digestive and sleep patterns will return with time, I'm told.

They will leave the next scan till late September at least, as the lymph nodes will remain inflamed from chemo, so no point scanning till then.

Archie explained that if they're the same size they'll do nothing, and if they're slightly smaller they'll do nothing! They won't be larger because of treatment. So we can't do any more than watch and wait. I've had all the treatment I can have for quite some time to come. They've done it all. I was glad, as I've absolutely had enough—and told him so!

So, the waiting game began again, and life gradually became as close to normal as it could be. I became absolutely determined to make the most of life—work, especially.

Through August and September, Lisa and I pressed on with work on the *Bible for Families*. I loved it. Much of my role involved writing Bible reading notes for inclusion alongside the Bible pages, and articles and features which would bring God's word alive. The Bible had been such a source of inspiration, guidance and nourishment for me in the preceding months that while the deadlines were tight and the workload huge, it was more of a pleasure than a chore.

Carlton TV took an interest in my diaries and made a string of short four-minute programmes as part of their *Illuminations* series. Filming was hilarious, with shots of me reading the diary, walking along the street, even stretched out on the bed scribbling away. I had to walk one particular stretch of path in our local park about 19 times, and at one point a little lady with a black-and-white dog was in danger of being featured more than me! The film crew used such wonderfully soft focus filming techniques in our kitchen, showing the children and me baking, that all the sympathy I needed from friends and family to ensure a desperately needed new kitchen soon evaporated!

But I continued to experience crushing tiredness, often sleeping in the middle of the day so that I was awake for the evenings spent with Richard and the children. I probably pushed myself too hard, but it was difficult not to. The days were too short to fit everything in. Life seemed too short.

Around this time, Richard began to get very down about work. He had known several miserable years trying to change jobs, to no avail. Having been backed into a corner in a job that was highly pressurized and deeply unrewarding, he became quite depressed, but battled on.

I found that the emotions I had buried about his situation, and the subconscious anxiety about my own, surfaced at the most unexpected times. It wasn't that we had stopped trusting God, just that we were unprepared for the way that those things 'put on hold' while I was very ill came back into our daily lives to ambush us with a vengeance. Neither had I been warned just what a fragile time 'post transplant' could be, physically and emotionally. An incident at a *Care for the Family* staff awayday was typical:

FRIDAY 6 OCT, AWAYDAY

Talked to Rob. He asked how R is. I told him how low he's getting with his job, and a bit how I felt up and down—that it was a tough time. Like so many others, he doubtless thought that if I looked a lot better, things must be fine. I hadn't really told anybody else much, so it was a bit of a confession. Then Rob had to rush off for some reason. It couldn't be helped and wasn't his fault. But I felt as if I'd exposed all my emotions and they'd been left raw, all my fragility exposed. Went and sat with Sheron and had a little cry and talked it through. I explained that I felt like a pot of yoghurt whose lid had been violently ripped off and the pot squeezed, leaving an oozing mess. I'm handing over the rawness to you before I sleep, Lord. I'm sure it won't be the last time I have to do that. Thank you for Sheron.

I duly went for my scan at the end of September, going through the motions as if I was popping down to Derriford for a pint of milk:

171

The radiographer asked me if I'd had a scan before and I said I'd lost count. 'Oh,' she said, in a business-like manner. 'Needn't worry about you, then.' Do these people really understand what a difference their attitude makes? I felt like callously replying, 'No, you needn't worry about me. I'll probably be dead in a few months.'

Black patches like that didn't happen often, but when they did they were disturbing. I found I got incredibly angry at any injustice or unfairness, any insensitivity to others' feelings, as if the world just had to be right if I was still living in it. It was another side of the recovery period for which I had been totally unprepared.

MONDAY 9 OCTOBER

12.33 pm. About two hours ago, Mike Hamon [the post-transplant haematologist] phoned. The two lymph nodes are still inflamed—smaller, but still there. They don't know if the treatment has made any difference.

We just have to wait and watch. Although the report gives a very tentative 'static', they can't see clearly behind the colours denoting different types of tissue on the scan to work out exactly what's going on. So I'll have a clinic appointment at the end of November and probably another scan late December or early new year. In the meantime I wait and watch for symptoms.

Waiting again. Watching.

WEDNESDAY 11 OCTOBER

Psalm 130 in my reading again…

> *I wait for the Lord,*
> *my soul waits for the Lord*
> *more than watchmen wait for the morning,*
> *more than watchmen wait for the morning.*

How appropriate!

CHRISTMAS DAY 2000

Another Christmas—what a bonus!

Woken at 6.45 by Benji with his new pen torch, creeping up to the bed, switching it on and saying, 'Give me the money!' Delightful child. Much hilarity followed, with me claiming that it was R who 'has all the money I'm afraid, Mr Burglar', and that I was just the one who spent it.

Had our usual Bucks Fizz for breakfast, and toddled somewhat drunkenly down the road to church. Drunk on euphoria more than anything, I suspect.

The oven is definitely on the blink. We need new everything in this kitchen. I just about managed to cook the Christmas dinner. It was like being on a game show where you have to cook 103 dishes in fifty different ways in record time on two gas rings and half a grill. A kind of 'Ready, Steady, Rush all over the place and fall down exhausted, Cook'. Kids have been brilliant fun today—I haven't thought 'I wonder if?' once.

Yet in true roller coaster style, Boxing Day in Truro with Richard's family was the exact opposite. I found myself struggling with anger and frustration for much of it. and wrote:

Today was so difficult. I'm not really sure why. On the way home in the car I kept thinking, 'It's going, Christmas is going and I won't see another one.' Silly.

But the roller coaster climbed once more. The next day we had a house full of friends, games and good food. Afterwards, and late, I collapsed exhausted in the front room with a new cookbook to browse through, thinking about what to attempt for New Year's Eve.

Quite unexpectedly, after falling asleep, I was suddenly seized with a conscious knowledge of the reality of God, overwhelming in its intensity, yet simplicity. I later wrote:

There has been a strange and clear 'spiritual edge' to this late evening that I can't really explain. I fell asleep on the front-room sofa reading Nigella Lawson, and woke thinking that I'd better go off to bed. Was suddenly very aware of the 'spiritual world' in a way I can't explain. Sounds kind of cranky—but it wasn't like that at all. It was just a sense of the triviality of earthly things and their impermanence. I felt my tiredness blend with a longing for heaven, which was almost tangible. It was as if God was saying, 'I'm here at the end of all this. This isn't what really matters.' It was amazingly wonderful. A breath, a foretaste, of the sensation of heaven.

31 January was the next scan day. I caught the bus to Derriford—another case of popping out for a pint of milk—but was determined to walk home. I had remembered that, while in hospital, I had vowed to walk home again! I wasn't quite up to it on that first occasion, but I could do it now. I was trying to prove something, I guess. It was a great feeling, walking the four miles or so back. My daily reading was from Psalm 28:7:

> *My Lord is my strength and my shield;*
> *my heart trusts in him and I am helped.*
> *My heart leaps for joy*
> *and I will give thanks to him in song.*

It was exactly how I felt as I paced along the road. Remembering the words was like musical accompaniment.

On Monday 5 February, I received the results of the scan, and in the evening I wrote:

Scan just confirmed no change. I had prayed for a miracle—but maybe this is the miracle. It hasn't grown. Who am I to say? All that matters is that your will is done. I'm peaceful and content if that's the case.

Several lovely e-mails tonight in response to my round robin giving everyone the news. Thank you, Lord, that I am still in your hand...

LATE MAY 2002

I'm hurriedly writing this in time for a much-needed new edition.

Since 5 February 2001, nothing has changed as far as that verdict is concerned. I've been told to be on the lookout for symptoms. I attend clinic regularly. The mass, whatever it is, still sits there. It doesn't tell us it is cancer; it doesn't tell us it isn't. We assume it's dormant cancer, sitting like a volcano in our life scenery, keeping its own secrets about when it might or might not erupt. But for now, it's quiet. The waiting continues.

Waiting is defined by what we do as we wait, and there's been plenty to do in the waiting time. I did have my new kitchen fitted—a long, laborious process which left us delighted with most of the tradesmen, not wildly impressed with the kitchen company, and an awful lot poorer!

Benjamin is in the second year of his secondary school, still playing tennis, and almost taller than me. Lois is halfway through her GCSEs, arty and fiercely independent, giving us all the challenges we'd expect from a 15-year-old, and lots more besides! Richard has recently begun a new job with Cancer Research UK, having been made redundant in December 2001. We grin at God's ways!

I'm busier than ever, more inclined to throw caution to the wind and 'go for it'. A bit more laid back about the children, overcome with love for them more often, inclined to focus on enjoying life rather than just plodding through it.

I continue in my role as Staff Writer within *Care for the Family*, and have become increasingly involved with Spring Harvest Christian event, planning and speaking in that role. I recently joined the 'Motherhood, a Roller Coaster Ride' team on tour with Dianne Parsons, which gave me the opportunity to share some of my personal roller coaster ride as a mother facing serious illness.

Freelance writing and speaking opportunities continue to grow and develop. God has plenty for me to do.

The *Bible for Families* was published at the end of 2001 and my friend and colleague Lisa and I spent a wonderful couple of days staying in beautiful hotels in Manchester and Belfast with the Hodder team, to promote it locally.

The trip to Belfast gave me the opportunity to see Berta.

Berta

One of the great things about the publication of *In the Palm of God's Hand* has been the number of postal and internet friends I've made, mostly with those who've read the book and written or e-mailed with words of appreciation. A few special friendships have developed as a result— not least with Berta. She and her husband Mark have three children, Benjamin, Joel and Ellen.

Berta and I 'met' when she e-mailed *Care* in London, having read the book, and asking if she could contact me. We began to talk to each other by phone, but more frequently by e-mail, often in the middle of the night when we couldn't sleep—about ordinary stuff like the films we'd seen and the books we'd read, but more frequently about our hopes and dreams for our kids. She taught me a lot about God's ways, especially those most difficult to understand. One day she wrote:

God has been talking to me about 'rights' for years. I heard a message when I was in college about how God, in Jesus, gave up his rights to be God, to be accepted, to be married, to have a family and a roof over his head and, at the very end, the right to life. At various times I've remembered it and felt God challenging me through it. The last couple of months, the bit about the right to life has been on my mind. In the garden, Jesus could have said, 'OK, enough is enough. I've sacrificed my whole life.' But he didn't 'cos he loved/loves us.

I shared it in Communion in church one day and since then have felt a greater strength and freedom. Don't misunderstand, I'm not about to curl up and die. My hope and prayer is that I will be around for years yet, but I realize that I'm now on the wrong side of the statistics. I just sometimes think that the Christian community finds us slightly difficult to deal with unless we are miraculously healed. I would love God to move in power in my life and I believe he does, but I know that not everyone is healed.

It was liberating for me to have someone with whom to echo such words. Berta seriously challenged me to present the 'alternative' view of cancer, and all that it offers by way of a glimpse of God, to the Christian community of which we're both part. I began to talk and write more about the experience of cancer as a journey that could lead to an encounter with God. We both experienced a richness in our relationship with him that we'd never known before—despite, and in the midst of, the suffering.

But we were rarely serious for long.

Berta's breast cancer had returned and she was about to embark on another round of treatment. We had both faced the kind of regime that makes you look like a Michelin man with sunburn, longing to return to normal. Everything in sight (and out of it) seemed to swell, thanks to the steroids. We longed for size 10 bodies, and knew they'd be available only by liposuction or in heaven.

How biblical we were doesn't matter. We understood each other, and dreamed of kitten heels and floaty bias-cut 'frocks'. I hid my pre-treatment size 10 clothes in the spare room wardrobe, and Berta kept her wedding and engagement rings—too small for her fingers—in her jewellery box. She told me one day in an e-mail that Ellen, then 5, had brought that jewellery box to her in bed one morning, asking Berta what the rings were for. Berta explained, 'That's the one Daddy gave me when he asked me to marry him, and that's the one he gave me on our wedding day.' She suddenly realized that she would probably never see Ellen married, and panic overwhelmed her. Like I had, often, she found herself weeping as she e-mailed to share the experience:

That's when the tears started, like they are now. I so much want to be there when she walks down the aisle, has her first boyfriend, starts wearing make-up. I want to go shopping with her and get her to help me pick out clothes, etc.

I understood. I frequently 'dramatize' future events happening without me in my head, my kids' wedding days among them. We can be cruel to ourselves, but somehow it's part of coming to terms with the separation.

I met Berta just that once in Belfast. We had lunch together, with Mark, and talked about meeting up again with the kids. But we never did. Berta died at the beginning of February 2002. I miss her. I wish we'd known each other longer. After a period of numbness, I wept buckets, uncharacteristically kicking the skirting-board in the kitchen in anger.

I wasn't able to be at her funeral, as I had pneumonia, but I soon remembered that God is Berta's God too. She was in his hand on earth. She knew where she was going. She is with him in heaven.

Our last words to each other were typical. Berta had been taken into the Marie Curie centre in Belfast in an attempt to control her sickness by having some fluid drawn from her stomach. Mark was keeping me in touch with how they were doing by text and phone. I texted Mark one afternoon to tell Berta, 'I don't believe a word of it—you're having liposuction!' to which she replied, via Mark, 'Of course—what did you expect?' They were our last leg-pulling words to each other. She died two days later.

A week after she died, Mark told me, Ellen looked up at him as he combed her hair, and said, 'Daddy, why do you always cry when you do my hair?' He was struggling with ribbons and bobbles, and had realized it was a 'Mummy' thing. I spent days afterwards wanting to catch a plane to Belfast to do Ellen's hair.

I mentioned the incident to hundreds of mums on the 'Motherhood' tour, asking them to remember the 'Mummy' things and try not to take them for granted.

I'm still in touch with Mark. We speak, laugh, and sometimes weep, on the phone together often. We hope to meet up this summer, so that the kids can meet and we can laugh and reminisce together—maybe even cry some more together.

But the great thing is—we'll all see Berta again. We talked of heaven often. We'll be there together. We may even get to wear some kitten heels and a floaty frock (well, Berta and I, anyway—Mark might decline).

Berta never stopped praying for those she cared about, and those alongside whom she received treatment. One such friend was Pamela. Pamela also had breast cancer. She and Berta received much of their treatment together and shared many of their experiences, but Pamela always wondered at Berta's strength and peace in the midst of her illness. So Berta shared something of her faith with Pamela and asked me to pray for her.

Berta's e-mail of 28 July 2001 read:

Another girl has been getting the same treatment as me since Christmas. She has been a real blessing, but is not a Christian—at least, her experience has led her to question if there is a God. She is always bright and breezy and Wednesday mornings were enjoyable… we were the 'h-babes/twins/terrible twosome', depending on who was speaking. She had asked me once why all this hadn't made me doubt. I never got to answer her fully, and now my drugs will be changed, and I'm going to miss her on Wednesdays—but your book explains so much of how I feel, I'm going to give her a copy.

In January, just weeks before she died, Berta wrote:

Can I ask you to pray for Pamela again? I gave her your book around September. She loved it and has since been talking about God. She has been reading her Bible and praying. I'm assuming she is now a Christian, but last week she e-mailed me to ask me about my 'peace'. She had a scan yesterday and is anxious about the results… she has been re-reading your book.

In fact, Pamela read the book several times, but we weren't to know that until much later.

After Berta died, Pamela also went into the Marie Curie centre. They had lost touch. Mark was unsure about Pamela and whether she had become a Christian. It seemed as if we would never know, as Pamela died a few weeks later.

Then, out of the blue, just as I was preparing this update, I received a letter from a lady I have never met, Elvira Lowe, who wrote to me from Belfast:

Dear Wendy, I was reading through the latest Care for the Family *newsletter this morning and was delighted to read that you are doing well at present. I wanted to write and tell you how much your book meant to a friend of mine called Pamela…*

My eyes could hardly cover the text that followed fast enough!

… I met Pamela a few years ago when she came to see me at the suggestion of her consultant. Pamela had just had a recurrence of breast cancer. I had had breast cancer twice… we had much in common. We kept in touch, then last year Pamela discovered that the cancer had spread to her bones. She was very positive, but eventually came to terms with the fact that she was not going to get

better… I wasn't sure where Pamela stood spiritually and prayed for wisdom to speak to her… she told me that she had found her faith again… someone had given her a wonderful book which had been such a help to her. It was your book. Pamela could identify with so much of what you had written and greatly appreciated your honest approach. She referred to the book often in conversation and kept re-reading it. Sadly, Pamela died in February this year, but I wanted you to know how much your book had impacted her life in the months before she died.

Elvira's Pamela just had to be Berta's Pamela. The details seemed to fit. I checked with Mark—he was sure too—and again with Elvira. We were sure. As Mark said, 'Praise God!'

'Well, there we are, Berta, babe,' I thought. 'That's what you call teamwork!'

Berta had not shrunk from the prompting to share God with Pamela. In sharing her faith and passing on the book, she had lived out until her final days—and allowed me to live out—those lovely words from 2 Corinthians 1:3–4: 'Praise be to the God and Father of our Lord Jesus Christ, the Father of compassion and the God of all comfort, who comforts us in all our troubles, so that we can comfort those in any trouble with the comfort we ourselves have received from God.'

For days afterwards I couldn't stop smiling. And what made me smile most was the thought of Berta in heaven, and Pamela arriving unexpectedly a few weeks later. What a party there must have been. The h-babes reunited—in kitten heels and floaty frocks!

For me, life goes on, at least for now. And because it goes on for me, but not for those like Pamela, Berta, Lucy and another friend who recently died, I often suffer from survivor's guilt. It's a very real thing. I can still go shopping with my daughter and 'pick out clothes'. I can still pin up her hair for her. I don't take those wonderful details of life for granted.

The only antidotes to such guilt are remembering that God has saved me thus far for a purpose. Life must be lived to the full, with not a moment wasted, let alone an opportunity. Sometimes that's exhausting and frustrating. But priorities have changed. My life should reflect that.

Recently, *In the Palm of God's Hand* won the biography category of the Christian Book Awards 2002. It was the cherry on the cake. More importantly, it was proof, perhaps, that God is expert at 'steering what he hates to accomplish what he loves'. I could almost see him clapping his hands in glee.

As I stood at the awards ceremony alongside other winners, I reflected on all that God had done through the book—on the dozens of letters I've received sharing how he has spoken to so many people through it.

Somebody said, 'Do you feel proud?'

'No, not proud,' I replied. 'Incredibly humbled, amazed and privileged that such a great big God could use a very small me to do everything and anything from making tiny differences to changing, even saving, lives—for eternity.'

Just recently I wrote a prayer poem as part of my work at *Care for the Family*. It sums up that feeling.

Father God,
Set a dream in my heart.
Help me trace its detail from small beginnings,
Colour it with bold brush strokes.
Engrave it on my heart in times of doubt.
Strengthen its design against the winds of impossibility.

Give me arms outstretched
To catch the dreams of others,
Help us sketch hope in the aftermath of pain,
Stand together in the shadows of disappointment,
Share in the celebration as dreams become reality.

Creator God, set a dream in my heart…
A dream of hope, a dream that will change a moment, a day, a life.
For eternity.

We live this life as the beginning of eternity. It is not all there is. That knowledge keeps me going when the 'what there is now' is difficult.

And what there is now is difficult. We still do not know what lies ahead. I am not in remission. Doctors will not even consider that longed-for phrase until five years after diagnosis. Lymphoma has a habit of turning up again at around the four-year mark. We're at three years plus now.

A recent check-up appointment identified a small lump on my neck—a 'raised' lymph node. It could have been nothing; it could have been something. Once again, the not knowing was tough. As a result there were good days and bad days, angry days and days full of trust and faith that could only have been a gift. But… the lump disappeared. It's likely to have been nothing but a blip caused by a low-grade infection. The consultant told me, 'Get out of my office and come back in three months' time, once you've enjoyed your summer.' Just watch me!

To the consultants working hard and watching with me, time and procedures matter. They matter less to God. He has his own time. For him, time both stands still and gallops. He has his dream for me, and for each one of us—a dream too marvellous for our comprehension. He measures the heavens with his hands, but our times and our lives and our dreams are also held there. That's a good place to be.

All four of us remain 'in the palm of God's hand'.

✣

'PAIN IN THE OFFERING'
Update for the 3rd edition

MARCH 2005

My haematology consultant tells me it is very unlikely that the lymphoma will return and that I should 'get out there and live life'. With a spring in my proverbial step we go to Spring Harvest at Minehead, where I am on the speaking team. Afterwards, to recover and for a bit of mum/daughter bonding, Lois and I spend a night in Bath, where the scene is set for the next instalment…

THURSDAY 7 APRIL

Lois and I are at the Ayrlington Hotel in Bath. We spent the day at the Bath Spa Hotel being 'pampered'. Lois loved it—I hated it. I was bored to tears and the massage was *agony*. Best bit was drinking tea and reading glossy magazines in the lounge after my release.

All this frippery was a prize from *Woman and Home* magazine—a reward for a published letter in which I congratulated them for highlighting the work of the *Look Good… Feel Better* foundation. I spent a jolly afternoon in a LGFB group when I had cancer. Seems a long time ago…

FRIDAY 8 APRIL, 7.43AM

About half an hour ago, while showering, I leant forward against one arm and felt something odd in my left breast. I felt deep into its depths. It's a hard round area—a huge lump.

I put my head against the tiled wall and wept unbidden, reactive tears as the water cascaded down. I whimpered, 'No, please, no, please, not again.'

The lump is quite large—about 2 inches across—and very hard. How have I missed it?

Lois is still sleeping… she looks so beautiful… my baby, even at 18. Today was supposed to be a happy day, choosing a dress for her sxhool prom…

Lord?

Evening

Public knowledge tells me that 90 per cent of breast lumps are benign— harmless. Insider knowledge tells me this one isn't. Is that neurosis or experience, Lord?

Yes, it was lymphoma that I had before, not breast cancer, but maybe once you've had cancer you develop a sixth sense—or a sick sense—I'm not sure which. I have spent the day hiding my shock and panic from Lois while shopping, fighting back tears and trying to stay sane.

By lunchtime I decided—as if I had a choice—that the timing just isn't on. Lois has A level exams in a few weeks and Benji has GCSEs. Neither Mum nor Dad is well and Richard is finding work difficult, hundreds of miles away from us.

Lord? I cannot believe that you would allow this. Haven't we had enough?

It's as if the roller coaster has plummeted down the fastest, sheerest slope after the briefest of steady climbs and taken my breath away.

SATURDAY 9 APRIL

Home. The lump is still there. Oddly, I keep expecting it to disappear. A miracle seems due. I trawled the internet today for info about it. Big mistake. It could be a cyst or fibro adenoma, but somehow this intruder doesn't exactly fit the description of either. Sounds like a police man-hunt. I'll give it a few days to get lost, and then take it to the surgery if it doesn't—kind of arrest by GP.

I sound lighthearted; I feel desperate. How can the two possibly go together?

Lord, I don't know how to pray or what to pray. I'm incredulous, fearful, lost, maybe even slightly insane with disbelief.

MONDAY 11 APRIL

Richard's birthday. I still haven't told him. Can't see the point until I know for sure. I'm just glad that he's in London this week and didn't pick up my angst over the weekend. No GP appointments left today—will have to ring again tomorrow.

Evening

Driving back from Tesco today, I was wondering if it's best to ignore it and hope it will go away, at least until after the children's exams. How can I do this to them?

Strangely, I feel as if I knew something like this was coming, but I'd dismissed it as neurosis. It's so easy, with our experience, to believe that the worst will always happen.

Broke the small, brown Hornsea pottery vinegar pot that Mum gave me when I went off to college. It was so precious, but it flew out of the pull-out larder and smashed on the floor. I wept. Crying over spilt vinegar? Or broken dreams?

Lord? You're silent. Isn't there anything to say?

Sometimes I wonder why I ask. I know you're there—I have known your love and faithfulness. It's just that you seem to have deserted me right now. Last time around, there was so much dialogue: I would ask and you would answer. And this time? Silence; hollow yet howling silence.

Sobbed in the bath tonight. Could hardly speak to R on the phone. He must think me very odd.

I am begging you to take this away, Lord, because if this is cancer and the lump is this huge, I must be in big trouble. My books talk about lumps of 1 and 2cm— this is the size of a large pickled onion, and it seems to have come from nowhere.

Lord, please give me your peace. Speak to me, reassure me. I am terrified.

TUESDAY 12 APRIL

It's 6.15am and I have just made a cup of tea. I'm sitting up in bed to do my Bible reading and pray, rather than toss and turn with worry. Somehow I've got to ring the GP's surgery bang on the dot of 8am (as required by the system) without the children knowing. Yet that's just the time they are leaving for school, and if I leave it even ten minutes all the appointments for today will be gone again.

Evening

By stealth and sleight of hand I managed to get a GP appointment for this morning.

'Blimmin' 'eck,' said my GP. I think that's medical speak for 'There is some cause for concern here.' Funny that. Something in me felt sure he'd say, 'Oh! Aren't you lucky to have one of these? Don't shout about it or everyone will want one and I'll be inundated!'

He was brilliant actually—as ever. No faffing, no fuss, just good humour, expertise and action. 'I'll phone the hospital straight away,' said he. 'With your history we can't be too careful.'

Why, when someone says 'with your history', do I always feel antique with the patina to prove it?

And why did it worry me that he was dialling the hospital as I left the room?

It'll be OK…

It will be OK—won't it?

THURSDAY 14 APRIL

Yesterday was our 20th wedding anniversary but R is in London. We are due to go away for the night on Saturday to celebrate—posh hotel, the works. How can I spoil that with news like this?

Lord, I really need to see indications of your love and sovereignty in this situation. As I've looked back over these past weeks, I have recognized little details that might have been you preparing me for this—speaking at Spring

Harvest about your grace in suffering; my grasp of the 'even if he does not' verses from Daniel 3:16–18. Strange, too, that Corinne rang yesterday, even though I wasn't here to take the call. We first met at Spring Harvest when she was recovering from breast cancer.

Lord, I don't understand your silence. Maybe there just isn't anything to say right now. Perhaps I have to wait. But you know my heart is breaking at the thought of all that might be ahead. As always, it's the not knowing and the waiting that's difficult.

FRIDAY 15 APRIL

'Blimmin' 'eck' (to coin the medical phrase), the hospital appointment's come already. That's what I call service, National Health or otherwise: Primrose Breast Unit, Wednesday.

Evening

R came home full of beans and chatted on about work and London. I tried to listen. Trouble is, I feel as if I'm carrying an incendiary device around in my bra, with which I will destroy the immediate settled emotional landscape of our lives at any moment.

When's the best time to tell him? Soon—it'll have to be soon. But how?

SATURDAY 16 APRIL

We're in a room at The Royal Clarence in Exeter, having driven up this afternoon. We're supposed to have a cathedral view but it is obscured by scaffolding and blue plastic net, due to refurbishment. Something apt in that.

I couldn't bear to spoil our lovely meal tonight, so waited until I was buoyed up by more than a couple of glasses of wine after dinner. As I explained the lump and the resulting GP trip, R just kept saying 'Yes?' in that terrible fragile way he has. The incendiary has silently exploded.

He doesn't deserve this. There was a certain déjà vu about our conversation—a 'here we go again' when we'd rather stay right where we are, thank you.

SUNDAY 17 APRIL

Evening

Crippled with numbness and fear in the bath tonight. I called for your help, Lord, but the empty silence pervades. Even the howling has howled itself hoarse.

Spent ages going through my life trying to work out if I had left any sin unconfessed, if I have been disobedient, if I have let God down. But I know it doesn't work like that. Maybe it's my way of trying to break down the barriers of silence.

Why so much pain, fear, illness?
Why so much silence from my God?

My God, my God, why have you forsaken me?
  But... you are still my God.

MONDAY 18 APRIL

Dreamt rich, emotion-filled dreams, but have woken feeling more at peace than for a long time.

Before Richard left for London this morning, he asked, 'How do you feel?' I just leaned against him and said, 'Very, very frightened.' I probably should have said, 'Oh, fine' but I think he prefers honest words to a brave face, which offers only dubious reassurance.

Jeff Lucas' Bible notes today[28] look at Jesus in Gethsemane contemplating his Father's will. It reminds me of Good Friday 1999, when I was facing all this before.

Do I have the courage to pray, 'Not my will but yours be done' in response? Is that what you are asking me to do, Father? It's hard to say 'I will lose a breast or I will die if that is your will', because pain and sickness are never really your will. Disease and suffering were never part of your plan for us—but you will transform the bad in them to good.

  So what do I say, Lord? (That's almost what Jesus said.) I don't want to go through what I think might be ahead, 'but you are the same Lord, whose nature is always to have mercy' (those words just slid into my head).[29]

If I really must face this dreadful disease again, I will, but please don't let it be. My prayer is a reverse of the one Jesus prayed—but I know you know it's all I can manage right now.

WEDNESDAY 20 APRIL

I have decided to go to Tavistock this morning, wander around the shops and then drive back to the hospital, calling in at 2.30 for my appointment as if on a whim.

Jeff's Bible notes are apt again—on John 18:11, 'Shall I not drink the cup the Father has given me?' Thanks, Jeff. I'd rather you weren't that spot on. But am I frightened, oddly reassured or challenged by it?

I know the taste of this cup. It's that familiarity which sickens me. But the notes end with, 'Finally be strong in the Lord and in his mighty power' (Ephesians 6:10).

You're speaking, Lord, just a little, just enough. You're a God of few, carefully chosen words. I am grateful for every syllable. Thank you.

Evening

As I walked through the familiar sliding doors of Derriford Hospital, Lord, I claimed your peace, strength and courage, and through your power I knew all three as I heard the doors swish and clunk behind me. Thank you, Lord—you were with me.

After dear old Birch Ward (where I had lymphoma treatment), the Primrose Unit is like the Ritz. It is well funded—largely by donations—and beautifully decorated.

It's odd how we women walk into the waiting-room full of other women, and avoid eye contact. Is it that we want to avoid the fear we know lies in each other's eyes?

For the men who've (mostly) accompanied their partners, it's even worse. They desperately try to avoid looking at the area between chin and waist of the women around them, while clearly struggling with their own fear and apprehension as well as sharing their partner's.

I spent three hours waiting between, and undergoing, tests. After a thorough examination in which the offending intruder was located ('Well, you certainly have a lump there'), I was sent off for a mammo-gram—an odd experience, like placing your boobs on a contemporary Perspex version of an old-fashioned behind-the-counter ham slicer, to be squashed. The gymnastics required to hold arms, hands and shoulders clear of the plate rival anything Olga Korbut ever did.

Next, an ultrasound. The two doctors in attendance, unsure about various features of the lump, decided they should do a core biopsy—an interesting procedure resembling a medical version of having an expert cheesemaker in a white coat slide his tube extractor into ripe Cheddar for testing. Except in this case it was the pickled onion being tested. (Why do I reduce everything to food metaphors?)

The whole experience was made much less uncomfortable by the banter between me, the nurse and the two doctors—one a Catholic—on everything from the newly elected pope (we are all disappointed that Cardinal Sin wasn't appointed) to the general election. I go back for the results next Wednesday—of the biopsy, that is. The election, like me, will have to wait.

THURSDAY 21 APRIL

In Jeff's Bible comment today, he's talking about mission statements: understanding why we are here and living with a mission and a purpose. The prayer at the end reads, 'Father, show me my purpose and help me to prioritize and choose as a result of knowing why I am here.'

Lord, I have the strangest feeling that something about this experience is linked into why I am here, to my 'mission'. Would you show me how?

As if in confirmation, the book I'm reading, *I Am With You*,[30] has the theme of God's love and the law of his universe, and says, 'For those who know and trust me, however, it is a state greatly enhanced, giving a unique sense of purpose and tranquillity.'

I feel sure that there is a purpose; there's just not much tranquillity.

FRIDAY 22 APRIL

J, the breast care nurse, phoned to say that she has chased my results and I can go in on Monday to get them. Rather different from last time, when I didn't have a clue what was happening for days on end.

I have nothing but praise and gratitude for my GP and the staff at the Primrose Unit. I know they feel particular sympathy for me—my situation is fairly uncommon—but once again the NHS in the shape of people comes up trumps when it's needed. Thank you for them all, Lord.

Evening

It's odd how I swing from defeatist gloom to joyous, trustful abandon. Today at one point I thought, 'Oh, whatever, Lord! I love you and I know you love me. That's all that matters!' I need to remember that everything God allows for our lives stems from the love he has for us.

MONDAY 25 APRIL

To Primrose for results.

My *I Am With You* reading[31] reminds me that God says, 'Pain is never my will and I am never remote from it… in bringing good out of chaos I am very much at work in the world's drama of alternating light and darkness… to bring about the spiritual gifts of compassion, patience, bravery and appreciation of myself. The only qualities that will ultimately matter. "Whoever endures to the end will be saved" (Matthew 24:13).'

Reassuring, if not exactly a bundle of laughs. Yet would I want such a bundle on a day like today? Reassurance is better.

Evening

Well, that's a blow—it's breast cancer.

Does writing those words make them easier to understand? That beautiful word—'breasts'—so closely linked to sex and lacy underwear, babies and femininity, gets hitched to the killjoy of them all, boring old cancer. (Let's have a bit less of the 'kill', maybe.)

I was told that there could be a wait at the Primrose Unit, so I took a thick book (Frank Delaney's *Ireland*—I wanted to be transported to a green and pleasant land) and settled down for a good read. I had only just flicked open the front page to board the plane when I was called.

Mr C the surgeon and J, the breast care nurse, had just come from the multi-disciplinary meeting that included my case. I took one look at Mr C's face and knew what he would say. Was that experience or intuition? He gently but clearly told me, with eye contact (that took bravery), that last week's tests show that I have breast cancer.

Immediately I seemed to be looking in at my own life from the outside, spending a minute or two floating above it all in an out-of-body experience. I hit the seat of reality again for the good news: evidently there is some. Although the lump is large, it is only a grade 1, stage 2 (by size) mucinous carcinoma—not too aggressive.

But as reality hit, tears spilled—not for me but for Richard, the children, my parents (so frail themselves) and all the friends who have stood by me and cheered me on and will now be asked to cheer again. How can I do it to them? I don't have an opt-out clause, but shouldn't they?

Mr C—such a lovely, gentle man—wanted to know where on my body I had received radiotherapy before, to ensure it could safely happen again. It can. Last time, RT was focused on the upper centre of my chest. I still have the tiny tattoo dot to mark the spot.

Surgery (a lumpectomy to remove the lump and lymph nodes for testing), followed by weeks of radiotherapy once the op site has healed, should do the trick. Hopefully chemo should not be needed, but it might be offered. I should avoid the hideous steroid-induced weight gain, constant sickness and baldness when I've only just had the nerve to grow my hair back.

The problem is *believing* all that, especially considering the history of the first cancer. Nothing was ever quite as simple as it seemed at first.

We spent some time talking things through—precious time, no doubt, but given willingly. Nurse J spent even more time answering questions in her office and loaded me up with booklets, having quickly discovered that, for me, reading takes away fear. It's just that I would have preferred to stick with *Ireland*.

I was given a choice of two dates for the op and chose Friday 13. It's the earliest but also the wackiest. I drag my sense of humour kicking and screaming into everything. Chances are, no other idiot will be daft enough to pick that day and I'll have the theatre and the surgeons all to myself. Ha!

I left the hospital stunned. Next to making a run for it and catching a plane for Acapulco—or Ireland—there wasn't a lot I could do.

Bizarrely, within minutes I found myself shopping for frozen peas in Tesco, thinking, 'I've got breast cancer.' Did other people notice? Was I now marked with a brand (not necessarily Tesco's)? How many other women in the same rocky boat, with the same wobbly trolley, had I passed in the supermarket without realizing their turmoil?

I couldn't be angry. I couldn't cry. I was numb. I phoned Richard—now out of an earlier meeting—from the car and told him the news. Do you know, I can't even remember what he said? How weird is that?

Late evening

I Am With You *reading*[32] *tonight: 'I am at work in any situation I permit.' Perfectly apt: you* are *speaking, Lord. Less than before, because perhaps there is less to say, but you are speaking, sending me to sleep with the words from John 16:33, '… that in me you might have peace'.*

TUESDAY 26 APRIL

It's 5.14am. I was woken by heavy rain just before four and don't expect to sleep again.

Have just turned to my reading for today and, well, look at that… Isaiah 49:16: 'I will not forget you! See, I have engraved you on the palms of my hands.'

On this first new day of another cancer journey, Lord, you are reminding me of all that went before, of your promise, of my security, with the exact words that gave so much of that security before. It's as if you are saying, 'Nothing's changed. I'm still here. Trust me.'

You are also prompting me to lie down and sleep in peace.

Later

(And I did.)

WEDNESDAY 27 APRIL

It's odd, but I just don't feel anxious. I keep thinking maybe I should, or that it will suddenly hit me, but I feel perfectly held in God's love—perfectly held in that tried and trusted hand.

The lump is stinging and digging a bit today from the biopsy site, but it doesn't seem to matter.

You, Lord, are in quiet control. There seems to be no point in worrying or fretting. Thank you for peace and assurance.

FRIDAY 29 APRIL

Have spent today helping my lovely friends Deb and Tim prepare for their wedding tomorrow. It's amazing how distracting it can be, looping ribbons on to champagne glasses, arranging flowers and trying to get candles to stand up in chinchilla sand (don't ask), not to mention seeing the happiness of people you love.

Later

What a roller coaster this is. The carriage began to trundle down the slope tonight as I chatted on the phone about it all to two friends—almost as if I was talking about someone else.

Then, as I sat quietly listening to some music, a huge sob welled up and I began to cry like a baby. It was as if all the sadness and disappointment needed to come to the surface.

Lord, despite the fact that you held me through it and comforted me in the depths of my sorrow, it is hard to take. Yet once again I hear you say, 'I know, I know.'

SATURDAY 30 APRIL

Have a new outfit for the wedding. Well, I deserve it really, don't I?

Never one to flash my cleavage before, I am suddenly proud of it! I have decided to flaunt it (subtly, I might add) while I can.

I will tuck a lacy camisole under a short cream jacket with pale blue linen trousers and glam myself up. Suddenly I want to be very girly. Do not want to be remembered (when everyone finds out) as 'that woman with breast cancer at the wedding'.

Later

Stood outside the reception venue in the early evening sunshine, watching blossom blow off the trees against a Botticelli blue sky and felt something of the preciousness and fragility of life. It was if God were in each piece of blossom as it fell. Is that an odd thing to think? No—it was a touch of his love.

All in all, a lovely, lovely day, full of friends and laughter: an oasis of joy.

SUNDAY 1 MAY, EVENING

By raging contrast, church today was awful. Slam goes the roller coaster carriage.

A few lines from one song had me slumping down next to Richard in floods of tears for several minutes. All the elders were lined up on the platform and we were surrounded by people, yet no one appeared to notice. No one asked if we were OK afterwards or offered to pray: I have never felt so isolated in the midst of such a crowd.

That comment alone reminds me that I am becoming increasingly angry. How ill-fitting that emotion is alongside a certain peace. Letting the anger out must be a good thing, though. It fuels me, somehow. I'm angry that this disease dares to come anywhere near me again; angry at the pain it causes friends and family; angry at the interruption of my life just when I was getting it back; angry that God's beautiful design is marred.

After the service, a couple of people whom I would like to have told and asked to pray for me wanted to tell me what was going on in their lives, so I said nothing.

I felt lost. Looking around, I wondered how I would get through again this time. Would everyone be bored? I just wish there was a way to keep it to ourselves. But we can't do that practically. It would hurt those who really *want* to care.

Cancer this time around is so different. I've 'been there, done that' with all the scary emotions before, and my faith transforms those feelings, without a doubt. But I am still fragile. This time the fragility hides behind a curtain of experience, making an appearance when I least expect it, my vulnerability creeping out from around the edges.

MONDAY 2 MAY

Chris and Kate came to pray with us tonight. At one point, Chris said, 'It's hard to tie up what's happened with a compassionate and loving God.' I honestly hadn't thought of that.

So what's my response? That you are loving and compassionate is a given. It goes without saying. I know it. I have seen and felt the evidence for that. You weep at our pain, agonize with us in our sufferings and writhe with us in anguish. I can only conclude that there must be a good reason—if 'good' or 'reason' are 'reasonable' words—why this has happened, even if we won't understand until we meet with you in eternity.

TUESDAY 3 MAY

Today is my 45th birthday. Cancer and birthdays seem ominously linked: last time around I struggled through my 39th just weeks after diagnosis.

Wind and rain stopped us walking along the coast and down to The Ship Inn at Noss Mayo for lunch as planned. Instead I did some work and then ventured into town to find the 'button front pyjamas' I need for hospital—not exactly my style.

I hunted around for an hour, increasingly depressed at the prospect of having to spend several days trapped in either blue checked sale-rail winceyette or pink sparkly satin embellished with Winnie the Pooh. How many more ways will I lose my dignity?

Couldn't find anything, so walked home in self-pity, arriving just as R had spread out a birthday tea in the conservatory, complete with flowers, pink fizz and lots of silly, childish eats. What a darling.

My e-mail box was full of messages, and friends trailed in and out with cards and presents and hugs. I spoke on the phone to the people who matter most and spent precious time with the kids and R. All this love is what matters. Utilitarian pyjamas can wait.

Jeff's Bible reading notes comment on Christians facing hardship and read, 'They do have the resource of faith and a friendship with God that will help them pick up the pieces. But they are still called to live in the shadowland that is our fallen world.'

Those words echo Chris's, that this 'does not tie up with a loving and compassionate God'. In the shadowland we live—and are ill—under the constraints of that fallen world. But God is still with us. He is our greatest resource. For now, we cannot leave the shadowland and all that it might bring us in terms of suffering. But one day we will! One day we will leap joyously into the light…

WEDNESDAY 4 MAY

I have decided to 'go live' with a cancer diary in *The Evening Herald*.[33] It will appear on Thursdays so that my usual Monday column can continue as normal. It means that my regular readers don't have to read about cancer if they don't want to, and it enables me to carry on writing about wider issues on Mondays.

I don't want to be accused of exploiting my experience, but I know that if I had read something similar the first time around it would have diffused the fear and decreased my sense of isolation. If my 'story' helps people to voice their own experience or understand what friends and family are going through, it's worth it.

But we will be so exposed. Protect us, Lord.

THURSDAY 5 MAY

General Election Day. I must have the only 15-year-old son who gets more excited with every edition of *Election Special*. Just as well he's doing A level politics next year.

I went to the pre-admissions department today for the usual round of pre-surgery tests, conveniently located at about three dozen venues across the hospital—enough paperwork to fell a tree for.

The doctor asked if I sleep well. I said 'Not really.' She looked concerned and I explained that I have a world championship snorer for a husband. She smiled and said she'd put it in my notes.

I am splashed over the front page of *The Evening Herald* tonight. The choice of words isn't great. I should have checked. They have given me a 'Why me again?' headline and a sense of 'It's not fair'. That's something I have *never* said or felt. My line has always been 'Why *not* me?' There is nothing fair about this disease; it doesn't care and it doesn't have an ounce of justice in its cells.

Evening

My friend Anita phoned tonight and read a beautiful piece she has written about the love of Father God. She wanted to share it as I have encouraged her to write. It was so moving and so relevant to my situation that I cried!

She also asked if the elders had offered to pray for me. I explained that it was up to me to go to them, but no, I hadn't. She asked if I would think about her praying for me together with Karine, another friend from church. I do like the idea of prayer for healing in the context of close relationship. The three of us have shared much about God. I said I would think and pray about it.

Lord, it's important that they both know where I am coming from—that I know you can heal miraculously if it fits into your purposes, but that it doesn't mean you will. We've been this way before, Lord, haven't we? It's your will first in all this. So please give me your guidance and wisdom.

FRIDAY 6 MAY

A Labour government is returned with a reduced majority and I must go pyjama hunting again. No connection between the two. Just life.

SATURDAY 7 MAY

Flexed the plastic in Truro: I've gone all girly! Pretty underwear (pale pink... when did I ever buy pale pink?!), some sparkly sandals and a couple of silky flimsy tops.

I am in danger of developing the taste and shopping habits of a footballer's wife in an attempt to hang on to my femininity.

Have found the Breast Cancer Care website and posted a comment on the forum about 'going pink'. Will be interesting to discover if anyone else out there has done the same thing.

Heard a quote on the radio today that supports this retail therapy: 'Crying is the refuge of plain women: pretty women go shopping.' Well, whether I qualify or not, that seems a good idea to me!

On a more serious note, I have thought hard about the healing issue and asked some wise men and women for their view. Have decided to begin with Anita and Karine—all girls together—so they are coming round on Monday night to pray with me.

SUNDAY 8 MAY

Church was tough again today, for different reasons. Several people had heard 'the news' and were upset. The weeping of others who care about me is hard, not because it upsets me but because I so upset them. There is something special about another person sharing my tears, but watching them weeping *because* of me is so much worse.

Tonight we went to the cinema to watch *Downfall*, about Hitler's last months in power. Harrowing yet strangely hopeful, it prompts consideration of the extremes of human character: the strength and power of compassion (which Hitler regarded as a weakness) against the true weakness of the power of evil, which he adopted as strength.

The mob rule, turmoil and blood-soaked casualty scenes certainly threw all this cancer stuff into perspective. At least I'll have an anaesthetic for my op on Friday!

My friend Hayley and I were noting that we are likely to be in Derriford Hospital at the same time for lump removal—hers a baby, mine a tumour. Mine's likely to be much less trouble once it's out. Not half as cuddly, though.

MONDAY 9 MAY

Went to see J, my breast care nurse, to ask questions and clarify details. I suspect, from what she is saying, that chemo is likely after all. Why do they always move the goalposts and start another game just when you've got your boots off?

Karine and Anita came round to pray this evening. We all wept buckets in the process and peeled off layers of how we were feeling about all this. Anita is struggling so much with why it should happen again, and asked, 'Hasn't she had enough?' We held on to God in the midst of that prayer and struggle and said, 'We trust you, Lord', even though we don't understand.

But I just feel numb and exhausted now, as if you don't care. I know that's not true, but it's how I feel. Wrung out, abandoned, isolated. Where are you, Lord? What is all this for?

TUESDAY 10 MAY

The mist of misery has cleared a little. Several cards arrived, two from different friends that contained (unknown to them) familiar verses from last time around: Isaiah 41:10, 'Do not fear, for I am with you; do not be dismayed, for I am your God. I will strengthen you and help you; I will uphold you with my righteous right hand.'

Preparation for Friday?

Evening

I have been spoilt rotten today. Alice took me for coffee and a snack in front of the vast blue that is Plymouth Sound and tonight Denise took me out for a girly dinner at Trattoria Pescatore. I just feel so cherished.

It was amusing leaving the house and tottering down the road to meet Denise, with Lois waving me off. I felt about 14. There I was in floaty top, heels that make me walk like a goat and lots of make-up—great fun!

It really is the best thing that either of them could have done. Normal, lovely, happy life in over-the-top dollops.

I am collecting breast cancer puns: 'This is an uplifting experience'; 'Look on the funny side'; 'Get it off your chest'; 'One lump or two?'; 'Keep abreast of the issues.' It's the unintentional ones that are the funniest. Like me saying, 'I'm going to milk this for all its worth.' Black humour is making me vulgar!

Breast Cancer Care forum girls are coming back with replies to my 'Are you going pink?' enquiry. Many have noticed that they've 'gone pink' too, choosing pink for everything from clothes to curtains. Oh joy! Pathological pinkness!

Text from Hayley to say that her lump has arrived as a beautiful baby called Robyn. I wept. What complex emotions wrestle with my soul…

THURSDAY 12 MAY

Was meant to go into Primrose at 2pm today in prep for tomorrow's op, but wangled myself a few more free hours. My goddaughter Judith has arrived from Birmingham to see me. I can't miss her.

The ward sister said I could have a few prelims on the ward and then go home for the night, as long as I return by 7.30am tomorrow and don't eat after midnight. Have visions of chip butties at 11.59. Instead we went to Pizza Hut and enjoyed an evening of fun and laughter with dear Judith.

My reading tonight is full of God's reassurance: 'Even when much is uncertain or threatening, know that you are much used because of my moulding of you.'[34] And Isaiah 49:3: 'You are my servant and will bring glory to my name.' Gulp.

FRIDAY MORNING, 13 MAY

Very odd driving into Derriford so early in the morning. Saying goodbye to R was awful. I just want to get this over with. Op is at 10am. Aim: to remove the tumour plus a healthy margin of tissue and a good snatch of lymph nodes from under my arm. These will be tested to see if the cancer has spread.

How do I feel? Fragile, hopeful, reasonably at peace... and as if at any moment somebody will come in and say, 'No, we've got it wrong. You've *had* your cancer. It's someone else's turn now!' That somebody must have got lost in the maze of corridors.

8.30am-ish

A doctor has just come to help me understand and sign the consent form, telling me all the things that could go wrong in graphic language. How did he know that black humour is the way with me?

Lord, go with me this morning. Protect me from infection. Give Mr C and the anaesthetist skill and judgment. Be with R and the kids today. Wrap us all up with your love and peace, Lord. I love you, and I know you love me. I trust you.

Evening

Well, I'm back, and as far as I can tell I appear to have two of all the bits I should have two of. There was always that niggling fear that I would come back one down, so to speak. The first thing I did on coming round was to plant my hand on my left boob to make sure it was still there. It is—and it hardly feels any different to me. I took a shifty glance when the nurses checked the wound. Can't really see much from my angle. I'll need to face the mirror later.

I went down to theatre first in the end, at 9am. In the rush I forgot to roll on my glam white anti-clot stockings, so my legs had to be clamped in blow-up tubes instead.

Am tired and drowsy after the anaesthetic, but not too sore—blocked up with pain-killers, no doubt. Have a very glamorous drain tube attached to my op site, which will travel everywhere with me for a few days.

Have just managed (illegally) to hobble down to the loo—better than facing the undignified gymnastics needed for a bed pan. My blood pressure was very low when I first got back and I've needed oxygen because of that, but otherwise I just feel tired.

Mr C, the surgeon, came to see how I was. He will explain what he's done tomorrow. He said, 'It all went fine' and told me to rest.

Lorenna has made me my first cup of tea. She is the kindest health care assistant I have ever met.

For now, I'm alive, and still have two (!). I feel fine-ish and am being cared for brilliantly. What more could I ask for? Thank you, Lord.

SATURDAY 14 MAY

Unexpectedly, I slept quite well.

Mr C came to see me again and gently explained that he has removed all of the lymph nodes as well as the lump, with a good margin of tissue. We just have to wait for lab results (around two weeks because a lot of 'pickling' has to be done) to prove that this margin was enough, and to tell us the state of the lymph nodes. If they are positive, the cancer has probably spread.

Lord, help me not to run ahead into the kind of fear alley that inevitably has a dead end.

My boobs are looking good so far. (Anybody would think I'd had cosmetic surgery!) Just one long arc line scar and virtually no change to shape or size. Miles better (well, inches, anyway) than I was expecting.

I got the feeling that Mr C was rather chuffed with the minimal cosmetic change he achieved. Obviously his priority is to remove the cancer, but making his work look good is an important psychological achievement for both of us!

Lois sat next to me this afternoon, revising for her history exam on Monday. Poor darling, what a setting to do it in, but both children seem so stoical. They have been here, done this, I suppose.

SUNDAY 15 MAY, LATE AFTERNOON

Today has been full of fun. A patient opposite tried to get to grips with her electric bed, with comical results. Feet skyward, head floorward, up a bit, down a bit. It was like the that old TV game show *Golden Shot*. It's a laugh a minute here. We are in danger of splitting our stitches in the process. Who would have thought I'd actually enjoy being in hospital?

I can go home later, once the nurses have showed me how to maintain and empty the drain. The occasional stinging pain on the top of my arm is particularly nasty. It's the nerve ending protesting. It should get used to its new life soon.

Evening

Home. Exhausted but happy.

Need to be back on Primrose in the morning to have the drain checked: it's me and my tubular shadow.

MONDAY 16 MAY

Richard has gone back to London this morning and Lois has her history A level exam today. Poor love, what a weekend she has had just before it. She and Benji have both had their revision and now exams disrupted, yet they never complain.

Lois and I had planned to go to Florence for a few days at the end of May. She went to Florence on a school trip around her 16th birthday and loved it so much that she wants to return to share it with me. I promised her that we would go for a few days before she went to university, as a mum-and-daughter trip. Then along came this and it has all had to be postponed. If I'm having radiotherapy from late July to September, I can't see how we'll manage it.

Lord, please work out the logistics. After all she's been through, I would love to be able to take her, but right now I can't see how.

Mandy is taking me to the hospital today to get the drain checked. I doubt they will remove it for some time, as it is still draining quite a volume of fluid.

This morning, I have been planning my work for the next few weeks. I have so much to do, and although I need to rest and recover, I always benefit from getting on with work when I can.

I also have the first practical exam (via telephone) for my Life Coaching Advanced Diploma today, after a year of part-time study. Will they notice that I'm slightly preoccupied, or will I just seem dazed and confused?

TUESDAY 17 MAY

Headline news is that Kylie Minogue has been diagnosed with breast cancer. She might have been original!

There is the usual media mix of accurate and careless use of language. When will we stop hearing that breast cancer is 'fine' if it's 'caught early'? Yes, it can be, but there are so many variations. Also, most breast cancer patients would say they are not 'bravely battling', they are just getting on with it. There isn't much choice!

Use of emotive and warlike language like 'battle' and 'win' doesn't help. It too often implies that you're weak or didn't 'fight' hard enough if you 'lose'. The prognosis for most women is increasingly good, but this disease still kills even those who 'battle' hardest.

The breast cancer charities will be overwhelmed with calls and, hopefully, donations.

Was reminded today that Delta Goodrun, another Aussie singer, had Hodgkin lymphoma—my first cancer—a while ago and now Kylie has breast cancer. Maybe this means I am actually an Australian girl singer but don't know it!

I still feel very tired. Several friends came round today. One did the ironing, but stayed for hours afterwards chatting, so I missed my sleep. I am really pleased to see everyone, but I do need to rest too.

WEDNESDAY 18 MAY, 4.30AM

I am overtired and not coping well. Woke very fearful—floods of tears. Feel no comfort. Wrote:

If I could write graffiti on the walls that curve around my path to heaven,
It would read 'No comfort'.
Even for those who love and trust in you.
'There is no comfort'.
Only the blackness of the night
And the emptiness of my heart.
'There is no comfort'.
Only my dreams of longing to be held.
'There is no comfort'.
Though I cry out against the wall, the dark, the tears, even the dreams
Through the long watches of the night
'THERE IS NO COMFORT!'

Best thing to do is to write. Words come, fast, spontaneous, angry.

I used to think there was a point in even the greatest suffering;
A glimmer of hope; some small triumph;
a victory cry running through the veins of pain.
But there is none.
There is no point but the stabbing point that wounds.
There is only God.
Yet even he hides himself in dark draperies.
He waits concealed behind walls of silence or lurks in the shadows of
hopelessness, so that I cannot recognize him.
Like Mary with tears that blur vision, I cry, 'Master?'
But I don't hear his voice.
Unlike her, I do not leap to my feet. I sink to the floor.
Lost.
There is no point:
only a hidden God.

I thought of the conference call I made today for my coaching exam. At the end, an automated voice told me that each person 'had left the building'. I feel as if God has left the building.

Today my God has left the building.
Taken his feet from beneath the conference table that is my life;
Finished his presentation and closed his portfolio.
I am no longer on the agenda.
Not even tagged on as 'any other business'.
He has become a sleeping partner.

Evening

Went into Primrose after a long, uncomfortable night to have my drain checked, and dissolved into tears on my favourite nurse, 'little sis' Steph. She gave me a hug and lots of good sense. Then I spent a long time talking to Mandy. If anyone knows how this feels, Mandy does, as she has lived half her life in the shadow of cancer.

Feel much better tonight. But this is such a roller coaster existence. One minute I'm grateful to be alive with two boobs, the next fragile, angry or self-pitying.

Wonder where Kylie is now? Was she doing what I was doing at 4.30 this morning? Drinking gin and tonic, unable to sleep, and writing self-pitying poetry?

Once again I'm learning just how precious my friends are. Just hope Kylie's got some like mine.

Thinking about the purpose of all this, what it's all about. Isaiah 41 keeps cropping up. I must look at it more closely later.

Later...

Isaiah 41:6: 'Each helps the other and says to his brother, "Be strong!"' (Exactly what a friend said in an e-mail the other day. I was a bit scathing in my response!)

Verses 9–10: 'I took you from the ends of the earth, from its farthest corners I called you. I said, "You are my servant"; I have chosen you and have not rejected you. So do not fear, for I am with you; do not be dismayed, for I am your God. I will strengthen you and help you; I will uphold you with my righteous right hand.'

Those verses keep recurring in so many forms... but I feel prompted to read on...

Verse 11: 'All who rage against you will surely be ashamed and disgraced; those who oppose you will be as nothing and perish.' (Does that apply to cancer cells?!)

Verse 12: 'Though you search for your enemies, you will not find them.' (Have they gone, then?) 'Those who wage war against you will be as nothing at all.' (Oh, if only!)

Verse 13: 'For I am the Lord, your God, who takes hold of your right hand and says to you, "Do not fear; I will help you."'

Then there are pictures of threshing—even of the mountains, the biggest, hardest obstacles—of desert springs, of trees and blossoming growth, until verse 20: '... so that people may see and know, may consider and understand, that the hand of the Lord has done this.'

Lord, I can't help thinking that this is all referring not just to your being in control of the cancer, but to what I must do with this experience. How I have wanted to combine the life-coaching training I've done with promoting cancer survivorship issues; to further the potential and positivity of cancer survivors; to start The One Life Company to coach, empower and equip cancer survivors to live their one life to the full.

Isn't this about good things blossoming out of bad because of the Lord's sustenance and protection? Then tonight I came across this: 'God loves with a great love, the man whose heart is bursting with a passion for the impossible.' [35] The idea of The One Life Company and what it will do is impossible. It would mean changing much of the negative perspective on cancer, prompting a rethink and working to bring good out of bad.

So often, I am in the depths of despair just hours before being lifted up and shown the possibilities ahead.

The roller coaster rumbles on. Which dips and climbs will we meet tomorrow?

THURSDAY 19 MAY

Drain removal day. Mandy and I are going to do a double act. She is going in for her MRI scan, so we are going to meet up around appointments as if at the beauty parlour.

I feel more rested and positive, as if God is back in the conference room and chairing the meeting.

Evening

An amazing day, full of wonderful surprises!

While I was waiting, Mr C, my surgeon, passed by in his operating theatre 'greens', very pleased to see me. I wasn't sure why. Then Nurse J popped her head around the door of the treatment room while Steph was removing the drain, to ask me to call in on my way out. 'Nothing to worry about,' she said.

My lab results were just back—early. Mr C had seen them, and as he had spotted me in the waiting room, he'd rung J to suggest that she give me the crucial details.

It's brilliant news! The tumour was removed with a good clear margin, but the best news is that the lymph nodes (Mr C removed all of them to be sure) were clear. They were distressed, which might be because of the lymphoma, but clear. This points to (although never guarantees, of course) no spread of the disease into the rest of my body. Even the tested blood vessels were clear! The cells are also hormone positive so they would respond well to hormone treatment if I want it.

My risk factor for recurrence (mainly due to the previous treatment) is 2.9 on a scale of 1–10. The news could not be better! Mr C will explain the detail at my Monday appointment.

I will have to have radiotherapy in July/August and will possibly be offered chemo—that will be up to the radiologist, Dr K. But it's looking good.

I have never received good news—and early—like this. Usually there are complications and delays. It means I'm happy, but weirdly cautious.

A friend had sent an e-mail today saying that he hoped the day would be full of surprises. Well, it certainly was! Thank you, Lord!

FRIDAY 20 MAY

The euphoria of relief continues, but my physical state reminds me that I mustn't think it's all over. I'm still tired from the op. The shooting pains down my arm are not fun. Stiffness and soreness in my arm and armpit will continue for some weeks: I do the prescribed exercises in some discomfort.

But the scar is healing well. The skin around it shows signs of the tissue underneath having been disturbed. It's soft, like dimples on the skin of cooling custard. Yeuk.

Coffee with my friend Teena. We talked about how we might ensure that we do what we really want to do in life.

I feel as if this is a second wake-up call. Maybe I didn't change my approach to life enough last time around, but picked up where I left off—inevitable to a certain extent?

I need to 'live' more. The challenge will be convincing my frugal accountant husband to live a bit more too! Lord, you came that we should have life 'to the full'!

I gather that Kylie had her op today. Hope she's not too sore.

SUNDAY 22 MAY, EVENING

Down goes the roller coaster carriage—a long, slow slide.

Richard has gone out. I feel very low. Have sat in the bath in tears again, feeling sore and tired and bewildered.

Tonight, all this seems so cruel. It is somehow made worse by everyone saying how brave I am and what an inspiration I am. I don't have any choice but to be brave and I don't want to be an inspiration—just normal and healthy.

When the outlook is so good, why am I so low? I feel more isolated this time. I feel that only the dear few want to be with me this time. Others sidestep the illness, sidestep me. It's as if I have been left to it because I know the ropes. I do, I suppose, but they are different ropes and they still slip through my fingers and burn.

I don't want R to go back to London tomorrow. I have hardly seen him to talk to this weekend.

The Breast Cancer Care forum has become my lifeline. There is space to be honest and real. But sadly, no hugs and no one to mop your tears when you cry. How self-pitying is that?

This up/down, up/down and rattle of the rails beneath is so disconcerting and bewildering. Help me to be strong, Lord.

MONDAY 23 MAY

There's lots of swelling above my scar this morning, which has been uncomfortable overnight. A nice fat fluid-filled seroma—it will need to be drained.

Later...

Saw Mr C as planned. He drained the fluid: first a couple of large syringes, then he added a little tap so that it poured out! It was like pulling pints. Yeuk again.

Much more comfortable now. Pints pulled, he explained the test results in detail: all the lymph nodes were removed because they seemed 'distressed' (weren't we all?) but they are clear. Losing all my lymph nodes means I will be at risk of lymphodoema—a painful swelling of the arm—basically for ever. Otherwise it's good news.

I still find the good news hard to believe. Why is that? Am I remembering last time when reassurance was so often followed by disappointment because something worse was discovered or a treatment hadn't worked? Am I wise to be cautious, or am I pessimistic?

The next step is referral to Dr K, the radiologist. Appropriately, as a blast from the past in more ways than one, he will arrange radiotherapy to begin in six weeks or so. He will also discuss chemo and post-treatment hormone therapy, on which I need to do some research.

Have made the Christmas cake recipe for Benji's birthday cake on 4 July. He loves it so much that I now make it in July too. The mixing was brilliant arm exercise.

TUESDAY 24 MAY

Breast Cancer Care's forum is amazing. I have never witnessed such love and care between people who have never met—and what laughs, too!

One girl asked how she should explain to her new boyfriend that one of her boobs was a prosthesis: a false boob. The next girl suggested she say, 'There's something I want to get off my chest.' (The old ones are the best!)

The advice seeker caught up later to say that just as she was sensitively leading up to her confession, things got a bit passionate. He suddenly made a grab for her and 'it' came off in his hand!

How we can all laugh at these things beats me, but thank goodness we can! I am grateful to be still in two (attached) pieces.

The forum is fast becoming my group of new best friends, especially as I contemplate post-radiotherapy hormone treatment. Help me make the decision wisely, Lord. I am very wary of Tamoxifen—even Arimidex — having read and heard so many horror stories about side effects.

Today, two people drew my attention to a book by Bernadette Bohan, who also had lymphoma followed by breast cancer. She 'went it alone' after basic treatment for a second cancer. There are quite a few girls in the forum who have done the same after their first.

I've stopped the HRT that I began five years ago to lessen my osteo-porosis risk, following a chemo-induced early menopause. I can't con-tinue feeding oestrogen-positive cancer cells with the oestrogen they need to grow, but I'll miss HRT. I have been so well on it, and we don't know that it caused this cancer.

I've researched the mucinous carcinoma too. It's a very rare type (only the most exclusive for me!) which only one to two per cent of women get. It's slow growing, invasive but not very aggressive. It has a good prognosis —a low rate of recurrence and resulting death—and rarely spreads to the lymph nodes, all of which points to a big question: if everything is clear and relatively low-risk, why take long-term drugs?

I can see the sense in the radiotherapy—it mops up well. But five years of hormones that are likely to give me a whole range of nasty side effects and other health risks? Several girls online said 'No'. Too many to count have tried Tamoxifen and given up, even those at high risk. It just gets too much for them to cope with.

I might be able to do this by diet—not cranky, but sensible. Have been researching phyto-oestrogens (which apparently safely mimic HRT) in diet.

So many decisions to make and I feel very alone with them at times. I just want life!

Bible verse from a friend today. There it is again: 'I have come that they may have life, and have it to the full' (John 10:10). A pointer to The One Life Company and survivorship? To God—not hormones—being the source of life? I wonder?

WEDNESDAY 25 MAY

I'm still stiff and sore and the exercises must continue, but there is a fun side to them. R and the kids keep coming across me apparently doing ballet or walking up the wall with my hands to stretch my armpit muscles. I also have to keep putting my hand up as if I'm asking to be excused. Benji calls it my tribal war dance.

Yesterday, while out with a friend, I suddenly realized I hadn't done my exercises for hours, so flung my arm in the air to do a bit of swinging and stretching—in the middle of Costa Coffee.

She says I'm still her friend.

I have certainly discovered who my friends are—more so than last time. Some people are just embarrassed; others don't understand how I can be upbeat. (They didn't see me last Sunday night!)

Some, it's obvious, are just plain bored—'Oh, Wendy and cancer again'—and have given it, and me, a miss this time. (I can understand that... wish I had the option.) Others, the 'dismissives', almost say 'And?' to the news, as if I should be used to this by now. Or 'It's good news anyway, isn't it? Just a *little* tumour?'

Yes, it *is* good news, and I am hugely grateful. I can never forget some of the women near me in hospital who have worse prognoses to face. How can I? I've been there too. But I can assure the 'dismissives' that the tumour wasn't little, and this is still bewildering, and it still drags me on to the emotional roller coaster.

At my bitterest moments, I wonder how the dismissive band would cope with 'just a little' second cancer? Or even a little first one? Especially if a surgeon approached their precious womanly bits with a nice sharp scalpel!

Sorry, Lord. My anger gets the better—or worst—of me too much.

The other day, Mr C (of scalpel fame) asked if it was easier or harder to deal with cancer the second time. I said, 'Both.' It's easier because I've dealt with the fear before: I at least know the form it takes, how it tastes, smells, ambushes—and this treatment is far, far easier than last time. But the fact that it's happened *again* and in an entirely new way is the rub. It shakes my faith in optimism. I feel I can't say, 'Well, it won't happen again.'

Also, I'm angrier this time, at the interruption of life (although this *is* life, of course)—angry at pettiness, at the waste of time and energy, gifts and goodness.

There's a lovely quote on the Breast Cancer Care forum tonight: 'Life may not be the party you hoped for, but you may as well dance while you're here!'

Oh Lord, let me dance long and hard till my feet are sore. Let me dance all the way to heaven… but not quite yet.

THURSDAY 26 MAY

I'm nervous about the cancer diary appearing in the newspaper again tonight. Are readers bored? Are they asking, 'Who does she think she is?' When I consider the number of journalists who've done this! There was even a *Sunday Times* article a while back asking, 'How many more cancer stories do we need?'

But as long as there is cancer, there must be cancer stories. We need to know we're not alone, to have someone to grab hold of metaphorically as we totter along the scary path that cancer is. The bored, who don't totter, can always do the crossword instead.

My wound is just very, very itchy under the plastic dressing now, but the underarm pain is improving. James 1:12 says, 'Blessed is he who perseveres under trial.' I have my own paraphrase: 'Blessed is she who perseveres under itchy plastic dressing.'

FRIDAY 27 MAY

A beautiful morning.

My wound now feels as if a credit card has been inserted under the surface, because of scar tissue forming underneath. Very odd!

Today I feel as if this whole experience is giving me greater confidence in you, Lord, and in life itself.

Jeff's Bible notes say, 'Faith takes risks and commits itself to relying totally on God.' In reference to Elijah, he says, 'Sometimes [faith] pours barrels of water on the sacrifice, then waits for the fire to fall. Taken any risks lately?'

As I begin to consider the perils and positives of further hormone treatment, I wonder how much I need to consider 'risky faith' and how much that idea could just be a cover for copping out of a sensible decision. Must do some research.

WEDNESDAY 31 MAY

I have passed my Life Coaching Advanced Diploma with a distinction! Feel quite proud, especially as I did the first practical exam the day after I came out of hospital.

There's a strange twist to all this. The main reason I did the course was to develop specialist skills, both one-to-one and in workshops and seminars, for helping cancer survivors to rethink their lives after treatment and to rebuild with a new perspective. How ironic that I should be rejoining that group just as I qualify. Who knows where it will all lead?

Evening

Mandy took me to Tesco this afternoon. It was like being 'let out'! I bought the new Coldplay CD, *X and Y*, as a treat and am playing it into oblivion. Coldplay have become very important to me: so many of their lyrics seem to fit life. I have a hunch that this new set will add to the soundtrack of my life, too.

Such a beautiful day today: it reminded me of the day in August 2000 when R picked me up to take me home after several weeks spent in hospital, mostly in isolation. I felt disorientated by all the busyness and traffic as we drove around Derriford roundabout. The bright sun, the blue sky and the yellow flowers in the flower beds seemed so shockingly vivid, after grey isolation unit walls, that they almost made me weep with joy.

What a beautiful world you have made for us, Lord. I wish there was a button I could press to remind myself to appreciate these simple, beautiful things. 'Live for today and enjoy it!' says Jeff in his Bible notes. Amen!

SUNDAY 5 JUNE

A beautiful sunny day—perfect for Cancer Research UK's Race for Life. Lord, you always use this event to speak to me. I am moved to tears by the cards filled in with handwritten names of friends and relatives and worn by runners.

'In memory of Mum' is seen often. One mum and young daughter both carried 'In celebration of…' cards, Mum with 'ME—I beat cancer' and daughter with 'MUM—she beat cancer and I am so proud of her'. Gulp.

Then there's the spectacle of watching the runners approaching the finish line. The race parallels the cancer experience—not because the fittest and fastest come first; far from it. Rather in the way that some runners struggle to get to the end, just as they so often struggle with the last few chemo treatments.

Two sisters ran the last 100 yards hand in hand, both laughing and crying at once. There were more mums and daughters racing together than I could count.

Three girls came along, arms around each other, almost dragging the middle one with them. 'Come on!' they were saying. 'You're almost there!' That was it for me. My eyes filled up at the parallel between those three and the way we women seem literally to hold each other up in this experience. It reminded me of the Breast Cancer Care Forum, and the way dozens of women will respond to the diagnosis, bad news or crisis of another, offering their love, support and sympathy, almost reaching out their hands online.

I felt very emotional—a mix of pride in the event and horror that it relates to me yet again, alongside a determination to find a way to bottle the positive action, love and team spirit of the event in some way. We could all do with a daily dose. And, of course, it always reminds me to 'run with perseverance the race' (Hebrews 12:1).

TUESDAY 7 JUNE

Have started reading John Ortberg's *The Life You've Always Wanted*,[36] which focuses on spiritual disciplines.

Lord, there is an interesting reference to something C.S. Lewis wrote, about the way in which you sometimes give us a strong desire to be with you or a strong sense of your presence, but that you also sometimes withdraw (at least from our conscious experience) all supports and incentives, as if to leave us standing on our own two feet, even if we will wobble and fall. It's then that we have to go forward in the kind of faith that almost relies on will alone.

That's exactly what seems to have happened to me. I have noticed how there is so much less of the dialogue between us than I knew last time. Yes, there are the occasional pointers, reminders and reassurances, sometimes when I need them most, but often absent when I need them most. It's as if you are standing at a distance, leaving me to learn to stand on my own two feet.

I have a clear picture of a father who has taught his daughter to ride her bicycle. He has held the back of the saddle and run along behind her for some time, but he must now let go and watch her wobble off into the distance. Sometimes she will wobble too much and fall, but he will always watch her, wait for her to get back on her bicycle and silently applaud as she does so.

That's a vivid, vivid picture, Lord. I am beginning to understand the isolation and the wobbling. And, strangely, I feel as if you are proud of me, especially of my metaphorically bruised and grubby knees.

Later

It's time to add small weights to the silly-but-necessary arm exercises that resemble tribal worship. Baked bean cans are too light, but two-for-one jars of Chicken Tonight sauce are perfect. I fear that the kids will post pictures of me on the internet, exercising in my nightie with two jars of 'honey and mustard'.

I have coincidentally spoken with two breast cancer friends today, both further on than I am. The first did not know that I was making the Tamoxifen decision but told me how she had decided against it. The second is taking the drug, but regrets doing so. She has been so ill and, to use her word, 'infirm' on it.

That's interesting, on the day before I see Dr K. How 'risky' will I let my faith be? And would it be faith? Or just risk?

THURSDAY 9 JUNE

Saw Dr K in the oncology department at the end of a day of friends and fun and feeling cared for. It's funny how it works like that, Lord. Some days it would be easy to feel forgotten and on others I feel as if you have prompted everyone to shower me with love and blessings. Thank you so much!

It was weird being back in oncology again, but I was met with so much kindness and recognition, before I even got to Dr K's office.

The lowdown is this. He is offering me chemotherapy (only three weeks' worth), radiotherapy (which could be tricky as I've had it before in a nearby area) and hormone therapy—the usual pathway. But I've done my research—and he knew it.

We looked again at an assessment scale which indicates the likely benefits and risks of each treatment in individual cases. Having the combined treatment will increase my already good chances of survival and non-recurrence by just seven per cent.

I don't feel that this significantly outweighs the disadvantages of chemo: possible long-term damage to organs (considering the previous high doses), hair loss, Pilsbury dough woman body, not to mention sickness, although it would be a doddle compared to last time.

Then add Tamoxifen, with its array of possible side effects—bone pain, nausea, weight gain, recurring menopausal symptoms for five years—and seven per cent doesn't seem like a lot.

So I've made the decision to opt for quality of life rather than slimly increased quantity, and will just have radiotherapy. Dr K is happy with that decision. He had promised to tell me that I'm an irresponsible idiot if he thought so—and he would. I am fortunate that my prognosis is good enough to be able to make the choice.

Because of my history, he wants to do some scans, including a full body scan and a bone scan, just to make absolutely sure there's nothing lurking anywhere else. I'm glad about that; I would want him to. But why does it make me feel nervous?

He also said that a second unrelated cancer at my age is very rare, and that makes me wonder what it's all about, not just in clinical terms but in life terms. I feel that this changes my wider life landscape. What's it all about, Lord?

So, the decision about treatment is made: risky faith. I go it alone with you, Lord—but then it's not bad going it alone with you, is it?

FRIDAY 17 JUNE

Days drag, waiting for radiotherapy, but there's something to look forward to this weekend. I am travelling 'home': to London first to meet up with R, and later to Kent to attend Sunday's 50th anniversary celebrations at the church in the village where I grew up. I'm hoping that it will be an opportunity to meet up with old friends and reflect on my 'spiritual heritage'.

Later, on the train...

Arm exercises + train travel = challenge. Where am I supposed to do them? In the aisle? In the loo? While waiting for my coffee in the buffet queue? I have only managed to lift my arm up and down a bit, and the looks I got for that were worrying enough.

Maybe I should just get to my feet, swing my arms and say, 'Excuse me, guys. I know you'll think I'm off my refreshment trolley, but this isn't a tribal war dance, it's a post-cancer surgery necessity. Just bear with me, avert your gaze or talk among yourselves. I'll only be a minute.'

At the very least it might have got me eight seats to myself.

SATURDAY 18 JUNE

We arrived 'home' last night to be met by my worried dad—and mum in terrible pain. I spent the next four hours waiting for a GP, cuddling Mum as she struggled in agony and packing her off to the hospital in an ambulance. Still no answers to her pain: this is always happening. I went to bed just as the birds were tuning up. It is a reminder that what's happening to me is insignificant in the scheme of things. Mum and Dad still need our care. My scenario is just a tiny, tiny part of life.

SUNDAY 19 JUNE

Beautiful, hot, sunny day: perfect for an anniversary.

I was disappointed that so few of the 'old crowd' made it back for the celebrations. Maybe my experience means that I give such days a higher priority. I have learnt how much people and memories matter: they are worth travelling the length of the country for.

Did catch up with a few old friends, though. It was fun spotting people and (in my imagination) peeling 25 years off their faces to see if they were who I thought they were.

Talking to people about this second cancer was interesting. I would have avoided it, but so many know already, or don't, but say brightly, 'You look well!' I try to play it down to save them from shock, and me from their sympathy. Telling them that mine is a rare carcinoma makes me feel like the cancer equivalent of a Hermès bag.

Richard and I wandered around the village last night. There is so much of me as a child and teenager wound up with this place. The recreation ground where we used to watch cricket on Sunday afternoons; the station where I caught the train to school every morning for six years and to which I returned, backpack heavy, as a student; the butchers and the bakers, not much changed; bus shelters where kisses were attempted; the shop where we bought tissues to stuff our bras before a night out; the houses where later we met for youth group Bible studies; the lanes we walked along on summer days as older, wiser teenagers deep in conversation about you, Lord.

I saw the bra-stuffing friend yesterday too. We have kept in touch since our Kleenex days and are planning a proper reunion soon. Neither of us will need tissues for our night out this time—me with a lot more relief than her!

MONDAY 20 JUNE

Children's exams are nearly over at last. They are, I'm glad to say, extra exuberant because of it!

I am due in oncology today for my planning scan and 'measuring up' for radiotherapy, but also need to book a dinner suit for Benji's school prom next Saturday. (Am I a proud mum or what?)

Later

We dashed into town to fit the suit and I went on to Derriford on the bus, arriving bang on time for my appointment. Still had to wait half an hour, but glad I did as I hadn't given myself time to think. Sitting there, I still refused to think and buried my head in a book.

Dear Myra on reception, with her mind on the diary in the newspaper, said, 'I won't call out your name—you don't want people to know who you are, do you?' A sweet thought, but I wasn't sure anybody would recognize my name anyway. So I said, 'Well, thank you, but don't worry too much. If I was Kylie Minogue there might be a problem!'

Then I was in for measuring. Flat out on the board to be marked up, my arms uncomfortably above my head, my brain began its familiar mutterings to my body: 'Excuse me, you've got this wrong. We've done this bit of our lives—we've had the radiotherapy. The lymphoma is all gone now.' Then body had to remind brain that, yes, lymphoma was gone but this was a new one, you see, so be a good brain and co-operate. It was like a parent taking a reluctant child to the dentist with a second toothache.

I was just beginning to feel very fragile when the radiotherapist approached and said, 'It's a bit much, this happening to you again, isn't it?' How I avoided tears, I'll never know. Instead, after a quick 'help!' prayer, I rabbited on about the way I am trying to take it in my stride, but in doing so I am blocking it out, which is probably not helpful because every time I go to the hospital to have something done, it hits me again. At least I was honest!

Somehow it was easier last time. The intensity of treatment meant that my every waking moment was filled with the cancer or recovering from the treatment. This time it's like living a dual life.

Once the measuring was done, I was sent off for my CT planning scan. Fitting my stiff arms up behind my head to go under the scanner was a bit of a challenge, but I did it in the end.

What do those pictures show? I know this was planning, not diagnostic. But next week I will have another CT that *is* diagnostic. Can the radiologists taking the pictures tell at a glance when there's trouble? I find it odd that complete strangers see pictures of what is going on inside my body long before I do.

I left the hospital feeling fragile and wondering what I should do with my emotions. Should I pop to Primrose Unit and cry on someone's shoulder? Go into the chapel and pray for help? Or just go home and get on? I chose the last option and got on the bus to trundle back, trying to focus on the beautiful day.

Wonder what Kylie's day was like. Bet she didn't have to catch a bus home…

TUESDAY 21 JUNE

Dr K phoned to ask me to go to Primrose on Thursday so that I can have another ultrasound. He said they can't quite see the area where the lump was removed, by looking at the CT scan. Seems a bit odd to me, but I'll do as I'm told.

Dr K phoned *himself*? I can hear the clanging of overused alarm bells.

THURSDAY 23 JUNE

Met Dr S for my ultrasound and he inadvertently gave me the news that Dr K had kept from me: the CT doctors had picked up a large round dark shadow just to the left of the scar and 'were having kittens'.

Off the bicycle I fly. It was a tough moment for Dr S and a wobbly one for me, but I was glad that Dr K had called me in on almost false pretences. What would have been the point of my worrying for 48 hours?

Dr S said that he didn't think it was anything sinister, but they must check. He showed me what the problem was on the screen so that I could see it for myself, and explained that it was likely to be fluid or lymph tissue. After a thorough exam, he concluded that it was indeed a normal bank of lymph tissue. The panic was a result of a problem with the 'cut through' pictures that the CT scans produce.

What's the physical effect of shock and relief so close together, I wonder? I am back on the bicycle.

Again I left the hospital feeling fragile. I know it was good news in the end, Lord, but it unnerved me. I can't seem to get my head around how I want to feel, respond or react to all this happening. I wonder if getting started on radiotherapy will help me get a grip. Maybe then I'll feel like a member of the 'proper cancer patient' club again, instead of someone who keeps coming in on a free ticket, reluctant to pay for full membership.

SATURDAY 2 JULY

Have just wept at the sight of Benji in his dinner suit, ready for his school prom, although I managed to hold myself together until he had walked out of the door! At a skinny 6ft 3 he looked wonderful.

Where has my golden-haired little boy gone? He'll be 16 on Monday.

MONDAY 4 JULY

Benji's 16th birthday. We enjoyed lunch out, chatting, laughing and leg-pulling, all four of us together. Last time around, I had prayed to be here for his 16th birthday, and here I am!

WEDNESDAY 6 JULY

Lois's school prom tonight. Having almost burst with pride at Benji, I have now done the same at Lo in a beautiful rose pink ballgown.

After the difficult hunt for a dress in Bath back in April, it took us a while to pluck up the courage to try again, but we found a gorgeous dress in a local boutique. The price necessitated a call to R, who happened to be at home. He met us at the shop, beamed at the dress and paled at the price tag! But he sensed that I was wondering if this would be the only 'big dress' I would see her in. Will I make her wedding day? So he paid—and tonight she looks like a model gracing the pages of *Vogue*.

I followed the same pattern as on Benji's prom night—waved good-bye, closed the door and burst into happy emotional tears of pride.

Lord, thank you. I am privileged to have witnessed these important days in my children's lives. I have known too many who haven't lived long enough to do so.

THURSDAY 7 JULY

I did the rare thing of switching on my phone at lunchtime, to find a text from Richard, sent earlier: 'Just to let you know I'm OK.' Odd message, I thought, so I phoned him and he told me that bombs had gone off across London.

The news is horrific. For once I was grateful for his early-bird habit of getting into the office before 8 in the morning. Dozens of others weren't so well protected, starting a very ordinary day with no inkling of what lay ahead. Today life and death seem very grim indeed.

Lord, when I asked you where you were today, you said 'There', and drew my attention to a picture of casualties and helpers comforting each other. You do not leave us in our suffering: you share it.

FRIDAY 8 JULY

Diagnostic scan today. The relevance of it is lost in my preoccupation with the far more serious events of yesterday, but it has to go on.

As usual, there was a struggle to find a vein to inject the gunk that lights up the picture. I have even less of a choice of co-operative veins now, as I must avoid needles in my left arm in case of lymphodoema.

The scan results will go on the 'urgent' pile.

I still have no date to begin radiotherapy and the waiting is beginning to get to me. I am tense, fragile and angry at myself for forgetting I am alive and well in relation to yesterday's dead and injured.

MONDAY 11 JULY

Yesterday afternoon, my right eye started to water, then hurt, but I couldn't find anything in it. I tried lifting the lid, blinking and eye baths, but nothing helped.

By bedtime I was being driven to distraction. I tried to sleep but couldn't close my eye comfortably.

Suddenly, I was hysterical. It was as if I had blown the safety valve on a pressure cooker. Out steamed all the emotions I had pressed down inside in an effort to control them.

I cried and yelled and clung to R, who just held me tight and let me sob out everything I was feeling. I begged him to make it all stop—not just the pain in my eye but everything to do with the cancer.

I cried out to you, Lord, from the depths, as if crying into a hollow tunnel. But there was no answer.

Eventually, calmed and all cried out, I managed to sleep, but my eye is still very uncomfortable this morning.

Later...

Went to the eye infirmary. With magnification, the doctor found a minute piece of glass attached to my cornea and whipped it out with the long edge of a needle. It probably blew in on a dusty breeze. My cornea is pitted with lots of little dents where the glass has moved around, and will be uncomfortable for a while. Antibiotic cream should, hopefully, heal it in a few days.

I can't help thinking what a whinger I am about one little piece of glass, considering the experience of London's bomb victims.

Lord, why is it that the kinds of blips I normally take in my stride are so hard to cope with right now? Anything that is beyond my control or ruffles the calmness is tough. Even the fact that I couldn't see to do the ironing was a source of distress. (Me? Worried about the ironing?!)

The key is the loss of control. The next six weeks will be dominated by radiotherapy (*when* it's finally organized!) There will be nothing I can do about it and it will completely dominate the summer. I will be tied to Plymouth and to the commitment of radiotherapy every weekday. I will see more of the inside of the oncology department than the eye infirmary staff saw of my eye. I long for it all to be over—but to be over, it's got to start.

Lord, this is so tough!

WEDNESDAY 13 JULY

As irony would have it, today was the day of my lymphoma check-up on Birch Ward. I met two of the nurses who took such good care of me last time around and told them what a gibbering wreck I am at the oddest moments—how I cried when a hospital security guard yelled at me because I was walking where I shouldn't be. 'You didn't read the X&%$£ sign, did you?' he snapped angrily.

I could hardly see the sign that said 'No pedestrian access', as my damaged eye is still watering badly in the sunlight. I had my sunglasses on and my head down to shield it. Does he not realize that people walking around a hospital might be preoccupied and vulnerable?

This experience is like trying to make all the pieces in a kaleidoscope stay in one place. You just manage to form a pattern and relax, and then something slips and there's another pattern to take in.

My haematology consultant expressed his sorrow at Round Two, and explained that he thought it unlikely that the massive amount of treatment last time around caused this time around. But he also admitted that 'we'll never know'. I walked back to the car with a heavy heart. Feel very low today.

Later

Have at least found a nurse consultant, at the Royal Marsden Hospital in London, who is interested in positive cancer survivorship issues and keen to share ideas. So that's a bright spot on the horizon… not that I can look at it with this eye.

The day ended brilliantly with me sitting in the evening sun (without looking at it too much) with Teena, drinking Pinot Grigio. I forgot all about cancer and spent much of the time laughing. I love it when the trivial takes over the terrible in such a wacky way. I need to do more of this: just walk away from the hospital, forget, talk about everything but this dratted disease, laugh myself helpless and enjoy special people.

WEDNESDAY 20 JULY

I sat up late last night reading Sheila Hancock's book *The Two of Us* [37] about her life with John Thaw, who died of cancer two years ago. I have ignored it before, thinking it would be a sentimental celebrity-fest. But it has had rave reviews. Quite rightly, because it is brilliant: an inspired mix of a brief social history of the 20th century, woven into an unsentimental story of both their lives. It's a poignant portrait of a man much adored, a marriage much treasured, and what happens when two flawed people love each other almost too much.

Sheila has known so much suffering and loss in her life that her sadness, completely devoid of self-pity, is almost palpable. This is real life that I identify with: there is so much personal pain in our wider circle at the moment. So many people have suffered accidents or illness, bereavement or tragedy. Somehow I can catch her mood and feel part of it, maybe because I feel so sad today.

Where are you, Lord? I feel as if you are hidden behind a dark curtain where I can't see you. Or are you watching me wobbling hopelessly to frequent halts on my metaphorical bicycle?

THURSDAY 21 JULY

Have arranged to meet up with Natalie, the nurse consultant from the Royal Marsden, next week, to talk about how we can raise the profile of positive cancer survivorship. We're meeting in Bath, where she has another appointment. Not a bad place to spend a day.

Will take the children and they can explore Bristol (more their scene) for the day. It's not exactly a holiday, but it might help to do something different. Once radiotherapy starts (will it ever?), trips together won't be so easy.

Lois and I will need a miracle and a very understanding holiday company—not to mention insurance—ever to manage Italy.

MONDAY 25 JULY

Travelled with the children as far as Bristol, where they spent the day being tourists. I carried on to Bath to meet with Natalie.

It was unnerving to get off the train at Bristol and come face to face with two policemen carrying rifles, in the wake of the London bombings. The children were reminded of what their dad sees in London every day. It made them extra effusive and affectionate in their goodbyes as we all set off in different directions.

I met Natalie over lunch to share our perspectives on the potential of cancer survivors, who have such a changed perspective on life. She is working on raising awareness of survivorship as a concept and promoting the potential of cancer survivors to give so much back to life. We are completely on the same wavelength and excited to have found somebody else banging the same drum. She thinks we have a fight on our hands similar to that of the early hospice movement.

Natalie is unique in her role, which means that she is often called upon to be a spokesperson. She has even sat on the sofa with Phil and Fern on *This Morning*! I bow down...

She gave me hope that we really can do something to make a difference: two formidable women with a cause! I don't think either of us will give up easily.

WEDNESDAY 27 JULY

At last! The oncology department rang to say that my preview for radiotherapy and final planning on the simulator is on Friday—bit of a challenge logistically, as my bone scan is on Friday too.

FRIDAY 29 JULY

I spent the afternoon radioactive after my bone scan injection: even the syringe appeared to be encased in protective lead.

I'm only dangerous if I cuddle babies and children, evidently. I wondered if I would walk around looking like one of the children from the old Ready Brek ads, surrounded by a hovering orange ring. Sadly, no.

I was told to drink loads all afternoon, go back at 5.15 for the bone scan and only use the designated secure loo in the nuclear medicine department. It isn't only what goes in that is radioactive!

Just before 3, I went into the radiotherapy simulation suite where the final measurements for radiotherapy are done. Basically, it's the gun without the ammunition. Two radiotherapists drew lines all over me so that I resembled an Ordnance Survey map of a low peak (in more ways than one!)

I'm a bit of a challenge because of the area where I had radiotherapy last time. It was difficult to angle the 'gun' to hit the right places from two different directions while avoiding my heart, lungs and the last radiotherapy site. A third radiotherapist, then Dr K, checked it out. The whole procedure took almost two hours.

While we were waiting for Dr K, I was given a chance to warm up and have a cup of tea. The fun started with the downside of my 'drinking lots' all afternoon. Would I have to trundle up to the 'nuclear loo' for fear of contaminating radiotherapy?

A call to nuclear medicine confirmed that as it was nearly the end of the day I could risk it. I was told that someone would check the loo with a Geiger counter later! So, feeling like a character from a sci-fi film, I was allowed to spend a penny—albeit a radioactive one.

Finally, Dr K checked that I understood that the radiotherapy beam will clip the edge of my left lung, but it should be fine. I signed the consent form, which confirms the expected side effects—burnt skin and extreme tiredness—and he went off on a well-deserved holiday. Mine, as yet a dream, will have to wait.

The bone scan that followed was a welcome rest. I just had to lie still on a table, flat camera immediately overhead, to be slowly dragged along a conveyor belt for 20 minutes. I felt like the cuddly toy on *The Generation Game*.

So, radiotherapy begins next Wednesday—at last!

SUNDAY 31 JULY

Now that I have my dates, I have been researching holiday insurance. I am determined to take Lo to Florence, even if it has to be the day after I finish radiotherapy.

Finding the holiday at a good price has been a dream (thank you, Cities Direct) but getting insurance has been a nightmare. The major insurance companies won't insure anyone who has *ever* had cancer. No matter that you're fit and well and probably healthier than the guy next to you on the plane, who is slobbering over his high fat / high carb intake and on the point of having a heart attack. No, you've had cancer, *that* disease.

Isn't it about time someone hit the insurance companies politely on the head and explained that the vast majority of cancer survivors are not about to expire?

Finally got some info from Breast Cancer Care and booked through an insurance company called Freedom. The policy covers both of us for everything. Better still, I was not treated by the girl in their office as if I was cerebrally challenged, breathing my last breath, or as if she needed to wear a mask and surgical gloves for her own protection.

Lord, please help the details fit into place. We need to book now in the hope that I'll have finished treatment in time, yet it's a risk. But what's life without risky faith?

WEDNESDAY 3 AUGUST

My first radiotherapy trip today.

Hideously expensive to park at Derriford Hospital, so I have arranged to park 15 minutes' walk away in the *Evening Herald* car park. That's going to be fun when I'm exhausted later.

Be with me, Lord. It's going to be very odd doing all this again.

Later...

It was a relief to be on the RT table for such a short time after last week's marathon planning session. I was introduced to my 'team', who will take care of me each day. Two of them look about 18. I must be getting old.

I was set up on the table, arms uncomfortably behind my head in arm rests (a contradiction in terms). The measurements were checked and the team left the room to the accompaniment of the 'bleep, bleep' warning.

It was then that I began to pray silently. After a few moments I heard the familiar high-pitched squealing, buzzing and drilling sound which signals that the zapping is under way. The treatment only takes a few minutes—it takes ten times longer to get to the hospital.

THURSDAY 4 AUGUST

R came with me to Derriford today—not for moral support, but because he has a curiously bent finger that needs unbending, and had his first appointment with the surgeon.

The contrast between our medical notes is hysterical. His file is glossy and brand new and contains one page. My buff and tattered tome is several feet thick: it looks as if it might take three strong hospital porters to lift it.

This is the first time R has ever needed to attend hospital for himself, having been to the GP only about five times in his adult life. We balance out NHS costs pretty well.

I sat with him before going to radiotherapy, and when we'd been waiting about ten minutes after his appointment time, he said, 'They keep you waiting, don't they?'

'Well, yes,' I said. 'That's what you're here for. Didn't you know?'

He has no concept of the amount of time patients spend waiting for anything and everything in hospitals, and no understanding of the way in which I have had to trail from pillar to post and wait hours everywhere over the last six years. It was an education for him.

SUNDAY 14 AUGUST

The second week of radiotherapy over, we have just spent a lovely night at The Royal Clarence in Exeter: a return trip to make up for our traumatic news-breaking last visit. And it was *fab*: food that tastes like food and a room so glamorous that we didn't feel as if we ought to sit down in it. What's more, this time we could *see* the cathedral!

Thank you, Lord, for special things!

MONDAY 15 AUGUST

'Are we on week 3 or 4 of radiotherapy?' I asked myself this morning. 'It's week 3, sweetie. Never could count, could you?' I answered.

'We' seem to be taking it all in our stride as a bit of an inconvenience. RT has become an annoying chore, like putting out the rubbish bags or cleaning the oven.

The social chit-chat with the team is the best bit. It's all I go for, really... Today they were trying to work out whether 'Bethlehem' was likely to be in the dictionary. It's a place name but, we wondered, would it also be listed as a metaphor in the same way as a 'new Jerusalem' or a 'personal Eden'? All this because the three of them had been working out conundrums to keep their minds active in between patients. How sad are they?

TUESDAY 16 AUGUST

My skin is still fine. I am slapping on pure aloe vera gel after every treatment and so far there's only a slight tinge of pink. It's like basting a turkey for the oven in reverse. The gel makes my skin stick to my bra, especially in the heat. Removing it later is like peeling clingfilm off a blancmange.

One breast cancer friend is going to greater therapeutic lengths to avoid soreness: she wears cabbage leaves in her bra, as apparently they absorb the heat. I asked her if organic cabbage makes any difference. It does. (If you were cleavagely challenged, I suppose you could always opt for sprouts?)

She told me a story about someone else who did the same, taking a cabbage to work for frequent changes. Not wanting to leave used limp cabbage leaves in the office bin, she took them home in a plastic sandwich bag and left them on the kitchen worktop to throw away. Her husband, arriving home hungry and hopeful, thought she'd bought him something of a delicacy for tea. He must have been disappointed when she told him what was really in the bag.

Now I know why 'brassica' sounds so much like 'brassiere'.

THURSDAY 18 AUGUST

A level results day for Lois and thousands of others the country over.

I sat outside the school, alternately praying and panicking, until she appeared with the ominous brown envelope. She's done it—two As and a disappointing B, but it's exactly what she needs for Warwick University. I feel more relief than anything else.

We broke open the champagne, demolishing half of the kitchen in the process (I can never open champagne safely), and greedily ate her chosen smoked salmon for a treat. Modest tastes, my daughter.

When it was all over and her shrieking was with friends rather than with us, I came up here to the bedroom to say 'Thank you, Lord' and count my blessings. Five years ago, just out of hospital after my stem cell transplant, I heard about a friend's son who had done well in his A levels, and wondered whether I would see Lois at this stage. It seemed such a simple thing to hope for at the time, yet an almost impossible thing too—but not for you, Lord.

Blessings pop up all over the place. I just have to take time to notice them. Thank you, you are indeed a great God, and today is a great day.

SATURDAY 20 AUGUST

Tonight Lois was chattering about university—all she'll need and what she'll do—without drawing breath.

I checked the dictionary for the radiotherapy team tonight and, no, Bethlehem isn't in the dictionary. 'Bursting', 'maternal' and 'pride' are, though.

MONDAY 22 AUGUST

Another week of exciting RT and today a bonus: a medical review with Dr K.

My bone scan is clear. The CT scan showed a small inflamed gland buried away in the centre of my chest. This very probably relates to the treatment last time around. A puzzling area has shown up there on my scans ever since.

Often, when a CT scan is reported, those who are interpreting the pictures don't know a patient's previous history and quite rightly report on every detail regardless. Dr K isn't worried. He will take a look at the scan picture himself, but hopefully it's scarring or a lymph node still in distress. (Help me! Help me!)

He located the site of the tumour beneath the scar, and, using a circular plastic disc, drew a circle round it with his indelible pen. Not 'X' marks the spot, but 'O'. This is to highlight the site where the final 'booster' treatments will be aimed: right on the spot where the tumour turned up. Hopefully it will eradicate any cancer cells still lurking about underneath the op site.

I now resemble a sale item that has been reduced because of a flaw or tear in the fabric, my 'flaw' circled in black pen to alert buyers. Good job it's not a low self-esteem day.

THURSDAY 1 SEPTEMBER

The booster radiotherapy treatments started today—three extra concentrated bursts around the scar area with something that resembles a Kenwood Chef mixer mounted on to a huge canopy.

Teena is driving me backwards and forwards this week, a lovely treat. She is insisting on doing so for the rest of my treatments. Somehow, when she insists, I don't feel smothered, just cared for. What's the difference? That she doesn't make a big deal out of it and fits it into the rest of her day, I think. I don't feel like an invalid. We chat away about anything and everything, and laugh loads.

MONDAY 5 SEPTEMBER

Hallelujah! Last day of radiotherapy. I said 'thank you' to the team and handed over much-deserved cards and chocolates before Teena and I had lunch out to celebrate.

Yet somehow I didn't feel as if there was much to celebrate. I still feel anticlimatic now: a kind of 'what was all that about then?' feeling.

WEDNESDAY 6 SEPTEMBER

Talked to J, my breast care nurse, to check there isn't anything else I must do now it's all over. She says the tiredness will continue for a while and I must give myself time to get over it, otherwise nothing. For now, I simply enter the limbo land that is wait-and-seeing, and hoping for the best. At least I know that territory.

I have a follow-up appointment in two months and a mammogram in a year. That timescale sounds hopeful. I should be jumping for joy.

THURSDAY 7 SEPTEMBER

Feeling a bit low, forgotten and self-pitying, and my pet hate is self-pity.

Lord, how would you have us live alongside this thin dividing line between life and death that we choose to ignore most of the time? I've been too close to it on too many occasions not to heed its warning, or its invitation—because there is an invitation hidden there too, an invitation to life.

Cancer is a hideous disease. The treatment is often worse, often harrowing. Scars and after-effects don't allow it to be forgotten. Despite all that, I wouldn't have been without either experience of cancer. My complacent world has been turned upside down. What really matters has come tumbling out to lie at my feet for attention. I daren't ignore those shining things.

In his first book,[38] Lance Armstrong, the *Tour de France* cyclist and cancer survivor, mentions the comment of a fellow patient who was some distance ahead of him—not on a bike, but in his cancer experience. Lance was at first puzzled, but later understood what this man meant when he said, 'You don't know it yet—but we're the lucky ones.'

I'm inclined to agree with him.

And what of you, Lord? These last few weeks have been strangely silent ones. I have read and prayed as ever, but there has been little in response.

I wonder if you are still standing back, watching the bicycle wheels spin off into the distance. I don't believe that you have ever taken your eyes off me. It's just that I'm a big girl now. I can do it. My faith has been stretched, and it fits over this experience, albeit tightly. Often it is threadbare, worn almost to transparency, but it stretches nonetheless.

It is risky, dangerous, fabulous faith, lived as if on an unpredictable roller coaster or that wobbly bicycle. Either way, I am perched precariously on top.

One song, played and sung often over these few months, echoes around this whole experience. It's a song about faith—faith whatever, faith 'even if he does not', faith for ever, faith that's fact.

It's about the fact that all I need is you, whether you are silent or engaging, laughing or weeping. It reminds me that your very name is blessed, and it sums up my summary of these past months like nothing else.

Blessed be Your name
In the land that is plentiful,
Where Your streams of abundance flow,
Blessed be Your name.
And blessed be your Name
When I'm found in the desert place,
Though I walk through the wilderness,
Blessed be Your name.

Every blessing you pour out I'll
Turn back to praise.
When the darkness closes in, Lord,
Still I will say:

Blessed be the name of the Lord,
Blessed be Your name.
Blessed be the name of the Lord,
Blessed be Your glorious name.

Blessed be Your name
When the sun's shining down on me,
When the world's 'all as it should be',
Blessed be Your name.
And blessed be Your name
On the road marked with suffering,
Though there's pain in the offering,
Blessed be your name.

You give and take away,
You give and take away.
My heart will choose to say:
Lord, blessed be Your name.

MATT REDMAN, COPYRIGHT © 2002 THANKYOU MUSIC

THURSDAY 15 SEPTEMBER

Lois and I fly to Florence this morning. Blessed be your name!

POSTSCRIPT

As I write, it is September 2006. Lois is just about to return to university for her second year of study. Benjamin, who (despite the trauma) did well in his GCSEs, has just begun the second year of A levels. He will som be applying to begin university this time next year. Richard continues to work for Cancer Research UK, which involves weekly commutes from Plymouth to London.

For now, at least, I am well. But I cannot be sure what lies ahead. There are positive responses to that knowledge: a desire to live life to the full, not to take the best things in life—friends, family, health and peace—for granted. But if I am honest, there are also, for me, frustrations: a desire to make the most of every moment, an odd kind of burden that causes impatience and a self-imposed demand to 'do womething worth doing' with the rest of my life. Survisor's guilt is a very real phenomenon: it often makes me very sad, even as I recognize that I am very blessed.

Increasingly I believe that those of us who have lived close to death are a peculiar band. We live life to the beat of a different ddrum. That beat is not an easy one; neither is it understood by those who haven't the experience to hear it. But God knows that. Indeed, he has led me through a desert place over these last weeks from which I have still to emerge. Sometimes I have more questions than answers, and know more tears than smiles. But that's OK with God. It's why Matt Redmans' song remains so close to my heart. Even as I say, 'My God, my God, why have you forsaken me?' I know he will always be 'My God'—and blessed be his name.

Whatever lies ahead and however the drum beats, I know that all four of us remain 'in the palm of God's hand'.

✣

AFTERWORD

Do not look forward to the changes and chances of this life in fear; rather look to them with full hope, that as they arise, God, whose you are, will deliver you out of them. He has kept you hitherto—do you but hold fast to his dear hand, and he will lead you safely through all things; and when you cannot stand, he will bear you in his arms.

Do not look forward to what may happen tomorrow; the same everlasting father who cares for you today will take care of you tomorrow and every day. Either he will shield you from suffering or he will give you unfailing strength to bear it. Be at peace then, and put aside all anxious thoughts and imaginations.
ST FRANCIS DE SALES

NOTES

1   Phillip Keller, *A Shepherd Looks at the 23rd Psalm*, Zondervan, 1970
2   Rebecca Manley Pippert, *A Heart Like His*, IVP, 1996
3   James Jones, *Fear No Evil*, Hodder & Stoughton, 1984 (p. 129)
5   John Diamond wrote a regular column in *The Times on Saturday* magazine, which followed his diagnosis and treatment for throat cancer.
6   John Diamond, *C*, Vermilion, 1998 (p. 10)
7   Diamond, *C*, p. 28
8   M. Craig Barnes, *When God Interrupts*, IVP, 1996
9   Eugene Greco, His Banner Publishing
10 Richard Daly, *God's Little Book of Calm*, HarperCollins, 1999
11 Hilary McDowell, *Some Day I'm Going to Fly*, Triangle, 1995
12 Robert Buckman, *What You Really Need to Know about Cancer*, Pan, 1995
13 *Encounter With God* Bible reading notes, Scripture Union
14 Bananas featured highly on the agenda of the 1998 bike ride. We had to collect what seemed like a ton from a sponsor, resulting in an acute lack of space in the van—and bananas with everything! Pete was my co-driver.
15 Diamond, *C*, p. 65
16 C.S. Lewis, *The Lion, the Witch and the Wardrobe*, Fount, 1950, p. 75
17 David Spiegel, *Living Beyond Limits*, Vermilion, 1993
18 Christine Leonard, *Affirming Love*, BRF, 1999

19 From 'Paracelsus' by Robert Browning

20 Fiona Castle, *Rainbows through the Rain*, Hodder & Stoughton, 1998

21 Rob Parsons, *What They Didn't Teach Me in Sunday School*, Hodder & Stoughton, 1997

22 Elisabeth Elliot, *A Path Through Suffering*, OM Publishing, 1990

23 Ron Mehl, *Surprise Endings*, Multnomah Books USA, 1993

24 Later I had a Christmas card from a *Home and Family* reader whose friend was ill with cancer. She had been encouraged by the article and was to share Psalm 130 with her friend. Letters like this one made me realize that God was at work in small ways which might make a big difference.

25 Oswald Chambers, *My Utmost for His Highest*, Oswald Chambers Publications, 1927, p. 12

26 Peripheral blood stem cell transplant or stem cell support enables very large quantities of chemotherapy to be given to patients who have responded well to first-stage chemotherapy. Such large doses suppress the bone marrow so severely that it would normally be unable to recover and reproduce sufficient numbers of blood cells. If healthy stem cells ('baby cells') are 'harvested' from a patient while the cancer is under reasonable control, they can be stored and given back once the high-dose treatment has been given and the bone marrow affected. In this way, the patient's own stem cells 'rescue' them from the damaging effects of a non-functioning bone marrow. Since the individual receives much higher doses of therapy, a better response to treatment is expected. However, stem cell therapy is arduous and risky. Nursing has to be done in isolation for several weeks because of the high risk of infection and it can take some considerable time for a patient to recover fully.

27 Peter Graystone, *Ready Salted*, Scripture Union, 1998

28 *Lucas on Life Every Day*, April 2005, CWR.

29 From the Anglican service of Holy Communion

30 Fr John Woolley, *I Am With You*, Arthur James, 1996, p. 104.

31 *I Am With You*, p. 109.

32 *I Am With You*, p. 111.

33 I write a weekly column in *The Evening Herald*, but this cancer diary was an additional insert, to appear every Thursday for 24 weeks.

34 *I Am With You*, p. 145.

35 Source unknown.

36 John Ortberg, *The Life You've Always Wanted*, Zondervan, 2004.

37 Sheila Hancock, *The Two of Us: My Life with John Thaw*, Bloomsbury, 2005.

38 Lance Armstrong, *It's Not about the Bike: My Journey Back to Life*, Berkley Publishing Group, 2001.